for **SANITY'S** sake

Lisa captures the essence of this phenomenon called "menopause" and offers encouraging insights as she challenges us women to overcome rather than succumb to menopausal symptoms. This book is a "must read" for every woman I know, whether she has reached menopause or not.

—Dr. Bonnie Novak, wife of founding pastor of Lakeshore Baptist Church

Menopause, or as my grandmother used to call it in a hushed tone laced with dread, "That Time of Life," is a time of hormonal havoc for most of us. Author Lisa S. Arnold offers Christian women the hope of Christ in her short, often humorous, and honest devotional, *For Sanity's Sake*. Menopause is often a neglected topic, but in this God-honoring book, the author focuses on it with a bold dignity we "woman of a certain age" will appreciate. She offers camaraderie, comfort, and reasons to celebrate who we are in Christ.

—Joy Dekok, author of the bestselling devotional, *Under His Wings (Lessons Learned From God While Watching the Birds)* and a woman in the middle of this malady we call menopause

Lisa S. Arnold has captured the essence, or, should I say the darkness of a woman and her menopausal ways in her daily devotional book titled, *For Sanity's Sake*. I love the way she adds humor to a not so funny situation, and her "Daily Hot Flashes" are like a cool drink of spring water. Anyone who is entering into this menopausal season of life will appreciate Ms. Arnold's honesty and candid approach to living a triumphant life before, during and after menopause.

—Sarah Martin Byrd, author of *Guardian Spirit, The Color of My Heart, The Manger Mouse,* and *The River Keeper*

Lisa's book of devotions is overflowing with true insights, advice and encouragement, offered by a woman who has served much time "in the trenches" of menopause and its many challenges. She navigates the reader through an exploration of how her own Christian walk has become deepened by the fiery physical trial of the "change of life."

For each day, she offers a scripture, followed by insights for the reading, topped with a "hot flash" of wisdom, and a prayer to get you started on your own daily internal cleansing and refreshing. As an author, I especially appreciated her reasons for writing this book. She asks an important question: "What good is experience if it isn't used to help someone?" Later in the book she says, "There is nothing you can go through that someone else has not experienced or will not experience some day. Share your struggles and become a source of wisdom to the next person. Write! And make a difference."

She has accomplished this with her book, and I know it will make a difference to any woman who reads it, and puts into practice the advice within it. As older women, we have traveled through many challenges, including the very hefty one of menopause. And passing through that challenge is just the beginning of renewal in body, spirit and strength. Thank you Lisa for pouring your heart into these pages. Your words will stand as a testament to God's love, care and guidance for all women, menopausal or not!

—Nancy Shew Bolton, author of *The Right Ingredients*

"And we know that in all things God works for the good of those who love him." (Romans 8:28a NIV) Just what is good about menopause? Lisa S. Arnold teaches us through Biblical women (and men), and through Scriptures, through current day circumstances and examples, that menopause is meant to draw us closer to God, who loves us personally and unconditionally, and through the emotional upheavals menopause brings. Lisa explains that God does not look at our changing outward appearance but at the attitudes and intent of the heart. She will teach you that because of God's love for you, you can endure and even embrace menopause.

—Judy Janowski, author of *Life Is a Garden Party, I & II*

for SANITY'S sake

Devotions for the Temporarily Insane: *otherwise known as the* MENOPAUSAL WOMAN

LISA S. ARNOLD

For Sanity's Sake

Devotions for the Temporarily Insane:
Otherwise Known as the Menopausal Woman

© 2015 by Lisa S. Arnold
All rights reserved

ISBN: 978-1-62020-502-0
eISBN: 978-1-62020-406-1

Unless otherwise marked, Scripture taken from the New King James Version®. Copyright © 1982 by Thomas Nelson, Inc. Used by permission. All rights reserved.

Scripture taken from The Holy Bible, New International Version®, NIV® Copyright © 1973, 1978, 1984, 2011 by Biblica, Inc.® Used by permission. All rights reserved worldwide.

Scripture taken from The Message. Copyright © 1993, 1994, 1995, 1996, 2000, 2001, 2002. Used by permission of NavPress Publishing Group.

Cover Design & Typesetting by Hannah Nichols
Ebook Conversion by Anna Riebe

AMBASSADOR INTERNATIONAL
Emerald House
427 Wade Hampton Blvd.
Greenville, SC 29609, USA
www.ambassador-international.com

AMBASSADOR BOOKS
The Mount
2 Woodstock Link
Belfast, BT6 8DD, Northern Ireland, UK
www.ambassadormedia.co.uk

The colophon is a trademark of Ambassador

ACKNOWLEDGEMENTS

My Lord and Savior Jesus Christ: Without Him there would be no book worth writing, no knowledge worth sharing, and no life worth living. To Him I give all the glory!

My husband, Duane, who believed in me and taught me how to believe in myself. I was a lost scared kitten when we met, you taught me how to soar to heights I never thought possible. God knew what He was doing when He brought you to me. Thank you for your never ending support.

My mother, Eileen Beth Pack, who painstakingly poured over every word of my manuscript. I couldn't have done it without you.

My children, Jessie, Carl, Auriel, Chris, Punky, Michael, Faith and Lilly, all who unintentionally provided great fodder for my book. You are all part of who I am, and I am a better person for having you in my life.

My editor, Brenda Covert, who, amazingly, was a kindred spirit after all. God brought my manuscript to the perfect person.

My publishers at Ambassador International for believing in my book. Thank you from the bottom of my heart.

INTRODUCTION

There **IS** life during menopause. In the midst of sporadic crying, uncontrollable screaming, or sweating like a momma combating intense labor pains, it is good to know that there is a sparkling spring at the end of the murky water.

Each day begins with a freshness never before experienced. Lamentations 3:23 offers that sweet, affirming promise that God's "mercies are new every day." God does not carry our mistakes of today into the newness of tomorrow. Great is His faithfulness!

Join me as we struggle, cry, sweat, and hopefully—in God's strength—regain control of our lives. With a determination on our part and a whole lot of help on the Holy Spirit's part, this can be the best time of your life. It is my prayer that through blood (Jesus' of course), sweat (ours of course), and tears (ours and probably everyone else's), we can make it to the other side—of menopause, that is—and step into a bigger, better, more abundant life.

With help from women in Scripture, significant women from the past and present, my own personal experiences, and the agonizing tales of friends and acquaintances, it is my hope that you come to a comforting realization that **you are not alone!** A massive army of women fights this battle every day. As you persevere through each battle and ultimately win the war, it will be your turn to share the vast wisdom you have accumulated to the next generation of poor, anxious (and I mean *really* anxious) souls just starting the climb. Here's to a merry menopause. God Bless!

JANUARY

JANUARY 1

READ: 2 CORINTHIANS 3:11-17

BRING ON THE NEW

Behold, the former things have come to pass, And new things I declare; Before they spring forth I tell you of them.

~ Isaiah 42:9

Change is inevitable. The arrival of a newborn baby reshapes the structured routine of first-time parents. That same baby must also suffer change as he is thrust from the comforts of the warm, safe confines of his mother's womb.

Death is a surety, yet it reigns supreme in its element of surprise. A newborn baby is expected; often death makes its entrance without warning or apology. Difficult adjustments await loved ones left behind.

"Behold, former things are come to pass, and new things I do declare." The onset of menopausal symptoms signifies the passing of former things and the declaration of something new. Often, women are thrust into its grasping tentacles of symptoms without any warning. Women who live full, invigorating lives suddenly visualize with horror the onset of old age and the proverbial rocking chair beckoning them on the front porch.

God has no intention of allowing you to rock your way into eternity. The refining fires of menopause will only strengthen you for the journey ahead. God has great things in store for you. What they are, only He knows; whether you will rise to the challenge is entirely up to you.

TODAY'S HOT FLASH:

The future is not something to fear, but something to spring into with great anticipation and excitement for what is to come.

PRAYER:

Father, whatever it takes, I'm Yours. May Your supernatural strength see me through even the hardest of days. Amen.

JANUARY 2
READ: 1 CHRONICLES 16:4–12

A TIME TO SEEK GOD'S STRENGTH

Seek the Lord and His strength; Seek His face continually!
~ 1 Chronicles 16:11

Once upon a time there was a woman, and she was in complete control of her life. Without warning, her world began spinning out of control. Fluctuating emotions and embarrassing physical changes plagued her. In her own strength, her emotional and spiritual stamina dwindled; it was time to seek supernatural intervention. Why had she waited so long? (Can you guess who I am talking about?)

The Creator and Sustainer of our bodies desires for us to seek His strength as we maneuver through the murky waters of menopause. Only through Him is it possible to stay afloat in the stormy hormonal seas of midlife.

The awesome fact that God uses me—a hormonally challenged woman—to accomplish His Kingdom work, is nothing less than miraculous. Each day as I "seek the Lord and his strength," He transforms me from an anxious menopausal victim to a confident woman of Christ. There are women He could use that need less transformation, but He chose me, and through my weakness His strength is magnified. Because I am hand-picked by God, I know He will supply the strength to accomplish His work.

You, too, are hand-picked by this Holy God to do a great and mighty work for His kingdom. In your own strength, frustration and failure will prevail. In His, success and contentment are promised.

TODAY'S HOT FLASH:

Our weakness is transformed to powerhouse strength when God is allowed to take control.

PRAYER:

Almighty Father, teach me to depend on Your strength in this time of change and turmoil. Transform my weakness into power through Your Holy Spirit. Amen.

FOR SANITY'S SAKE

JANUARY 3

READ: MATTHEW 6:25-34

RESOLVE TO SEEK THE THINGS OF GOD

But seek ye first the kingdom of God, and his righteousness; and all these things shall be added unto you.

~ Matthew 6:33

Self-absorbency can be a byproduct of menopause. It is easy to become consumed with our feelings, our bodies, and our desperation to stay young. Others fade into the distance as "me, myself, and I" draw dangerously close to the surface. Jesus met His fleshly opposition in His time of desperation with intense prayer and unwavering focus on His Father. His human side could have easily disregarded the needs of the people and walked away from the torturous events soon to come. But, praise the Lord, the God side won, obtaining for us eternal security.

We, too, have a human side (the flesh) and a God side (the Holy Spirit). All the power Jesus had as God, we have through His Holy Spirit. But only as we choose to "seek first the kingdom of God and his righteousness" will self-motivated desires evaporate and God-motivated desires take precedence.

Resolve to seek the things of God above everything else, regardless of the sinful inclinations provoked by fleshly hormonal attacks. As we put Him in the center of our thoughts and deeds, our desire for "self" will slip away, and service to others will again become a part of who we are in Christ.

TODAY'S HOT FLASH:

When God is placed on the highest pedestal of your life, the anxious "me" attacks will depart and God and others will replace the vacancy left in their wake.

PRAYER:

Righteous Father, don't let me get caught up in the me, myself, and I's. May they fade into obscurity, and may only who I am through You shine brightly for all to see. Amen.

JANUARY 4
READ: GENESIS 1:26–31

THE LURE OF POWER

Then God saw everything that He had made, and indeed it was very good.
So the evening and the morning were the sixth day.

~ Genesis 1:31

Eve—the mother of all mankind—was perfect in every way. She had a gorgeous body, a sweet temperament, and perfectly balanced hormones. So what happened?

The cunning words of a fascinating creature lured her to a dangerous place. His offerings of power and prestige intrigued her. Was she suffering from PMS? No. Somewhere deep inside her a simmering began, and as the serpent lavished his enticing words on her, that simmering turned into a rolling boil. Yes! She wanted to be like God! And with one swish of her arm, she captured that forbidden fruit in her grasp and chomped down.

Life would never be the same again for Eve, or for the rest of humanity; sin entered the picture. Eve couldn't blame run-amok hormones for her sinful behavior. It was a decision of the will that led her down such a destructive path.

Hormones make an easy scapegoat, but as we witnessed with Eve, they are not always to blame. God expects us to take responsibility for our wrong choices. He doesn't buy the temporary insanity plea, and neither should you.

TODAY'S HOT FLASH:

Vigilance is the key to holiness. Menopause does not give us license to misbehave, but rather a forewarning to draw near to God before the serpent has time to strike.

PRAYER:

Father, teach me to take responsibility for my sin and seek forgiveness as soon as my heart is convicted. Amen.

JANUARY 5

READ: EXODUS 15:1-21

THE HIGH TIMES

And Miriam the prophetess, the sister of Aaron, took a timbrel in her hand; and all the women went out after her with timbrels and with dances.

~ Exodus 15:20

Whenever the Israelites experienced a great deliverance from God, they reacted with jubilation. When Miriam and the Israelite women experienced their high, "they went out with timbrels and with dances." The great and mighty God delivered them from certain death, and they joyously worshipped Him. They soared with their emotions, doing the right thing by using their excess energy to praise their Deliverer.

Like Miriam, our emotional highs should catapult us to decisive faith action. We can't anticipate how long the mood will last, so there is no time to lose. Grab your timbrels and dance; lavish God with your praise and service while the energy thrives. You'd amazed at how much you can accomplish. This new phase of life is the perfect opportunity to build new dreams, begin new ministries, enlarge short-sighted visions, and set out for new adventures. It is a time to praise God with newfound excitement. Don't waste a second; enhance to its fullest this special time God has graciously given you.

TODAY'S HOT FLASH:

Menopause is not the ending of something good; it is the beginning of something greater than you can ever imagine.

PRAYER:

Praiseworthy Father, I know that I can't have these high emotions every day. Help me not to waste a second when they come. Amen.

JANUARY 6
READ: EXODUS 17:1-7

WATCH YOUR BACK

So Moses cried out to the Lord, saying, "What shall I do with this people? They are almost ready to stone me!"

~ Exodus 17:4

I have to chuckle at Moses' desperate plea to God. On my most agitated days, my husband proclaims to anyone listening, "You better watch your back." He's indicating that those knives I am washing may end up somewhere other than the drawer. Thank God, through the Spirit, I can claim some semblance of self-control.

When I am in the midst of sever hormonal surges, I have a hard time finding the humor in them (but my husband sure can). How do I remain godly when no one else understands my struggle? I can run and cry (I've done that). I can stand and scream (I've done that, too), or I can find comfort in God's reply as Paul did when he pleaded for Him to remove his thorn in the flesh.

"Three times I pleaded with the Lord to take it away from me. But he said to me, 'My grace is sufficient for you, for my power is made perfect in weakness'" (2 Corinthians 12:7).

When you feel out of control, activate your inner power—the Holy Spirit—and remember, His grace is sufficient, and in your weakness His power is revealed.

TODAY'S HOT FLASH:

Our weakness provides the opportunity for the Holy Spirit's power to magnificently radiate through our otherwise hopeless situation.

PRAYER:

All sufficient Father, I need Your grace for today. Override my weakness with Your Holy Spirit power. Thank You for using me in spite of myself. Great is Your faithfulness. Amen.

JANUARY 7

READ: LUKE 24:33–43

PLEASURES IMMEASURABLE

And they gave him a piece of broiled fish, and of an honeycomb.
And he took it, and did eat before them.

~ Luke 24:42–43

Have you ever noticed how often food is talked about in the Bible? Eating is one of our favorite ways of fellowship. With this delightful mode of entertaining sometimes comes an undesired aftereffect. Avoirdupois! That's French for *excess weight*.

This "avoirdupois," which I like to call it because it sounds better than "fat," creeps up on us in little increments. So slowly does it ease into our lives that we are shocked when one day we step on the scale and it reads . . . well, you put in the number. Disgusted, we go out and buy new scales; after all, wasn't it just last week that it said 135? Darn it! These scales are broke too! And off we go.

How wonderful to know that we are not forever trapped in these sin-cursed, easily tempted shells. There will come a day when our enjoyment won't be hampered by guilt-ridden emotions and uncontrolled temptations. *Avoirdupois* will be a word from the past.

Cravings and desires such as we experience now will become nonexistent. Selfish desires will evaporate. With breathtaking awareness, our eyes will focus on the one who gave His life for us. On this side of heaven, immeasurable pleasures consist of chocolate cake and donuts. On the other side, we will feast our eyes on the Savior. Only then will our hunger be fully sated.

TODAY'S HOT FLASH:

Immeasurable pleasures exist for us in heaven. Don't get discouraged about what you can't have. It won't last forever.

PRAYER:

Giver of immeasurable pleasures, give me strength to endure temptation on this side of glory, knowing I can indulge in the desires of my heart on the other side. Amen.

JANUARY 8
READ: EXODUS 32:1–6

PATIENCE, PLEASE

Now when the people saw that Moses delayed coming down from the mountain, the people gathered together to Aaron, and said to him, "Come, make us gods . . . for as for this Moses, the man who brought us up out of the land of Egypt, we do not know what has become of him.

~ Exodus 32:1

Menopause has a way of illuminating those "little sins." Often we blind ourselves to our flaws; God unveils them with shocking clarity.

Take patience, for example, something the Israelites lacked. In self-righteous frustration they murmured to Aaron, "This Moses, the man that brought us up out of Egypt." They separated themselves from God's servant in an attempt to separate themselves from God.

Sometimes my frustration at my husband is so overwhelming that I find myself saying, "This man, the one that lives in my house." I separate myself from him emotionally so I can justify my wrong feelings.

This is when the Holy Spirit reminds me of His life-changing fruit that dwells within me. "But the fruit of the Spirit is love, joy, peace, LONGSUFFERING, gentleness, goodness, faith, meekness, and self-control" (Galatians 5:22–23). God allows no exceptions; either we are walking in the Spirit, or we are not. The evidence lies in our behavior. This spiritual fruit is to be present in our lives at all times, hormonally balanced or not.

TODAY'S HOT FLASH:

Longsuffering is more than patience. It is bearing with something or someone even to our detriment. This can also be called unconditional love.

PRAYER:

Oh, Father, magnify this characteristic of longsuffering in my life that I may be like Your Son Jesus. Thank You for being so longsuffering with me. Amen.

JANUARY 9

READ: 1 SAMUEL 25:5–42

SAINTLY SUFFERING

And David said to Abigail, blessed be the Lord God of Israel, which sent thee this day to meet me: and blessed be thou, which hast kept me this day from coming to shed blood.

~ 1 Samuel 25:32–33a

Abigail lived with an obese, drunkard of a man. Life must have consisted of daily challenges living with such a wretched creature. We don't know if Abigail suffered from extreme hormonal problems, but we do know she was a woman under substantial duress. Hormonal or not, Abigail's situation was bleak.

Interestingly, we don't find Abigail wallowing in self-pity, whining over bad circumstances, or attempting to rid herself of her wretched husband. She remains a loyal wife.

In the midst of a horrible home life, Abigail's charm and wisdom prevailed. She served the Most High, and that knowledge fortified her resolve. She chose to remain a saint even while living with a sinner.

Whether it is hormones or bad circumstances, our reaction is a choice. David praised Abigail for her quick actions and wise advice. He gives her full credit for saving lives that day. "Blessed be thou who has kept me this day from coming to shed blood."

David recognized God's character in Abigail. If God gave Abigail the strength to remain poised and godly in the worst of circumstances, He will do it for you.

TODAY'S HOT FLASH:

A wise woman of grace and poise exhibits a balanced and even temperament. It is achievable, as Abigail demonstrated, in the worst of circumstances.

PRAYER:

Father, I want to be a godly woman, regardless of my circumstances. Keep me strong and dependent on Your Spirit, no matter what. Amen.

JANUARY 10
READ: JOSHUA 15:15-19

GIVE ME MORE

Who answered, give me a blessing for thou hast given me a south land: give me also springs of water, and he gave her the upper springs, and the nether springs.

~ Joshua 15:19

Achsah's father promised her as a wife to whomever captured the city of Debir. Othneil was the lucky man. He not only won the hand of Achsah, he also was given the south land as part of his dowry. He was content.

Achsah, on the other hand, was not. She wanted more. "Give me also . . ." was her request to her father—not once, but twice. The more she accumulated, the more she desired. In Achsah dwelled a dominant characteristic of selfishness.

As I struggle through this time in my life, selfishness reigns supreme as one of my great character flaws. I don't desire big things. I desire more me time and less time with family and friends. I want to go out for dinner, not slave over a hot stove. Instead of sharing my love with others, I demand others to love me more. When I think about the person I am becoming, I am ashamed.

God said, "Look not every man on his own things, but every man also on the things of others" (Philippians 2:4). I need to do some work in this area; how about you?

TODAY'S HOT FLASH:

Each day we have a precious opportunity to touch someone for Jesus. Let's not waste that on ourselves. What reward is in that?

PRAYER:

Forgiving Father, remove this selfish tendency that hovers near the surface all the time. Forgive me when I fail. Help me to look to the things of others first. Take my life and use it to touch someone for Jesus today.

FOR SANITY'S SAKE

JANUARY 11

READ: PSALM 46

A WOMAN OF GRACE

And she was a widow of about fourscore and four years, which departed not from the temple, but served God with fastings and prayers night and day.

~ Luke 2:37

What a lovely example Anna is of a committed woman of grace. Widowed after only seven years of marriage, she chose to dedicate her life to the Lord rather than seek another husband. Anna remained steadfast because God was her strength and her shield, her "very present help in trouble" (Psalm 46:1).

How did Anna manage to spend eighty-four years in the temple without going bonkers? It was an attitude of the heart and mind. She "served God with fastings and prayers night and day." Because her heart was totally devoted to her God, she was able to ward off attacks from Satan and the flesh that could have destroyed her spiritually. Anna climbed her mountain of difficulties with grace, and so can we.

Isn't it great to know that—if we cling to the Lord— there is a peace that passes all semblance of understanding on the other side of menopause? This peace comes through prayer and fasting. Graceful women are not born; they are divinely sculpted, created by years spent basking in the presence of the Lord. Don't wait another second. Wrap yourself in His calm assurance and don't let anything pull you away. You, too, can have a peaceful transition.

TODAY'S HOT FLASH:

Bask in the awesome presence of the Lord and become a divinely sculpted, graceful woman.

PRAYER:

Divine Lord, I want to be like Anna, a graceful woman devoted to serving You. Help me to cling to You so I can have a peace-filled transition to the other side of menopause. Amen.

JANUARY 12
READ: GALATIANS 5:16–26

OVERRIDING ANXIETY

This I say then, walk in the Spirit, and ye shall not fulfil the lust of the flesh.
~ Galatians 5:16

Menopausal women are often anxious women. If asked what is wrong, we can't give a definite answer. We are experiencing one of the frustrating symptoms of overactive hormones called anxiety. We know it is hormonal because we can feel the familiar unsettling emotions fixating themselves into position for an indefinite stay.

Anxiety is a fleshly emotion and is conquerable through the power of the Holy Spirit. The sharp, penetrating edges of the flesh become dull and useless as we learn to "walk in the Spirit." The impenetrable shield of the Spirit offers unconditional protection for those desiring relief from fleshly attacks. The Holy Spirit's protection is sure, but He will not take action without a personal invitation.

We have a choice; even when that horrible feeling wells up inside us bursting for an outlet; we can counterattack with the Word, prayer, fasting, and praise. There is no penetrating the fortification set up by the Holy Spirit when we allow Him to protect us from the wily attacks of the flesh.

TODAY'S HOT FLASH:

Fortify your emotions with an impenetrable Holy Spirit shield. Only as we "walk in the Spirit" can we ward off the attacks of our fleshly desires.

PRAYER:

Thank You, Lord, for the gift of Your Holy Spirit. Release His power within me to fight the sin of my flesh activated by my hormones.

JANUARY 13

READ: 2 CHRONICLES 22:8-12

WHO ARE YOU BECOMING?

But when Athaliah the mother of Ahaziah saw that her son was dead, she arose and destroyed all the seed royal of the house of Judah.

~ 2 Chronicles 22:10

Athaliah had serious hormonal issues (my interpretation). Not surprising since her mother was Jezebel. She was so driven by her passion to be queen that when her son died, she killed all her grandsons, removing any possible heir to the throne. Little did she know that God, in His great wisdom, hid one special grandson away for safekeeping.

We've read the tragic stories of mothers killing their children. A hormonal disorder is often blamed. In the midst of extreme hormonal distress, their lack of self-discipline pushed them to commit horrendous crimes.

I can relate, and I am sure you can too. My husband steers clear of me when my eyes glisten with villainous intent and the knives are uncomfortably close at hand. The frightening truth is that it only takes one act to become like Athaliah.

If we are weak in certain areas, our hormonal surges will magnify that weakness. Take heed lest you become known for your evil deeds at this time. Only you and the Holy Spirit can control who you become. Let it be like Christ, not like our enemy the devil.

TODAY'S HOT FLASH:

Great passion is desirable when controlled by the Holy Spirit; when it is controlled by Satan, it can be deadly.

PRAYER:

O Holy One, protect my mind and thoughts. Let my passion be Christ-driven. The only person I want to become like is Your Son, Jesus Christ. Amen.

JANUARY 14
READ: PSALM 1

LIKE A TREE PLANTED BY THE WATERS

And he shall be like a tree planted by the rivers of water, that bringeth forth his fruit in his season; his leaf also shall not wither; and whatsoever he doeth shall prosper.

~ Psalm 1:3

Balance and self-control in the hormonal woman's life doesn't come easy. Scripture gives us insight as to how to achieve it. It isn't cutting the amount of coffee we drink (although that will relieve some of the anxiety). It isn't exercising more frequently (although that increases our energy and improves our attitude as well as helps with unwanted pounds). It isn't repeating a mantra one hundred times a day (although if it is a Bible verse, it can't hurt).

Psalm 1:2 says, "But his delight is in the law of the Lord; and in his law doth he meditate day and night." This inspiring verse reads so simply, yet the difficulty in living it defies reason.

Satan will construct every possible barrier and implement every conceivable distraction to keep us from becoming like a "tree planted by the rivers of water," unmovable and ever thriving in our Christian walk. Only through determined vigilance can we fight off his attacks.

Balance and control in our lives will come when we stubbornly cling to the promises of God. When we believe He will do what He says, we will begin to live it. When we begin to live it, everything we do will prosper.

TODAY'S HOT FLASH:

Only those deeply imbedded in God's Word will remain strong and resistant when the attempts of Satan seek to uproot them.

PRAYER:

All-important Father, I want to love You more. Help me put You first in my thoughts. If I do this, I will become as unmovable as a tree planted by the rivers of water, and no hormonal surge can move me from my firm foundation. Thank You for that promise. Amen.

JANUARY 15
READ: PROVERBS 3:1–13

FLAWED UNDERSTANDING

Trust in the Lord with all thine heart; and lean not unto thine own understanding. In all thy ways acknowledge him, and he shall direct thy paths.

~ Proverbs 3:5–6

When my hormones are raging mightier than a crazed bull, I don't see things clearly. I attack the red cape because my perception is flawed, just like the misled bull. There is a difference; a bull is a bull, an animal, unable to differentiate. I am a human being, a person created in the image of God. If I take time to listen to the rationality of what I know and to the nudgings of the Holy Spirit, an intelligent decision will follow.

In our own strength, it is impossible to follow God's chosen path and natural to act in accordance to our own understanding.

To "trust in the Lord with our whole heart" is to go beyond the motivations of our feelings. Jeremiah tells us the "heart is deceitful above all things, and desperately wicked: who can know it?" (Jeremiah 17:9).

Think with all your mind, not with your heart. Do what you know is God's will for you today, regardless of what your flawed understanding tells you, and He will "direct your paths." With God in the driver's seat, you can never take a wrong turn.

TODAY'S HOT FLASH:

Deceived by her flawed emotions, unchecked by the Word of God, the hormonal woman becomes like that raging bull, out of control and heading for trouble.

PRAYER:

Omnipotent Father, I know my understanding is flawed and my emotions are often irrational at times. Help me to obey Your Word over my feelings every time. Amen.

JANUARY 16
READ: MATTHEW 7:1-6

A CRITICAL SPIRIT

For with what judgment ye judge, ye shall be judged: and with what measure ye measure, it shall be measured to you again.

~ Matthew 7:2

"You sound more like your grandmother every day," my husband accused. How could he say that? My grandmother was miserable, critical, and unloving. It took me years to realize that she would never love me—couldn't love me—for her bitterness had grown deep and diamond hard. Not at me, but at the world, and she allowed no one close enough to penetrate that hardened shell. Could some truth resonate from my husband's accusation?

Almost in total abandonment, my words fly from my mouth unchecked and harmful. I hate this person I often become and cringe when I fall into the snare set by Satan and my hormones. My excuses are feeble and my intemperance downright disgraceful. My surging hormones aren't to blame; they only enhance the negative feelings already present. Before menopause, they remained hidden below the surface, safely out of everyone's view.

Jesus said with what "judgment ye judge, ye shall be judged." Fear courses through my veins as I read this, for I know my judgments are biased and critical and I have no excuse. In moments of desperation, I run to the loving Word of God and saturate myself in His counsel. My goal is to start sounding like Jesus instead of an incarnation of the evil one himself.

TODAY'S HOT FLASH:

Don't fall into Satan's snare. There is no excuse for biased and critical judgments. Saturate yourself in the Truth until you start replicating Him in every word and deed.

PRAYER:

Merciful Father, forgive my judgmental attitude, my finger pointing, and my nasty remarks. I want to become like Jesus in everything I say and do. Amen.

JANUARY 17

READ: EPHESIANS 2:1-10

THANK GOD FOR GRACE

For by grace are ye saved through faith; and that not of yourselves: it is the gift of God: Not of works, lest any man should boast.

~ Ephesians 2:8-9

I often lie awake at night trying to remember at least one good deed I've done or an encouraging word I've said during the course of my day. Sometimes I have to dig deep to find even a smidgen of something redeemable.

Why does God love me? Especially now, when my hormones are raging and I already feel useless, fat, ugly, and unneeded. Why does God tolerate my outbursts? He is God! In a split second He could (and probably should) squash me, humiliate me, and disown me. Instead, His compassion overwhelms me.

God's Word tells me He loves me because He chose to love me. He didn't choose me because of my outstanding feats of merit, my tremendous abilities, my perfect body, or my highly intelligent mind (thank God for that). He chose me because of His awesome grace. "For by grace are we saved through faith, it is the gift of God."

Thank God for His grace. I don't deserve it. I can't earn it. I can't purchase it. It is a free gift. Unworthy that I am, I will ever be grateful to the One who picked me up out of the mires of sin and made me His adopted child—just because.

TODAY'S HOT FLASH:

Where would we be if perfection was the requirement for receiving God's grace? Can anyone come close to the perfectness of God?

PRAYER:

Father of grace and mercy, thank You for Your saving grace, for new mercies every day, and for the wonderful truth that each day brings with it a new beginning. Amen.

JANUARY 18
READ: ECCLESIASTES 1:1–11

VANITY OF VANITIES

Vanity of vanities, saith the Preacher, vanity of vanities; all is vanity.

~ Ecclesiastes 1:2

Favour is deceitful, and beauty is vain: but a woman that feareth the Lord, she shall be praised.

~ Proverbs 31:30

What menopausal fears do you harbor? For some, it is the undeniable fact that old age is fast arriving. Many women view menopause as the beginning of the end. The question, "How did I get so old?" enters their minds frequently, and the answer is elusive at best.

We spend money on wrinkle cream, buy clothes that make us look thinner, and dye our hair to cover the gray. Forever youthful is a concept embraced by millions in our culture. Billions of dollars are spent and made attempting to defy the effects of time.

The world continues to seek new and improved creams, lotions, exercises, and surgeries, but age is not respecter of persons. When Eve bit into the forbidden fruit, she sealed the fate for all humanity.

We can waste thousands of dollars attempting to stay young, and God may call us home tomorrow. It really is as Solomon said, "Vanity of vanities, all is vanity." Vanity is a trap that deters our eyes from God and onto ourselves. How is God getting the glory in that?

TODAY'S HOT FLASH:

God first, God only. Forget about the things this world has to offer. Choose the best; choose God. Your service done in Jesus' name will never grow old.

PRAYER:

Lord and Determiner of my time here on earth, help me to keep my eyes and heart focused on You alone. I want the best out of life, and You are it. Amen.

JANUARY 19
READ: PSALM 23

COME REST A WHILE

And he said unto them, Come ye yourselves apart into a desert place, and rest a while: for there were many coming and going, and they had no leisure so much as to eat.

~ Mark 6:31

Fatigue's ever constant company overwhelms many menopausal sufferers. Couple this with insomnia, its frustrating counterpart, and you have a concoction as impractical as fire and water, yet still present. As a pastor's wife, I constantly struggle to live up to other's expectations. Only when my mind refuses to function and my body sputters to a stop like a car void of gas do I take time to rest.

Those who have not experienced menopause cannot understand the full implications of it. It is known as the "old lady's disease." Compared to most women experiencing their "change," I am not old. My pre-menopausal symptoms began at about thirty-five. My doctor's reaction when I told him I was going through menopause was patronizing at best.

The redeeming factor in all this is that God understands and he bids us to "Come ye yourselves into a desert place, and rest a while." God knows we need a time of quietness by the still waters so our souls (and hormones) can be restored to some semblance of normalcy. Go ahead; lay your weary head on His shoulders and rest a while. Restoration comes in the quiet moments. Don't let anyone rob you of this much needed respite.

TODAY'S HOT FLASH:

If fatigue plagues you, take time to rest. It is in the quietness of the still waters that God's presence is magnified.

PRAYER:

Lord, Creator of who I am, teach me to unashamedly take the rest needed. Help my family and friends to understand. Amen.

JANUARY 20
READ: PSALM 25

DEFEATED ENEMIES

O my God, I trust in thee: let me not be ashamed, let not mine enemies triumph over me. The troubles of my heart are enlarged: O bring thou me out of my distress.

~ Psalm 25:2, 17

The most formidable enemy (other than Satan) I've ever battled is my out-of-control emotions. I am ashamed when I think of the times my temper, tears, and sarcasm have blasted forth without restraint. When this happens, I am allowing the sin of my flesh to usurp control that rightfully belongs to the Holy Spirit.

The greatest power in the universe resides within me, and I allow Him to get kicked around by a few stray hormones with nothing better to do than cause havoc. The Holy Spirit is all-powerful, but truly I am weak. I am like a baby fresh from the womb, having no control over his newly discovered emotions.

In our weakness we are made strong when we cry out to the Lord as David did. "Let not mine enemies triumph over me. The troubles of my heart are enlarged; bring me out of my distress."

Our heavenly Father can't resist responding to the agonizing cries of His beloved children. Deliverance is always sure.

TODAY'S HOT FLASH:

Every new day requires a new prayer for help. He is faithful and will hear your cry. Relief is just a prayer away.

PRAYER:

O Lord, my strength and my Redeemer, I am so weak. Thank You that You are strong. Fill me with Your Spirit that I may ward off the onslaught of Satan and the reactions of my sinful flesh. Amen.

JANUARY 21

READ: LUKE 14:28-35

UNDERSTAND AND PREPARE

Or what king, going to make war against another king, sitteth not down first, and consulteth whether he be able to with ten thousand to meet him that cometh against him with twenty thousand?

~ Luke 14:31

What is a battle but two opposing sides fighting against each other to gain the victory? Isn't that what our emotional struggles consist of? Spirit warring against flesh? As a king wouldn't go into battle without first determining his plan of action, neither should we. God, in His Word, has established His principles for preparation. Victory is possible if we seek to understand what menopause and raging hormones are all about. Once we educate ourselves, we must then prepare for the coming onslaught.

In preparation for war, the king seeks wise counsel. Often this counsel is made up of more than one person, each specializing in specific areas. In preparation for menopause, the process is the same.

First, it is important to seek out a good doctor. One who specializes in menopause and its related issues. Don't settle for a doctor who says, "You're getting older. Deal with it." We know our bodies, and we are the best qualified to know when help is needed.

Second, seek friendships with other women who are experiencing or have experienced menopause. No one else will understand like they do. Spend time together, sharing struggles and victories.

Finally, saturate yourself in God's Word and prayer. Preparation in these three areas will make the climb a little less treacherous.

TODAY'S HOT FLASH:

It is not weakness to seek help; it is wisdom in action. Become passionate about helping other women while remaining godly in the process.

PRAYER:

Dear Lord, help me to swallow my pride and talk to doctors and other women about my needs. Keep me focused on Jesus so I can help others stay focused on Him as well.

JANUARY 22
READ: ISAIAH 26:1–15

SECRET TO STAYING YOUNG

Thou wilt keep him in perfect peace, whose mind is stayed on thee: because he trusteth in thee.

~ Isaiah 26:3

Many women have a tendency to draw physical comparisons. If someone our age looks younger than we do, we become depressed and experience bouts of jealousy. If they look older (have a few more wrinkles or more gray hair), we silently rejoice in their misfortune. How women age is as different as each person's unique personality.

Our inescapable genes play a part in how we look, but culture, atmosphere, care, and spiritual attitude play a much larger role. Women who have learned to cast all their cares on Christ experience a peace that is evident physically and emotionally. They are secure in their identity as children of God, and they allow Him to carry the burdens that would otherwise drag them down.

True peace deflects worry lines and fights off debilitating health problems such as stomach ailments, headaches, and depression. It allows women to remain calm in stressful situations and to laugh at the small stuff. How do we obtain this perfect peace? "Thou wilt keep him in perfect peace whose mind is stayed on thee (God)." When we forfeit our concerns to God, life suddenly becomes bearable—more than bearable, a downright joy to live.

TODAY'S HOT FLASH:

With our minds focused on the Lord, we won't notice if a little gray has crept in around the roots. We will be too busy living life more abundantly in perfect peace.

PRAYER:

Father of peace, forgive me for my preoccupation with staying young. Help me to keep my mind stayed on You that I may experience Your perfect peace. Amen.

JANUARY 23

READ: PHILIPPIANS 4:1-8

SWEET MOMENTS

Finally brethren, whatsoever things are true, whatsoever things are honest, whatsoever things are just, whatsoever things are pure, whatsoever things are lovely, whatsoever things are of good report; if there be any virtue, and if there be any praise, think on these things.

~ Philippians 4:8

How do we keep our negative thoughts from consuming us? Philippians 4:8 is our one size fits all answer. Write it down, hang it up, type it out, read it when you feel like it . . . and when you don't. In this wonderful verse, we find the key to enjoying the sweet moments of every day. Even when life's pressures pursue, sweet moments are waiting to be found.

If you're having a fuzzy brain day, find your sweet moments in quiet music and a time of relaxation. If people are driving you crazy, find your sweet moments in a hot bubble bath with an uplifting book of encouragement. Feeling lonely and blue? Find praise in the ones you love by relaxing in a comfy chair and browsing lazily through the photo albums. Think of the sweet thing someone did for you the other day—just because. There are always good and lovely things to think about.

Think on things that are true and real. Don't weigh your mind down with the "what if's" and the "if only's." They are not true and real for today. You are a child of God—loved, forgiven, adopted, protected—these things are true and real. Think on these for a while.

TODAY'S HOT FLASH:

What makes your life complete? Think on these things and you will learn to find the sweet moments of each and every day.

PRAYER:

Wonderful Father, help me dwell on things that are good, lovely and pure. Thank You that You are always faithful even when I am not. That is the sweetest thing of all. Amen.

JANUARY 24
READ: PSALM 139:14-24

EMBRACE THIS TIME, DON'T FEAR IT

I will praise thee; for I am fearfully and wonderfully made; marvelous are thy works; and that my soul knoweth right well.

~ Psalm 139:14

We may feel like our minds are in the throes of Alzheimer's and our bodies have sunk to new levels, but in all of this it is a comforting reminder that we are "fearfully and wonderfully made, and marvelous are his works."

"Ugh," you say. "That doesn't describe me. I've gained ten pounds, I can't remember a thing, and I am as cranky as the wicked witch of the east. God's 'works' don't seem so marvelous right now!" Isn't it great that the truth of this verse is not determined by how we feel?

Aging is inevitable, unchangeable, and universal. We can waste precious time fretting about it, or we can embrace this God-given gift of time with genuine fervor. What have you always wanted to do but never dared? Go ahead and take the plunge. Now is the time to become the person you've always wanted to be. There's power in maturity. A glorious and exciting time awaits you, if you dare. God has given you a gift; don't throw it away with miserable thoughts and actions. Run, run, run, and then take a giant leap for womanhood. It only gets better; it's all a matter of the mind!

TODAY'S HOT FLASH:

The most exciting part of life has yet to be lived. What are you waiting for? Have at it, sister!

PRAYER:

Gracious heavenly Father, I am ready to experience the greatest time in my life. Take away my fear; make me bold for You. Take me places I've never been. Bless this time in my life. Amen.

JANUARY 25
READ: JUDGES 4:1-11

JUST ANOTHER CHALLENGE

And she said, I will surely go with thee: notwithstanding the journey that thou takest shall not be for thine honour; for the Lord shall sell Sisera into the hand of a woman...

~ Judges 4:9a

Deborah was the fifth of the judges that led the Israelites before the time of the kings. When war against Sisera was inevitable, she sent for Barak, God's chosen military leader. But in all his manliness and bravery, Barak refused to go unless Deborah went with him. She didn't hesitate for a moment; she said, "Surely I will go with thee." It was a task that needed to be done, and if she had to go, so be it.

Deborah is a good role model for women. Faced with a challenge, she didn't back down. You and I are faced with a mighty challenge, and we are involved in another kind of war. Throughout history, women from every station of life have proved their endurance and bravery. Barak (a man) wouldn't go to war unless Deborah (a woman) went with him.

We may not face an army, but menopause is almost as unpredictable and often as harrowing. Like Deborah, we will face the challenge and persevere. Don't shy away from it or be ashamed of it. Learn all you can, seek a doctor's help when necessary, and lean heavily on the Lord. Let the challenge begin!

TODAY'S HOT FLASH:

God will carry us when we need carried, wrap us in the warmth of His arms when we need rest, and never, ever leave us alone.

PRAYER:

Ever-present Father, You have brought this challenge my way, and I know You will never leave me or forsake me. Lift me up; give me Your strength to meet the challenge head on. Amen.

JANUARY 26
READ: 1 CORINTHIANS 10:1–15

DELIVERANCE

There hath no temptation taken you but such as is common to man: but God is faithful, who will not suffer you to be tempted above that ye are able; but will with the temptation also make a way to escape, that ye may be able to bear it.

~ 1 Corinthians 10:13

My self-control problem has gained momentum since the onset of menopause, but that doesn't make God's promise in 1 Corinthians 10:13 any less real. I often remind women during counseling sessions of God's promise to strengthen them when times of temptation strike. To these women who have placed their trust in me, I appear steadfast and sure in my advice.

In my secret corner of the world, when there is no one to advise, no one to convince, and no reason to carry on my perfected façade, I am weak and unsure. Praise God for the reality of God's precious promise. I don't have to sin, I don't have to allow these hormonal uprisings to control me or my life, and dear sister, neither do you.

He will not give us more than we can bear, and He always prepares a way of escape. If we refuse to take it, the blame lies solely on our shoulders.

TODAY'S HOT FLASH:

How do I escape something that is inside me, follows me, and goes wherever I go? By claiming the ever faithful promises of our great and wonderful God and living according to His Word.

PRAYER:

My Great Deliverer, I feel like screaming today. Calm my spirit and please don't let anything unholy escape from my lips. Keep my eyes and heart focused on You so my mind won't wallow in the mires of sin. Amen.

FOR SANITY'S SAKE

JANUARY 27
READ: ACTS 9:1-22

THE "CHANGE"

"Isn't he the man who raised havoc in Jerusalem among those who call on this name? And hasn't he come here to take them as prisoners to the chief priests?" Yet Saul grew more and more powerful and baffled the Jews living in Damascus by proving that Jesus is the Christ.

~ Acts 9:21a–22

Menopause is often referred to as "The Change." That's okay, because that is what it really is, a change in life. Not in and of itself better or worse, just different than it was before. The better or worse is up to us. There are many physical and emotional changes that take place in this phase of life. Our bodies become more demanding of attention, it is harder to keep the weight off, and childbearing years are slipping by. Believe it or not, there is a good side; we often gain a new sense of boldness and confidence in our abilities and in who we are as individuals.

Paul endured a change every bit as challenging. He went from hunting Christians to becoming one. He received the same reaction we get when we do new and crazy things. They asked, "Isn't he the man who raised havoc in Jerusalem among those who call on this [Jesus] name?" His friends tried to kill him, and the Christians feared him. He wasn't about to relinquish his newfound faith; he would boldly and actively prove himself. He "grew more and more powerful," and it happened all because of "The Change."

TODAY'S HOT FLASH:

I decided to become a writer and wrote this book. How is your "Change" going to transform the world for Christ?

PRAYER:

Changeless Father, I will rejoice and thank You for this time of my life. Help me to embrace it with everything You created me to be and go forward boldly without fear. Amen.

JANUARY 28
READ: ACTS 5:12–29

HOT FOR JESUS

Then came one and told them, saying, Behold, the men whom ye put in prison are standing in the temple, and teaching the people.

~ Acts 5:25

The new Christians in the book of Acts were "hot for Jesus." Filled with absolute confidence in their faith, they boldly shared the Good News to everyone. The Holy Spirit had come, and they were free indeed to spread His truth to all who would listen. And listen they did. Thousands of souls accepted Christ and experienced that same burning desire.

We women, as menopause sisters, experience a different kind of burning. We call them hot flashes. One minute goose bumps and chattering teeth overwhelm us, the next we are tempted to strip off anything that can be removed! (I recommend you don't do this.) We are on fire! What is a woman to do with such a frustrating demonstration of "The Change?"

I try to handle this with a good sense of humor. When the sweat starts to pour down my brow, I excitedly proclaim, "I am hot for Jesus!" Those present during my outburst stare at me incredulously and assume I have lost it for good this time.

Don't just say it—live it! This is a great time to become "hot for Jesus!" The hot flashes are inconvenient, but turn them to your advantage and keep the fire burning as you serve the Lord each day.

TODAY'S HOT FLASH:

Learn to laugh at yourself. Make the best of your inconveniences, find humor in them, and get on fire for the Lord!

PRAYER:

Keep me on fire for You, Lord; teach me to find humor in all my circumstances and to use them to serve You in a more fulfilling way. Amen.

JANUARY 29

READ: JEREMIAH 30:1-17

WRITE IT DOWN

Thus speaketh the Lord God of Israel, saying,
Write thee all the words that I have spoken unto thee in a book.

~ Jeremiah 30:2

From the very beginning God used the written word to spread His truth. We have His private love letter to us in the form of the Holy Bible. Throughout Scripture, God instructed His servants to write His Word on door posts, hearts, and scrolls. It is His main way of revealing Himself to His most precious creation.

If God is in it, it is worthy to remember. How do you think this book started? I was struggling with my very extreme symptoms of menopause and started scribbling down my feelings, experiences, and what God was saying to me through His Word about them. It kept me focused, helped me realize I wasn't alone, and gave me incentive to do more. I decided if I was having such a struggle, there must be millions of other women fighting the same battle. Maybe I could help and encourage them to look at the whole process differently—with a sense of excitement instead of a feeling of despair and defeat.

Look at me—in a new phase of my life and with a new career. Who knows what God has planned farther down the road? Write down your experiences. When the time comes, God will use it for His glory.

TODAY'S HOT FLASH:

Every experience is worth writing about. There is nothing you can go through that someone else has not experienced or will not experience some day. Share your struggles and become a source of wisdom to the next person. Write! And make a difference.

PRAYER:

Father, You are great and greatly to be praised. Open my heart to writing my experiences and feelings so I may share them with others. Use it to draw me closer to You. Amen.

JANUARY 30
READ: PROVERBS 31:10-31

THE WISE WOMAN

She openeth her mouth with wisdom; and in her tongue is the law of kindness. She looketh well to the ways of her household, and eateth not the bread of idleness.

~ Proverbs 31:26-27

The wise woman stays focused on her calling, regardless the struggle. She shares her wisdom with the younger women and is a strong tower to those just beginning the journey. She speaks kindness even if nastiness threatens to pour from her lips. She never allows the temptation to bear fruit.

The wise woman looks "well to the ways of her household" even when she doesn't feel like it and fatigue overrides energy. She doesn't stop doing the necessities because she is having a hormonal day. If there is laundry to do, she does it. If there is dinner to cook, she cooks it. If the Sunday school lesson needs studied, she studies. It is never a matter of "how she feels." She determines her actions by the necessity of the job.

A wise woman doesn't become Wonder Woman. She learns to balance the essential with the nonessential. She will not let criticism determine what she does or how she spends her time. She will know what is right for her and what God requires of her; nothing else matters. She walks in peace because she has learned to choose the greater need, and she finds satisfaction in that.

TODAY'S HOT FLASH:

Wise women are in tune with their bodies, families and, most importantly, God. They take what they know—not what they feel—and accomplish the greater need. Are you a wise woman?

PRAYER:

Blessed Father, make me a wise woman. Teach me to look after my household according to their needs. Give me the strength to accomplish all You have for me today. Amen.

JANUARY 31
READ: TITUS 2

TEACH THE YOUNGER WOMEN

Then they can train the younger women to love their husbands and children, to be self-controlled and pure, to be busy at home, to be kind, and to be subject to their husbands, so that no one will malign the word of God.

~ Titus 2:4–5

When my first menopause symptoms hit, I was lambasted. No one told me what to expect or what I was going to experience and feel. I was only thirty-five, and it was the last thing I expected. The dreaded "change" only happened to old ladies; that counted me out, didn't it?

It's a different world today. Menopause is probably the only thing our girls haven't learned about. Titus exhorts the older ladies to teach the younger ladies to be "self-controlled and pure." This gives us a perfect opening to sneak in that which they won't want to talk about but need to know. If it were sex, homosexuality, or STD's, they'd gladly embrace the subject, but not the "M" word. Ugh!

Teach them anyway. Teach them that even if self-control isn't an issue now, it may be down the line when they enter into this new phase of life. Teach them what to look for and how they can offset the inevitable. They will thank you someday, even if it is forty years down the road. But for some, it will be much sooner than that.

TODAY'S HOT FLASH:

In order to teach the younger women, we first have to accept the fact that we are aging. Get over hindering hang-ups. Then go share what you know with those who don't have a clue.

PRAYER:

Lord and Teacher, give me the strength and ability to boldly teach the young women what no other woman is willing to do. Give them the ears to hear and the grace to listen. Amen.

FEBRUARY

FEBRUARY 1

READ: LUKE 6:1–12

CAN'T SLEEP? CAN PRAY!

And it came to pass in those days, that he went out into a mountain to pray, and continued all night in prayer to God.

~ Luke 6:12

If you haven't experienced it yet, you will. That dreaded symptom of menopause called insomnia. It took me a while to realize why I was suffering from it. Before, I had only to lay my head on the pillow and I was in Dreamland. Suddenly, out of nowhere, everything changed. I took over-the-counter sleeping pills, put on soft music, read until I couldn't keep my eyes open, and stayed up late, but to no avail. The minute I settled down to sleep, my eyes popped open.

There were times Jesus couldn't sleep either, but he didn't thrash back and forth praying for sleep to come. He did just the opposite. He went to a quiet place and prayed. Instead of wasting hours in the night, he talked to His Father.

When sleep evades, take time to pray. Pour your heart out to a God who is ready and willing to listen. Pray for the president, vice president, and governor of your state. Pray for a closer walk with Jesus, a revival in your church, your pastor and his family, Iraq, Iran, and victims of natural disasters. God has given you a special opportunity to talk to Him for hours without interruption. Are you going to waste it by feeling sorry for yourself, or grab hold of it and become the prayer warrior you've always told God you wanted to be?

TODAY'S HOT FLASH:

God allows every symptom of menopause for a purpose. Learn what that purpose is, and life as you know it will begin to change.

PRAYER:

Lord, I've always said I wanted to pray more. Remind me, when insomnia strikes, that You have given me an opportunity to spend time with You. Amen.

FEBRUARY 2

READ: RUTH 1:1–5, 4:13–16

RESTORATION

Blessed be the Lord, which hath not left thee this day without a kinsman . . .
And he shall be unto thee a restorer of thy life, and a nourisher of thine old age.

~ Ruth 4:14–15a

With a horrific soul-splitting bang, Naomi faced her wilderness experience: her two sons and her husband dead with no hope of remarriage. She resigned herself to the prospect of a dry and thirsty life. Ruth, her daughter-in-law, had other plans. With faithful abandonment, she declared her loyalty to Naomi.

Naomi had a kinsman named Boaz who owned a field, and she obtained permission for Ruth to glean the remnants after the harvest. Determined to provide for her mother-in-law, Ruth faithfully trudged the fields every day. Boaz' interest was aroused, and it wasn't long before the dreariness of the day turned to jubilation when he asked Ruth to marry him. What joy this brought to Naomi and all who sympathized with her plight. "Blessed be the Lord who hath not left thee this day without a kinsman." Naomi's reprieve had come. Sadness turned to rejoicing.

Our journey through menopause resembles Naomi's tumultuous trek. The long dreary days seem to lag on forever, but how wonderful it is to know that green pastures await us just around the corner.

TODAY'S HOT FLASH:

The probability of years seems like an eternity. But someday we will look back and thank God for the lessons learned as He molded us into mature women.

PRAYER:

Lord, You are my life-sustainer; help me endure these long years with dignity. Lift my heart when the days are dark and cold. Amen.

FEBRUARY 3

READ: EXODUS 15:22-27

THE LOW TIMES

And the people murmured against Moses, saying, What shall we drink?

~ Exodus 15:24

Isn't it amazing how everything that was so perfect yesterday can be so wrong today? The Israelites experienced ups and downs frequently. It wasn't long after dancing for joy because of God's goodness that they began murmuring and complaining over God's lack of attentiveness. "What shall we drink?" they whined. Within a matter of days, the great and mighty miracles dimmed in their memories, and they unabashedly fussed over something trite. Didn't they know that the God who parted the Red Sea would provide water to drink?

God does not give us the luxury of using our hormones as an excuse to murmur and complain (See Philippians 2:14). He expects us to step beyond the temptation of flesh-oriented discontentment and to replace it with God-honoring gratitude and satisfaction.

The lows are inevitable, but godly actions and words are not optional. Bite your tongue, sing a song, leave the room, do whatever it takes to remain holy. God does not give us a free pass just because we are having a hormonal moment.

TODAY'S HOT FLASH:

Christ refrained from lashing out at His persecutors in the midst of His pain and suffering. We should do the same.

PRAYER:

Ever-patient Father, forgive my sinful outbursts. Help me remain in control of my emotions. Give me solitude when it is most needed and rest in time of turmoil. Thank You for Your tender mercies. Amen.

FEBRUARY 4
READ: 1 SAMUEL 2:9-23

BE PATIENT WITH ME, DEAR

Now Hannah, she spake in her heart; only her lips moved, but her voice was not heard: therefore Eli thought she had been drunken. And Eli said unto her, How long wilt thou be drunken: put away thy wine from thee.

~ 1 Samuel 1:13-14

Most men are naïve where women and menopause are concerned—bless their hearts. They don't have a clue what is wrong with their wives, and many don't want to know. Hannah wasn't going through menopause, but she was confronted by a man who had no clue what her problem was. Jumping to conclusions, he assumed she was drunk. "How long wilt thou be drunken?" he asked. Had he taken the time to inquire first, he would have realized Hannah was a heartbroken woman seeking God's favor.

Our husbands are a lot like Eli. Hannah didn't lose her cool; she patiently informed Eli of the truth. Once he understood, his attitude changed. Our husbands need to learn about menopause. They need to learn what the symptoms are, what the remedies are, and how they can help. They need reassurance that every time we cry, it doesn't mean they did something wrong.

Ask his forgiveness when you do attack and follow it with a "please be patient with me, dear; it won't last forever." He will understand. Remember, he loves you.

TODAY'S HOT FLASH:

Your husband wants to understand you. Help him. Buy books, share your struggles, and call on the Holy Spirit's help. You're both in this together.

PRAYER:

Help me to love my husband, Father. Help him to understand and patiently endure. Use this to make us stronger in our relationship. Amen.

FEBRUARY 5

READ: ROMANS 2:1-11

TRUTH OR CONSEQUENCES

But unto them that are contentious, and do not obey the truth, but obey unrighteousness, indignation and wrath, tribulation and anguish, upon every soul of man that doeth evil, of the Jew first and also the Gentile.

~ Romans 2:8-9

I've always considered myself a happy-go-lucky person, easy to get along with, smiling all the time, and not easily offended. But recently that has changed; my husband tells me I scowl in my sleep. I hate to admit it, but I am becoming a contentious woman.

A contentious women disregards God's Word and replaces it with her own distorted truths. When she does this, she invites tribulation and anguish into her life and the lives of all those around her.

Even in the midst of menopause, God expects us to be gracious women. The Holy Spirit's mighty power can strengthen and empower us to win the battle of our emotions if we give Him permission to do so.

Do you really want to become like your crotchety grandmother or the old biddy down the street? Put a stop to the contentious behavior before it defines who you are. You have the Holy Spirit within you; He will divinely shape you into a gracious woman.

TODAY'S HOT FLASH:

If you act contentious, hold on to bitterness, and spew out wrathful words, you will begin to look like the person you don't want to become. Now that's a scary thought!

PRAYER:

Precious Lord, forgive me for being a contentious woman. Give me strength through Your Holy Spirit to overcome the negative emotions of my hormones. I can't do it alone. Amen.

FEBRUARY 6

READ: ACTS 1:1-4, 2:15

WAITING FOR THE WONDERFUL

And, being assembled together with them, commanded them that they should not depart from Jerusalem, but wait for the promise of the Father, which, saith he, ye have heard of me.

~ Acts 1:4

How many times do we jump into things before we are ready or before we understand the full picture? How many times do these rash actions lead only to discouragement or defeat?

In this fast-paced world, we dread red lights, slow drivers, and annoying commercials. Dial-up is replaced with Road Runner, and our TV's can play three shows at once. Waiting with serenity has become a long lost art.

For the menopausal woman who is always anxious, waiting does not rank high on her list of favorite things to do. The seemingly nothingness of what she is accomplishing grates on her nerves and enhances her anxiety.

The disciples were commanded to "not depart and wait for the promises of the Father." Not in case they came, but because they would come, in His good time. God's promises are true for us as well. If we learn to wait on God, we will fly like an eagle, walk and not be wearied and best of all, come to the end of our journey intact and better than before. Patience, my dear friend; God will do great things with you—in His time.

TODAY'S HOT FLASH:

God is not on our time schedule. As we walk with Him, we will accomplish everything He has planned for us to do.

PRAYER:

Oh Lord, You know I don't like waiting. Calm my spirit and help me to relax in Your goodness and perfect grace. Amen.

FEBRUARY 7

READ: EPHESIANS 1:1–24

FLAWED BUT USABLE

In whom we have redemption through his blood,
the forgiveness of sins, according to the riches of his grace.

~ Ephesians 1:7

Joseph was a spoiled brat who flaunted his privileged status in front of his brothers. Jacob was conceited and conniving and didn't care whose toes he stepped on. David was an adulterer and a murderer, and many people died because of his arrogance. We love these Bible characters and hate to hear them talked about so negatively. The truth really does hurt.

Sarah was jealous and uncaring of other people. Abraham too easily found himself in the arms of another woman for the so-called sake of the inheritance. Peter was hot-headed and attempted to do Jesus' bidding in his own flesh.

Why am I bringing up the sordid details of these people? Because in spite of their obvious failures, each one loved and served God. And because we love God, He will use us in spite of our uncontrolled hormonal outbursts.

Some days I wonder if I have blown it for good. But He reassures me I "have redemption through His blood, the forgiveness of sins." If God can take these saints and do great things through them in spite of their failures, He will do it with me and you. After all, they were flesh and blood, just like we are.

TODAY'S HOT FLASH:

God's chosen ones in Scripture were not superhuman or super perfect; they were moldable and willing in spite of their many failings.

PRAYER:

Father, mold me and make me into a usable vessel just as You did Rahab, Sarah, and the hundreds of others You have told us about in Your Word. I am willing. Amen.

FEBRUARY 8
READ: MATTHEW 6:19-24

SOUGHT AFTER TREASURES

But lay up for yourselves treasures in heaven, where neither moth nor rust doth corrupt, and where thieves do not break through nor steal: For where you treasure is, there will your heart be also.

~ Matthew 6:20-21

Peace of mind, a good night's sleep, healthy sexual relations, even temperament, and a slim, trim figure are little more than sought after treasures for women in the throes of menopause. We can only remember the "used to be's," and they come to mind with visual clarity although everything else is unclear in our hormonal fog.

We do our devotions and spend time in prayer and wonder why it doesn't work miracles in our lives. Our symptoms become opportunities to throw blame at God.

God never promised us total healing, absolute mind control, skinny bodies, perfect relationships, and eight hours of sleep. He promised to carry us through the storms and strengthen us for the battles, not erase them from our lives.

Jesus said, "Where your treasure is, there your heart will be also." Many of us find our treasure in this life, which will never satisfy. Focus on things above; it is an attainable and perfect treasure and one you will never lose.

TODAY'S HOT FLASH:

When we are consumed by the struggles we face in these mortal bodies, our work for the kingdom is greatly hindered. Where is your treasure? Wherever it is, there your heart is also.

PRAYER:

Lord, Keeper of my treasures, I am so consumed with battling these symptoms that I am neglecting my time with You. Forgive me. Amen.

FOR SANITY'S SAKE
FEBRUARY 9
READ: ROMANS 8:28-39

WHO AMONG US?

Who shall separate us from the love of Christ? Shall tribulation, or distress, or persecution, or famine, or nakedness, or peril, or sword?

~ Romans 8:35

Can the most powerful earthquake or death-gripping tsunami keep us from receiving Christ's love? Persecutors attempt to force us to deny our God by torturing us, starving us, depriving us of our necessities, but they cannot keep Christ's love from us.

Even today, as men and women are killed for Christ's sake, little do their tormentors know that they are catapulting them directly into the arms of a waiting Savior.

Can the throes of menopause remove Christ's love from us? Migraines, heart palpitations, hot flashes, and aching joints prevail at times. But never do they manage to take His precious gift of grace and mercy from our grip. Hormones may thrust us momentarily into the depths of despair, but His Spirit will win over our flesh, and Christ's love will remain steadfast.

Who among us has lost the love of Christ over wrinkles, gray hair, and occasional irritability? Or who can say, "He has gone and left me" when their behavior has not been as it should be? Through all our fleshly battles, Christ remains true and His love endures forever.

The highest mountain cannot keep His love from us, and the deepest sea can't compare with the depth of His love for us. Isn't Christ's love wonderful?

TODAY'S HOT FLASH:

Absolutely, positively nothing can separate us from the love of Christ. His love is as sure as it is secure. Find comfort in that.

PRAYER:

Precious Father, I just want to thank You and praise You for Your love. You are wonderful and worthy of all glory, honor, and praise. Amen.

FEBRUARY 10
READ: 2 TIMOTHY 1

IN SEARCH OF A SOUND MIND

For God hath not given us the spirit of fear; but of power, and of love, and of sound mind.

~ 2 Timothy 1:7

Sometimes my fuzzy mind makes it impossible to concentrate, and truly my dark days are at their peak when this occurs. As I wait for the blessed clearing to return, my impatience turns to guilt as I dwell on my piles of incomplete work.

When I attempt to use my brain for more than simple and uncomplicated thoughts, confusion sets in, and my brain transforms into a jellified mass. Thank God this doesn't happen all the time, or life would come to a screeching halt.

Imagine what this does for my time with God. Sometimes I sit at my desk with my hands on my forehead, muttering, "Oh God, just help me through today." I realize the self-centeredness in this little prayer but feel useless to say anything different at the time.

In my confusion, it is great to know that through God's Spirit, He has given us the "power of love and a sound mind." God has promised that as we cling to Him, the sound mind will come, and when it matters most, we will be able to stand firm in the wonderful knowledge of Jesus Christ and his blessed faithfulness to His promises.

TODAY'S HOT FLASH:

Do what you are called to do; depend on God to lead you where you need to go. Your clarity of mind will come with obedience.

PRAYER:

My Lord and Shepherd, help me to let Your Spirit guide me when I don't feel like I can make a wise decision. Let me find rest in the comfort of Your love. Amen.

FEBRUARY 11

READ: ROMANS 8:14-27

EXCESSIVE GROANINGS

Likewise the Spirit also helpeth our infirmities: for we know not what we should pray for as we ought: but the Spirit itself maketh intercession for us with groanings which cannot be uttered.

~ Romans 8:26

Through the muddledness and confusion of hormonal imbalances, I often groan to God distorted prayers and misconstrued suppositions. There are times when "God, help me" is the only rational request I can lift to the Father.

Whether it was because of hormonal fuzziness, a broken heart, sickness, or exhaustion, most of us have felt depleted and unable to utter a word to God.

God isn't tallying our prayers. He isn't pointing an accusing finger and reprimanding us for imperfect communication. Our guilt for missed or sometimes senseless prayer is misplaced guilt; it has nothing to do with God.

Enter in the precious Holy Spirit. When our prayers are stifled, He is "making intercession for us with groanings which cannot be uttered." He knows us intimately and is taking the liberty to translate our hurt, pain, confusion, and inadequacy into perfect petitions. Where would we be without divine intercession?

TODAY'S HOT FLASH:

God hears our cries even when we can't utter a word. The Holy Spirit knows us intimately, and He sends our petitions to a loving Father in spite of us.

PRAYER:

Thank You, God, for the intercession of Your Holy Spirit. It is wonderful to know my true needs and desires are delivered to You perfectly and unhindered by my sin. Amen.

FEBRUARY 12
READ: JOHN 12:3A

PRIZED POSSESSION

Then took Mary a pound of spikenard, very costly, and anointed the feet of Jesus.
~ John 12:3a

A few years ago, I spouted youthful looks, physical ability, brain smarts, and independence as my most prized possessions. It took my four-year-old grandson to remind me of my priorities and encourage me to refocus my thoughts.

When he showed up for Sunday school with a gallon size bag of change, I questioned him as to what he was going to do with it.

"Give it to Jesus," he proudly stated.

"All of it?" I asked.

"All of it!" He determinedly proclaimed.

I was reminded of another person who gave her all. Mary Magdalene came to Jesus with her most prized possession, a bottle of expensive perfume. Out of her love, she offered it as a sacrifice at the altar of Jesus' feet.

The things I prized most were quickly fading away, and I was powerless to stop it. With total abandonment, I decided to offer everything I am, wrinkles and all, to Jesus Christ. He alone is my prized possession. Who or what is yours?

TODAY'S HOT FLASH:

What prized possession do you need to offer at the altar of Jesus' feet?

PRAYER:

Most Precious Savior, help me to always remember that there is no other prize greater than You. Teach me to cherish You for the worthy King that You are. Amen.

FOR SANITY'S SAKE

FEBRUARY 13

READ: MATTHEW 5:21-26

TAKE TIME TO MAKE IT RIGHT

Therefore if thou bring thy gift to the altar, and there rememberest that thy brother hath ought against thee; Leave there thy gift before the altar, and go thy way; first be reconciled to thy brother, and then come and offer thy gift.

~ Matthew 5:23-24

As I get older, I can't help but think about all the friends and family members I haven't seen in years. My mind wanders to my sister who lives in Colorado and my brother in Florida. Different belief systems and stormy relationships in our youth have kept us apart. Suddenly, I have a desire to reconnect.

Time has a way of mending old wounds and forcing us to put our differences behind us. I began searching for ways to connect with them without being overbearing and self-righteous—one of their claims from my immature Christian years.

Reminiscing reintroduces us to the tucked away offenses we have pushed far into the dark corners of our minds. Jesus said, "If you enter your place of worship and, about to make an offering, you suddenly remember a grudge a friend has against you, abandon your offering, leave immediately, go to this friend and make things right. Then and only then, come back and work things out with God" (Matthew 5:23-24, The Message). Who is it you need to make amends with? Make it right today; tomorrow may be too late.

TODAY'S HOT FLASH:

Get things right before it is too late. You don't know when your last tomorrow will be, or for that matter, when theirs will be either.

PRAYER:

My God, reveal to me any person I have wronged, not just recently, but in my past as well. I want to make things right. Give me the boldness to do what You ask me to do. Amen.

FEBRUARY 14
READ JOHN 6:30–40

JUST AS YOU ARE

All that the Father giveth to me shall come to me; and him that cometh to me I will in no wise cast out.

~ John 6:37

Charlotte Elliott struggled with bitterness in her life and although convicted to come to the Savior, she was convinced she must wait until she made things right in her life. A minister by the name of Dr. Caesar Malan of Switzerland came to visit her while she was gravely ill; he asked her if she had peace with God. This angered her. But a few days later she called to apologize and said she would like to become a Christian after taking care of some things in her life. The minister assured her she could "come just as you are," and that is exactly what she did.

It wasn't until fourteen years later that she wrote the beautiful encouraging song, *Just As I Am*. This song comforts the troubled hormonal soul as well; pay close attention to the third verse. "Just as I am, tho' tossed about. With many a conflict, many a doubt, fightings within, and fears without, O Lamb of God, I come."

What a perfect illustration of the turmoil experienced by menopausal women. Bring the conflicts, doubts, restless fighting and fears, and lay them at the feet of Jesus for He "wilt welcome, pardon, cleanse, relieve." This wonderful song fits every circumstance. Claim it, sing it, and believe it today.

TODAY'S HOT FLASH:

In every circumstance, during every tumultuous time, Jesus is standing with arms open wide. Run to Him and find the relief you need for today.

PRAYER:

Thank you, Lord, for Charlotte Elliot and the wonderful song You impressed upon her heart. May it continue to soothe souls for generations and may it soothe mine for today. Amen.

FEBRUARY 15

READ: GENESIS 8:15–22; 9:1

SILENT AND STRONG

And Noah went forth, and his sons, and his wife, and his sons' wives with him.

~ Genesis 8:18

Not much is said about Noah's wife. So we must assume that she plays the part of his helpmeet, silently offering support and encouragement without need for recognition. I envision her as having the grace and poise of a queen and the humbleness and submission of a godly woman.

Noah was 600 years old when he entered the ark. When God commanded Noah to build an ark, we hear of no spousal opposition. With endurance she withstood the mean words and gawking eyes. With dignity she stood up to those who thought her husband was insane and proclaimed her belief in his God. She trusted Noah, and therefore, she followed him in his endeavors.

Any man in the ministry knows how hard it is to minister with a wife who does not share his love for service. Noah was able to accomplish his task because he truly had a soul mate. She labored with him while he built the ark, while on the ark, and after the ark landed on Mount Ararat.

Yes, Noah's wife was a woman of poise, grace, humility, and submission. Sculpted through years of hardships and trials, but also by her love for her husband and belief in her God.

TODAY'S HOT FLASH:

Through our years of menopausal hardships and trials, God is sculpting us into women of poise, grace, humility, and submission. It will only happen when we decide this is the type of woman we desire to be.

PRAYER:

Almighty God, I want to complete my menopause with dignity and be a far better person than I was when I entered it. Please help me. Amen.

FEBRUARY 16
READ: 2 SAMUEL 11:1-17

BATHSHEBA THE REDEEMED

And David sent and enquired after the woman. And one said, Is not this Bathsheba, the daughter of Eliam, the wife of Uriah the Hittite?

~ 2 Samuel 11:3

Was Bathsheba the innocent victim touted by good Bible scholars? David sent for her, and she came. It doesn't say she begged him not to defile her or that she refused to come. It appears that she came, a willing participant.

The reputation of the king was widely known. He was not unjust or given to evil tendencies. She most likely could have denied the king access to herself without any grave repercussions. But instead, she heeded his lustful call.

Even if she did fear for her life, there is the question of integrity. If she was an honorable woman, she would have said no, regardless the consequence. Death or punishment will not sway a woman of integrity. She failed to the utter core of her being.

We may not have stepped over such boundaries as she did, but if you are like me and in the midst of menopause, your failings often number into the dozens (in one day).

God did not cast Bathsheba aside because of her sin, He fully forgave her. Whatever our sins of the past, we are redeemed by the blood of the Lamb. Completely forgiven!

TODAY'S HOT FLASH:

Bathsheba attained redemption through the blood of Jesus, just as you and I did. What a blessing to know He is the same yesterday, today, and forever.

PRAYER:

Lord and Redeemer, take my many mistakes and outright sins and use them to get me to where You want me to be. Amen.

FEBRUARY 17
READ: JOB 3:1–3

TUMULTUOUS TIMES

Let the day perish wherein I was born, and the night in which it was said, There is a man child conceived.

~ Job 3:3

Granted, our plight is not comparable to the intense agony, grief, and shame that Job experienced. But often we place ourselves in the same category. There are times when the ability to survive another minute seems unbearable. Our head pounds, our heart races, our senses are magnified, and irritability reigns supreme. It is during these tumultuous times that we murmur that same cry, "Let the day perish wherein I was born," commonly said, "I wish I was never born."

In comparison to Job's suffering, my problems are trite, my symptoms bearable, and my discomfort trivial at best. But in moments of weakness, I am tempted to feel used and abused and to wallow in my self-pity.

Life may rain showers of moodiness on my head, trip me up with anxious moments, and topple me with headaches at inopportune times, but daily blessings surround me as I confront every obstacle. When compared to Job, the words from my lips should unequivocally be "This is the day that the Lord hath made, I will rejoice and be glad in it."

TODAY'S HOT FLASH:

Make it a practice to rejoice out loud even if the emotions aren't there. The right attitude will come with the right action.

PRAYER:

Lord, You are my present help in times of trouble. Help me to find You in all that comes my way. I know You are always with me. Teach me to rejoice in Your faithfulness. Amen.

FEBRUARY 18
READ: ECCLESIASTES 1:1–11

THERE'S SOMETHING FAMILIAR ABOUT THIS

The thing that hath been, it is that which shall be; and that which is done is that which shall be done: and there is no new thing under the sun.

~ Ecclesiastes 1:9

Intense hormonal surges are déjà vu to most women. As teenagers and as pregnant women, we suffered from hormonal imbalances, pimples, irritability, bloating, and weight gain. With the familiarity of the situation, why do we react so differently? The previous episodes represented significant but positive changes in our lives—adulthood and motherhood—two very important and much yearned for events in every woman's life. Menopause is different. It forces us to face the reality of old age. Our immortality suddenly looms over us with a newfound realization.

For those with no hope, the future is scary and uncertain. But for those of us who have that precious hope in Jesus Christ, it represents adventurous times as we work toward the end of our journey here on earth. Don't lose steam; forge forward with renewed momentum. With that blessed hope ever before us, living for the Lord becomes an exciting adventure.

Solomon commented that there is nothing new under the sun. The hormonal surges are old hat; what comes next is up to us.

TODAY'S HOT FLASH:

It is in the perspective of what happens next that women get caught up in despair. Don't be afraid; you have nothing to lose and everything to gain.

PRAYER:

Dear Lord, help me to realize that this is the beginning of something new and wonderful. Open my eyes to where You are leading. Renew my passion for life. Amen.

FOR SANITY'S SAKE

FEBRUARY 19

READ: 1 CORINTHIANS 2

STAND FOR THE RIGHT CAUSE

For I determined not to know anything among you, save Jesus Christ, and him crucified.

~ 1 Corinthians 2:2

The front page of our local newspaper was recently adorned with pictures of two well-known movie stars and two popular politicians. They were posed in a setting of a lush green forest, with the intentions of making a bold political statement.

Three of the four were over fifty. Why are they taking a stand now? Why not twenty years ago? Interestingly, something happens to men and women when they are faced with their own immortality. They desire to make a difference, to leave a lasting imprint, so they embrace a cause.

I respect their desire to do a good thing. How sad that it will all come to naught. As Christian women facing our sunset years, it is imperative we choose the right cause.

Paul said, "I determined not to know anything among you, save Jesus Christ." Jesus was Paul's cause, and He is to be ours as well. We can get so focused on good things that the best thing is left undone and unspoken.

Let someone else save the whales and the rain forest. We have a more important calling. His name is Jesus! Don't choose the good or the better—choose the best! Choose Christ!

TODAY'S HOT FLASH:

The greatest cause of all is to bring a lost world the Good News. Jesus Christ loves them and died for them. If they grasp this, all the rest will fall into place.

PRAYER:

Loving Father, in the remaining years of my life, let me focus on the greatest of all things—sharing Your Son Jesus to a lost and dying world. Amen.

FEBRUARY 20
READ: ROMANS 14:13-23

SOMEBODY'S ALWAYS WATCHING

Let us not therefore judge one another any more: but judge this rather; that no man put a stumbling block or an occasion to fall in his brother's way.

~ Romans 14:13

I have five children between the ages of twenty-six and forty-four, as well as three children between the ages of six and ten. I also have three daughters-in-law, two sons-in-law, and fourteen grandchildren. I can't forget my mother, father, step-mother, and numerous nieces, nephews, aunts, and uncles. Add to that a congregation of approximately one hundred people and an entire community that we minister to. What's my point? Somebody is always watching.

Every word and deed we say or do is carefully analyzed by the most important people in our lives. It is a daunting but necessary task to keep ourselves under control during these menopausal years, but it's one God has entrusted us with. He also has privileged us with the duty of teaching the younger women. I pray we do not disappoint Him.

TODAY'S HOT FLASH:
A major slip up in our behavior can have drastic effects on the very ones we love the most.

PRAYER:
Gracious Father, remind me often of the people who are watching me. I do not want to become a stumbling block to anyone, especially those I love. Amen.

FEBRUARY 21

READ: MARK 15:6–15

CHOOSE WHAT IS RIGHT

But the chief priests moved the people, that he [Pilate] should release Barabbas unto them.

~ Mark 15:11

In the midst of a growing and deliberately fanned passion, the people of Jerusalem turned their backs on the Truth and joined in the frenzy as they cried "Crucify Him." They were so determined to see this man die that they risked the safety of their families by allowing a murderer to go free in place of an innocent man.

It is easy to succumb to the seductive wiles of passion. Betty, in the midst of her "change," allowed her passion for something new and different to destroy her marriage. Her consuming, negative thoughts betrayed the very man she had promised to love forever. In her passionate desire for a more exciting life, she divorced him.

Just like the people who condemned Jesus, Betty allowed something terrible to happen because she followed her heart instead of the truth of God's Word.

When we are in a highly emotional and irritated state of mind caused by the effects of menopause, we need to be on the alert for Satan's persuasive arguments.

Make a commitment now to remain true to God's Word no matter how you feel. God will honor your efforts and peace will once again be restored.

TODAY'S HOT FLASH:

Don't let your emotions win the sin battle. Stay true to God's Word. The right feelings will come with the right actions.

PRAYER:

Righteous Father, help me to react toward others in the manner that is glorifying to You. Help me to be obedient to You in all things. Amen.

FEBRUARY 22

READ: EPHESIANS 1:1-11

MY PLACE IN THIS WORLD

Having predestinated us unto the adoption of children by Jesus Christ to himself, according to the good pleasure of his will.

~ Ephesians 1:5

With harsh reality, menopause catapulted me into midlife, but deep within there still remains an unsevered connection to the child I used to be. My mind and heart still cling to that young girl desperately trying to find her place in this, big, cold world. Because this child part of me still exists, I find it hard to look to the future as an older woman.

There is a part of me that is still searching for the why's of my existence. The significance of who I am. The importance of what I do. Theologically, I know the answers: I am here to serve God, to worship God, and to exist for His pleasure. I understand that, so why do I continue to yearn for more concrete answers? Will I accomplish God's will for my life? Have I lived up to God's expectations? Will I disappoint my Almighty Father? These are only some of the questions that plague me as I approach my golden years.

Are you still that little girl searching for your place in this world? Branch out and grasp your faith with a newfound fervor. When you do make it to the end, God will reveal the true picture of who you are and what you did for Him during your years on this earth. Listen and follow. He knows all the answers even when you don't.

TODAY'S HOT FLASH:

Give control of your life to God; the exact details are not important. Obedience in your daily walk is imperative.

PRAYER:

Wonderful Father, keep my inner little-girl eyes on You. You are the only One who will never misguide. Teach me to trust in You with all my heart. Amen.

FOR SANITY'S SAKE

FEBRUARY 23

READ 1 THESSALONIANS 5:8–24

PRAY WITHOUT CEASING

Pray without ceasing.

~ 1 Thessalonians 5:17

Continue in prayer...

~ Colossians 4:2a

Praying always with all the prayer and supplication in the Spirit...

~ Ephesians 6:18a

Enlightenment has finally arrived. I have grasped the meaning of "Pray without ceasing."

"Lord, don't let me say something stupid."

"Lord, don't let my stomach act up while I'm up front singing."

"Lord, one night without hot flashes would be nice."

"Lord, don't let me be irritable with my husband."

"Lord, I'm so fat and ugly; why do you love me?"

"Lord, I wish he'd shut up—forgive me for thinking that, Lord."

"Oh, Lord, I am a needy person."

"Lord, Help!"

Don't deny it. I know you are there too. If you truly have a relationship with Jesus Christ, He becomes the shoulder you lean on, the person you complain to, the one you curl up with on a dreary February day. God has changed me from a fifteen-minute habitual prayer to a twenty-four/seven beseecher. I guess He knows what He is doing after all.

TODAY'S HOT FLASH:

God may allow difficult times in our lives because it is the only way He can get us to draw near to Him. How much closer can you get than twenty-four/seven?

PRAYER:

It's me again, Lord, asking for a measure of Your perfect grace and wonderful mercy. Wrap Your arms around me and help me make it through today. Amen.

FEBRUARY 24
READ: EPHESIANS 6:18–24

SHARE YOUR TROUBLES

But that ye also may know my affairs, and how I do, Tychicus, a beloved brother and faithful minister in the Lord, shall make known to you all things.

~ Ephesians 6:21

Many women hide themselves inside a tiny emotional cubicle during their menopausal years, fearing the worst of their symptoms, afraid to seek help or guidance. A recent story I read told of a woman who hung herself because her menopausal symptoms became unbearable. Had she sought out help or talked to a friend, she might have made a different choice.

Don't harbor your fears deep inside. They may culminate someday to a horrendous ending or send you spiraling into a long, lonely menopausal existence. Millions of women walk this same path. Look around: in your church, your grocery store, movie theaters, and job locations, everywhere you turn, there are women silently suffering. Reach out and touch a menopausal companion with understanding hands. You may be the one who saves her from spiraling over the hormonal edge and falling into a state of miserable existence.

TODAY'S HOT FLASH:

Everybody needs somebody sometime. It is only the proud or scared person who is afraid to admit it.

PRAYER:

Healing Father, lead me to someone today who needs a friend. Help me to swallow my pride and share my emotions and needs to other godly women. Amen.

FEBRUARY 25

READ: PSALM 16

LINED WITH WISDOM

The lines are fallen unto me in pleasant places; yea, I have a goodly heritage.

~ Psalm 16:6

Okay, so maybe it's not talking about my wrinkles, but that was my first thought when I read this verse. To me, wrinkles are to be shunned, and no place would be a good place for their appearance. Someone once told me they can tell how old a woman is by the wrinkles in her neck; I am now an obsessive neck checker. I count the creases on my brow and compare them to other women my age. "Hers are more pronounced than mine. O yes! I look younger than her." This confession of mine reveals the foolishness that still lingers within me.

Women who have soared past this obsession of youth deserve our admiration. They have learned the true meaning of contentment: an intimate relationship with Jesus Christ. In them true beauty is found. The confidence they radiate can't be compared to any façade of beauty touted by the media today. When others need advice, she is the one they come to. She recognizes her lines as a "goodly heritage" and is not ashamed of her age.

Wrinkles are not shameful reminders of old age; they are well-earned medals of valor for life lived and wisdom gained. Are you counting the lines on your face? Think of every line as a lesson learned and another step closer to God.

TODAY'S HOT FLASH:

Life is not about us! It is about Jesus who gave His life for our obsessions and fleshly lusts. Transfer your desires to Him. These fleshly shells are not worth the stress.

PRAYER:

My Lord and my God, I am sorry that I obsess so much about aging. Teach me to turn that obsession onto Your Son Jesus. He deserves it all. Amen.

FEBRUARY 26
READ: 1 TIMOTHY 4

A YOUTHFUL AND EXPERIENCED EXAMPLE

Let no man despise thy youth; but be thou an example of the believers, in word, in conversation, in charity, in spirit, in faith, in purity.

~ 1 Timothy 4:12

Paul exhorted Timothy to stand firm in his teaching. Often when a younger person is blessed with wisdom beyond their years, those who are older stubbornly refuse to accept what they have to say.

I get that reaction when I tell other women I am writing a devotional for women struggling through menopause. They look at me with mouth agape and ask how I could ever know about such things.

My menopausal symptoms surfaced around the age of thirty-five; I am now fifty-two, but for about ten years, menopause ballooned to monumental proportions. Believe me; I knew what I was talking about, regardless of what the "older" women thought.

Timothy didn't allow the reaction of other people to dissuade him from following God's calling, and with sheer determination, he persevered.

When God gives you a message to share, don't hesitate. Many will decide that you are not the one to deliver it. But if you are called, people will listen, and God will be glorified in your weakness. Stand up and be heard.

TODAY'S HOT FLASH:

There will always be the "no way" crowd, but you're not doing it for them. It is for God alone that we go boldly forth in whatever we have been called to do. Nobody can take that away.

PRAYER:

Heavenly Father, give me the wisdom of an older woman, that I may earn their respect and trust by my actions and words. May they see You working through me. Amen.

FOR SANITY'S SAKE

FEBRUARY 27

READ: LUKE 21:25–34

KEEP ALERT!

And take heed to yourselves, lest at any time your hearts be overcharged with surfeiting, and drunkenness, and cares of this life, and so that day come upon you unawares.

~ Luke 21:34

Samantha cut her hair and dyed it pink. Jackie left her husband for a younger man. Debbie started drinking again after twenty years of sobriety, and Linda surfed the Internet for "harmless" chats.

Menopausal women have been known to do strange things. Samantha, Jackie, Debbie, and Linda were active members of their church; when confronted, they blamed it on their inability to control their emotions.

God is not mocked; these women will reap just rewards for their actions. A hormonal imbalance is never a free pass to sin. A woman's ability to remain holy in the toughest of times is determined by her personal relationship with Jesus Christ. Her love for Christ and her desire to spend eternity with Him is her motivation for remaining holy in the midst of temptation.

Jesus said "take heed." No one knows the day or the hour of His return. What a horrific surprise if Christ returns while we are reveling in the lusts of the world. Will it be worth it when it is all said and done?

TODAY'S HOT FLASH:

Excuses do not fly with a Holy God. With the Holy Spirit's help, we can remain godly. It won't be easy, but nothing worthwhile ever is.

PRAYER:

Lord, help me say no to the sinful pleasures Satan thrusts before my eyes. Put Your loving arms around me and protect me from evil. Amen.

FEBRUARY 28

READ: 2 CORINTHIANS 1:1–11

COMFORTING OTHERS

Who comforteth us in all our tribulation, that we may be able to comfort them which are in any trouble, by the comfort wherewith we ourselves are comforted of God.

~ 2 Corinthians 1:4

Menopausal women often suffer the dreary Februarys even in the middle of hot summer days. While others are finding pleasure in the daffodils and daisies, the hormonally challenged are often trapped in a deep pool of depression that won't allow them to see the flowers for the dreariness of the soul. The brightness is hidden for the clouds that are in the way.

This midlife trauma is not a cruel joke set upon us by an all-powerful God. It is, like so many other trials in life, a training session. The experience we gain as we walk this stormy path will give us the wisdom needed to help other mid-lifers stay the course. Through our insight and hands-on experience, we can help them bypass the dangerous detours Satan has prepared to trip them up.

Only those who have walked the winding path are qualified to lead others down it. No one else can empathize with the emotional, physical, and spiritual turmoil that threatens to drive the hormonally challenged woman temporarily insane.

We suffer so we can someday "comfort them which are in any trouble." We don't have to wait until we reach the finish line. Every day affords us new knowledge. Use it to help the menopausal needy as they strive to survive one hormonal day at a time.

TODAY'S HOT FLASH:

Find a fellow menopausee and offer her hope. Together you can tread the course and gain insight and friendship that can only be shared by those suffering the same plight.

PRAYER:

Lord, don't let me waste my experience. Bring someone who needs my help my way. We can climb the mountain together and in one accord cross that blessed finish line. Amen.

FEBRUARY 29

READ: ISAIAH 43:18–19, 21

DWELLING ON MEANS FRETTING OVER

Behold, I will do a new thing; now it shall spring forth...
~ Isaiah 43:19a

I like new clothes, new adventures, and even new and intriguing ice cream flavors. But when God said, "Behold, I will do a new thing," adopting three small children was the farthest thing from my mind. Who would have ever guessed?

Truly, the former things have passed. New things like lack of sleep, noise (lots of it), TV dinners, family vacations, and disorganization appeared almost instantly.

Why did I give up calm for chaotic? Peace for pandemonium? Romance for regularity? The answer is simple: God asked, so I answered. What was I supposed to say? No? To Almighty God? I don't think so!

Your new thing may not be adopting children, but it will most definitely be something every bit as challenging. I doubt it will be what you have your heart set on. God loves to take us outside our comfort zone. Your only job is to say, "Yes, Lord." Trust Him to take care of the details.

You are at a turning point in your life. It is a place of new beginnings—new blessings. Don't close your heart to God. His plan for you is beyond your wildest imaginations.

TODAY'S HOT FLASH:

To reject God's leading is to refuse His best—and with it untold blessings.

PRAYER:

Master of my life, Your plans for me are not those which I would have chosen—nonetheless, I will follow. Amen.

MARCH

MARCH 1

READ: PSALM 117–118:1

PRAISE HIM FOR THE CALM

O praise the Lord, all ye nations: praise him, all ye people..

~ Psalm 117:1

I woke up this morning with no major events on my calendar, no kids to babysit, and no place to go; it is my day to do whatever I want. I could scrutinize my house and fret over all the work that needs to be done, but I refuse to fall to the temptation. God has given me a day of calm amid the storms of life as a reminder of His love for me. I am not going to waste a second!

Because He offers me this time of refreshing, I will praise Him. When I think I can't take anymore, He calms my restless heart; therefore, I will praise Him. Because He knows my need before I do, I will exalt His holy name.

Maybe you feel you need that precious calm in your life. You have been told countless times that God never gives us more than we can handle, but you are beginning to wonder. Don't fret, my friend. My God is your God too; He is your Father; He is your ever-present help in time of trouble, and He will deliver you into the calming springs just when you need it most. Because this is true, you too can praise Him. You can exalt His name. He sees your need and meets it in His perfect way "for his mercy endureth for ever."

TODAY'S HOT FLASH:

Because His mercy endures forever, He will reach down and pluck you out of the storm just when you need it most. For that reason you can praise Him for the calm. It will come.

PRAYER:

Dear Father, my Rescuer from the storms of life, I thank You for the calm that replenishes me and gives me strength to make it through the hectic times. Amen.

MARCH 2
READ: ESTHER 4

FOR SUCH A TIME AS THIS

For if thou altogether holdest thy peace at this time, then shall there enlargement and deliverance arise to the Jews from another place, but thou and thy father's house shall be destroyed: and who knoweth whether thou art come to the kingdom for such a time as this?

~ Esther 4:14

Esther uncovered a plot of murderous treachery against her people. Their only chance of survival was for her to enlighten the king as to the source of this diabolical plan. After all, she was queen; his last queen was exiled for refusing to dance in front of his drunken friends. He could exile her, or worse, have her killed. She feared her husband.

Her Uncle Mordecai's wisdom encouraged her. "How do you know that you were not put in this position for such a time as this?" He asked her. Esther was young, but she boldly faced possible death for her people, and God blessed her obedience.

You may not be so young, but your relevance is every bit as important as Esther's. God has strategically placed you where you are for a purpose. I don't know his plan for you, but be assured; there is someone who needs you desperately. Maybe it is a grandchild, a co-worker, a stressed-out mother, a lost soul seeking hope. Whatever His purpose, you were put in their lives "for such a time as this," and only you can make the difference.

TODAY'S HOT FLASH:

God doesn't make mistakes. Where you are right now is where you are supposed to be. You may be the missing link that God uses to bring someone to Jesus.

PRAYER:

Lord, lead me to my assignment, whatever or whomever it may be. Don't let me miss out on making a difference in someone's life today. Amen.

MARCH 3

READ: PSALM 107:6

OUR SECURITY BLANKET

Then they cried unto the Lord in their trouble, and he delivered them out of their distresses.

~ Psalm 107:6

My three-year-old grandson strolls around with his dingy, stinky blanket as if the world would topple and life would come to an end if it left his presence. My nose crinkles as I must endure it in order to cuddle him in my arms. To him, his blankey is what keeps him safe; it keeps him warm, and as long as he has it in his possession, all is well. Someday he will learn the truth, and his sense of security will be shattered, but for now, he is content.

Jesus is our security blanket. When we need comforting, His loving arms wrap around us. When we need protecting, He redeems us "from the hand of the enemy" (vs.2). As a mother hen gathers her chicks and cuddles them in her protective bosom, so our Savior does for us. When we sin against Him and cower in fear of divine retribution, He calms our spirit and forgives our trespasses, "for his mercy endureth for ever" (vs.1).

What gives you security? Your job? Your money? Your spouse? Your family? Your degree? As we age, these tangible security blankets shrivel up and fade away. Spouses die. Retirement comes. Money dries up. And then what? Wrap yourself in the security blanket of Jesus. He will never die, never retire, and never dry up.

TODAY'S HOT FLASH:

Jesus "satisfies the longing soul, and fills the hungry soul with goodness" (vs. 9). What more does anyone need?

PRAYER:

Father, You alone are my security. Help me to let go of the things I cling to. You have promised to always be there for me. Help me to believe that. Amen.

MARCH 4
PSALM 119:1-16

BUILDING STRONG BARRIERS

With my whole heart have I sought thee: O let me not wander from thy commandments. Thy word have I hid in mine heart, that I might not sin against thee.

~ Psalm 119:10-11

A town between two rivers finds itself in deep water if no dike exists to protect it from the raging floods. Once the rivers break through, it is too late to begin construction of a barrier.

Because of the town's neglect, the waters let loose a fury of destruction. All things not secure are demolished. Things remaining are sullied and forever stained.

So it is with us if we have not resurrected strong barriers against the torrents of emotions and physical changes coming our way. Sin and Satan will rain destruction and mayhem around us and through us. We will end up hurting ourselves and especially the ones we love most.

Now is the time to prepare. The psalmist declares that he has hid God's Word in his heart. Why? So he will not sin against God. When temptation comes, when the enemy strikes, when emotions run wild, it is the Word of God that comes instantly to our mind and provides us with the strong barrier needed to protect us from falling into sin's sway.

It is the precious Word of God that covers us with divine protection. Make memorization a part of your daily devotional routine. Learn one verse a week and see how God uses that to keep your emotions in check and your mind on Christ.

TODAY'S HOT FLASH:

Building strong barriers now through our relationship with Christ, and His Word will protect us from the raging floods of life.

PRAYER:

Lord, You know how hard it is for me to memorize. Fill me with a special measure of Your grace so that I can implant Your words in my heart. Amen.

MARCH 5

READ: ZEPHANIAH 3:14-20

HE REJOICES OVER ME

The Lord thy God in the midst of thee is mighty; he will save, he will rejoice over thee with joy, he will rest in his love, he will joy over thee with singing.

~ Zephaniah 3:17

It is hard to fathom the Lord rejoicing and singing over me. My bad attitude and quick judgmental tongue make me less than desirable company. I can't stand myself when I am like this, and I feel unworthy of anyone's love.

How comforting it is to know that we are unconditionally loved by the Lord our God. He rejoices over us, he sings with joy over us—in other words, we are the source of His happiness. He is a lovestruck suitor wooing His beloved.

My friend, this is exactly what it is—the perfect romance. The perfect lover making holy love to his precious loved ones. Imagine yourself in front of a fireplace on a cold, stormy night. Everything is perfect, for you are resting in the bosom of the One who loves you immensely. His arms surround you, and in His beautiful tenor voice He serenades you with the most beautiful love songs you've ever heard. You wish this time would never end. It doesn't have to. His overflowing love never ceases. His joy over you never disintegrates. His love songs never fade away. You are His. As He rests in His love for you, so rest in that very same love. It will carry you through the worst of times.

TODAY'S HOT FLASH:

Is God romancing a stone? Are you cold and unresponsive to His love? Loosen up; cuddle in His tender arms as He lovingly sings of His love for you.

PRAYER:

Lord, it is hard for me to understand why You love me. Help me to rest in that love and accept it. It is wonderful to be romanced by You. Don't ever stop. Amen.

MARCH 6
READ: REVELATION 19:7–10

FAIRY TALE ROMANCE

Let us be glad and rejoice, and give honour to him; for the marriage of the Lamb is come and his wife hath made herself ready.

~ Revelation 19:7

Once upon a time there was a handsome Prince. This Prince lived with the knowledge that He would one day be King. Not just any King, but the greatest of Kings and He would rule the entire universe. But He didn't want to rule this universe alone, so He chose for Himself the perfect bride. The Prince was so enthralled by this bride that nothing she did could cause Him to toss her aside. He loved her. He cherished her. He groomed her for the day that they would come together. This provided Him with much joy. And so it continues today.

The marriage of the Lamb, which John talks about in Revelation, is our marriage. We are His beloved bride. Your fleshly romance that once burned hot and heavy may be sizzling out, but our romance with Christ will only gain momentum. He whisked down to this earth, sacrificed His life for us (isn't that what we dream our prince will do?), and continues to woo us with His never-ending love.

The greatest news of all to this fairy tale romance is that someday our Prince will come, and when He does, all other semblances of romance will pale in comparison.

TODAY'S HOT FLASH:

Lack of romance in your life got you down? Then look to the only Prince that promised never to leave you or forsake you. His love never diminishes.

PRAYER:

My Prince in shining armor, someday You will come. And when You do, I want to be ready to ride off into the sunset with You. I can't wait, Lord; come quickly. Amen.

MARCH 7

READ: PROVERBS 16:1–9

SHATTERED DREAMS

A man's heart deviseth his way; but the Lord directeth his steps.

~ Proverbs 16:9

Little girls dream big dreams. They dream of being mommies and having husbands like their daddies. As they get older, they dream of Prince Charming on his white steed, rescuing them from a life of misery. In early adulthood their dreams switch to all the great things they can accomplish in life. The perfect career, the perfect husband, perfect children, a beautiful house, and amid all this, they want to change the world. Then life happens and reality comes crashing in.

By midlife, we have experienced myriads of shattered dreams. For some of us, Prince Charming never materialized. Loneliness and solitude have been our only companions. For others, he came but turned into something far removed from a prince. We've lost children through death or rebellion, or never had them because of barrenness. The list of heartaches goes on and on.

Here we are, way beyond the little girl stage, and life has not turned out as we planned. My friend, the problem has always been our unwillingness to discover God's plan for our lives. We have spent forty or fifty years fighting against the goads and as a result bypassed God's best. Stop insisting on your will and give yourself completely to God. Don't you think it is time to place your remaining years in His hands and leave the directing to Him?

TODAY'S HOT FLASH:

We suffer unnecessarily because we leave God out of the planning stage. Haven't we suffered long enough?

PRAYER:

Precious Father, forgive me for leaving You out of my plans. From this day forward, may I seek to do Your desire for my life, not my own. I abandon myself to You. Amen.

MARCH 8
READ: GALATIANS 5:1-15

LITTLE SINS

Stand fast therefore in the liberty wherewith Christ hath made us free, and be not entangled again with the yoke of bondage.

~ Galatians 5:1

I told a lie today. Not a big one. One that won't even really affect anyone, but it affected my conscience. Just when I think I've got my act together and start patting myself on the back, I slip up again. How discouraging to realize I have a long way to go before I come close to Jesus' example; still, I am encouraged that my spirit is so sensitive that it kicks the stuffing out of me when I fail.

As mature Christians, it is easy to think we have already arrived. That God has taught us all we need to know. Unfortunately for us, God has a way of thrusting us back to reality when self-righteousness rears its ugly head.

How about you? Are there little sins you struggle with? Little sins that don't really make a difference in the bigger scheme of things? These tiny "flaws" will separate you from enjoying an uninterrupted relationship with the Savior. You see, He gave His life at the cross to free us from the bondage of ALL sin. Not just great big, life-affecting mess-ups, but the insignificant ones as well. Ask God to reveal these little sins so nothing drives a wedge between you.

TODAY'S HOT FLASH:

Don't be disheartened when the Holy Spirit pricks your spirit over some little sin. Be reassured in your salvation, repent, and draw near to God.

PRAYER:

Lord, thank You for my sensitive conscience. Reveal to me any "little sins" I've blinded myself to. I praise Your name for the wonderful mercy You bestow upon me every single day. Amen.

MARCH 9

READ: PSALM 18:30

AM I NOT STILL GOD?

As for God, his way is perfect: the word of the Lord is tried:
he is a buckler [shield] to all those that trust in him.

~ Psalm 18:30

"Lord, today I found out my mother has cancer. Why are You doing this?"

"Am I not still God?"

"Lord, I look in the mirror and see wrinkles; my bones are starting to ache. I am afraid of getting older."

"Am I not still God?"

"Lord, I watch the news; thousands die every day from what we call 'acts of God.' How can I explain why You allow such pain?"

"Am I not still God?"

"Yes, Lord, You are still God, and I will put my trust in You. For who is God save the Lord? And Who is my rock save my God? When doubts invade my thoughts, when the world questions my actions, when pain overwhelms, I will remember that I can trust in You."

TODAY'S HOT FLASH:

Don't forget, in the midst of turmoil, that God is God. We cannot understand all that He does. Even so, come what may, we can trust in Him.

PRAYER:

Forgive me, Lord, when I sometimes forget who You are, a mighty God who loves His children. When doubts surface, help me to turn my eyes to You. Amen.

MARCH 10

READ: SONG OF SOLOMON 2:1-7

HIS BANNER OVER ME IS LOVE

He brought me to the banqueting house, and his banner over me was love.

~ Song of Solomon 2:4

Imagine my joy when I realized this beautiful love story told in Song of Solomon was more than a story of King Solomon and his love for the Shulamite maiden. What a difference it made in my relationship with Jesus when I realized it was a description of His love for me. It is a striking picture of Jesus lavishing love on His bride (us)—an all-consuming love that envelops all who dare venture into His presence.

This precious book helped me understand the fullness of who I am in Jesus. Even though in my eyes I am not the beautiful young maiden wooed by her lover, in Christ's eyes, I am never more beautiful, never more loved than I am right now. He doesn't see my wrinkles, my hormonal surges, or my graying hair. He sees a beauty queen. "Behold, thou art fair, my love; behold, thou art fair, thou hast dove's eyes" (SOS 1:15).

When is the last time someone poured such loving acclamations over you? The promise of His unfeigned love is yours to claim. Read Song of Solomon and let His words saturate your entire being. It is the greatest love letter ever written, and you are its recipient. No matter who you are, what you look like, or what you have done, "His banner over you is love." Bathe yourself in those precious words. Aren't they the words every woman longs to hear?

TODAY'S HOT FLASH:

Whenever you are feeling unloved, ugly, and worthless, comfort yourself with this beautiful love letter, from our Lord to You.

PRAYER:

My precious Bridegroom, oh how I know I don't deserve Your love, and oh how glad I am that You offer it to me, in purity and unconditionally. Thank You, my precious One. Amen.

MARCH 11
READ: ACTS 20:28-38

IS THIS ALL THERE IS?

I have shewed you all things, how that so laboring ye ought to support the weak, and to remember the words of the Lord Jesus, how he said, It is more blessed to give than to receive.

~ Acts 20:35

I look around me. What do I see? The same old house. The same old people. The same old routines. Sometimes I am caught in the melancholy of monotony. In these down times, I often ask, "Is this all there is? Am I doing anything worthwhile?" And because I am already in a discouraged state, I can find no hope in my human answers. That is why I cannot depend on my emotions to determine my worthiness or the worthiness of this life I live. I must look beyond the surface of these questions.

It is in this same old house that I have given so much of myself. To my children, my grandchildren, my foster kids, church members, and so many more. It is to these same old people I have given myself: nurtured, disciplined, taught, and protected. These same old routines have been the source of much comfort to children long gone and grandchildren seeking solace in the midst of life's storms. I have given until there was nothing left to give.

Christ said, "It is better to give than to receive." Why am I surprised when He is always right? Christ wanted me to find out the secret for myself. It is in the giving that you receive the most.

TODAY'S HOT FLASH:

Life becomes monotonous when we stop using what God has given us to touch others with the healing balm of Christ's love.

PRAYER:

Lord, forgive me for murmuring and complaining. When I look deeper than my own emotions, I know that I am truly blessed. Continue to use me to bless others. Amen.

MARCH 12
READ: 1 JOHN 1:1-9

PROMISED FORGIVENESS

If we confess our sins, he is faithful and just to forgive us our sins, and to cleanse us from all unrighteousness.

~ 1 John 1:9

I admitted the other day that I told a lie. I wish I could say that it was a rarity, but the sad truth is that I sin every day. I don't mean to. I don't wake up thinking "What can I do to make God cringe today?" Sometimes I make it through the entire day with no major slip ups; just when I am prepared to pat myself on the back, God's still small voice intervenes.

"Okay, Lisa," He whispers, "you didn't tell any lies, you didn't swear, you fulfilled your responsibilities, but through all your good works, where did I fit in?"

When forced to stop and evaluate my day, I realize my thoughts were on doing good, not on Jesus Christ. I didn't focus on His sacrifice for me or my gratitude to Him. I was just working my way down a list. Again He has humbled me. Thankfully, I don't stay discouraged long, because the wonderful truth is, even in my self-absorbance, there is forgiveness. When I confess my sins to my Lord, He forgives me. Always! He faithfully cleanses me from all my dirty deeds. This act of loving kindness makes me want to do better. How about you?

TODAY'S HOT FLASH:

Christians should never live in a perpetual state of defeat. God supernaturally cleanses us from every sin, every time. What a great God we serve.

PRAYER:

Forgiving Father, reveal to me any unconfessed sin in my heart. Thank You that You are faithful and just to forgive me. Where would I be without You? Amen.

MARCH 13
READ: LUKE 24:1-5

THE RISING OF THE SON

And as they were afraid, and bowed down their faces to the earth,
they said unto them, Why seek ye the living among the dead?

~ Luke 24:5

I'm one of those people who need warmth and sunlight to thrive. Cold, dreary weather activates my hibernation mode. But sometimes, just as the gloom begins permeating my body, I am rewarded with a bright yellow kiss seeping through my window. The sun is shining! Immediately revitalization begins, and I feel like a new person.

It reminds me of the wonderful life-changing story we tend to consider passé. It began in a garden, preceded to a courtyard, and ended on the top of a lonely hill called Golgotha. The Son of God — tortured, tormented and hung to die on a cursed cross. Gloom and doom seeped through many frightened and confused souls. But the gloom and doom turned to blazing radiance when the rising of the sun revealed the RISING OF THE SON in all HIS glory. Darkness turned to light, for the SON was shining and continues even to this day.

TODAY'S HOT FLASH:

The Son truly does bring new life to all who have been kissed by His shining glory. Take time to ponder on the RISING OF THE SON today. It will invigorate you.

PRAYER:

Hallelujah to the Lamb: the wonderful Lamb of God. You lived, You died, and You live again — forever and ever. May that truth change my life. Amen.

MARCH 14
READ: 1 JOHN 2:7-11

ARE YOU WALKING IN DARKNESS?

But he that hateth his brother is in darkness, and walketh in darkness, and knoweth not whither he goeth, because that darkness hath blinded his eyes.

~ 1 John 2:11

Midlife, complete with run amok hormones and the realization of growing old, has a way of bringing out the worst in us. The bitter reality of what we haven't accomplished strikes hard. Names of people who we believe thwarted our goals come vividly to mind. Our fingers begin pointing in their direction.

Often this mindset is ignited by fear of what the future holds, of having to face past failures, and of death. The old adage "misery loves company" rings true to the bitter heart. Rather than embracing their remaining years, many women spend the rest of their lives clinging to their anger, oblivious to the fact that there are many new paths to cross and new mountains to climb. If we allow hate to fester and grow, we waste precious living time. God says "he that hateth his brother is in darkness . . . because that darkness hath blinded his eyes."

If we desire to experience the more abundant life God promised, then we first must learn to forgive others and love unconditionally, no holding back. Bitterness is an abundant life killer. When hatred occupies the heart, the paths of our future are darkened and life is stifled. You cannot walk in an unlit path. Fill the remaining years of your life with light. This light is the love of Jesus illuminating through you.

TODAY'S HOT FLASH:

If we love God, we will not hate our brother. We cannot belong to Him and walk in darkness. We are only deceiving ourselves.

PRAYER:

Oh, Lord, help me to forgive those who have hurt me. Open my blinded eyes that I may see any darkness in me. Cleanse my heart from this sin. Amen.

MARCH 15

READ: PHILIPPIANS 4:10-14

THE WILL TO OBEY

I can do all things through Christ which strengtheneth me.

~ Philippians 4:13

In the movie, *Ella Enchanted,* Anne Hathaway plays a young woman "blessed" with the gift of obedience. This gift soon turns to a curse and gets her into all kinds of trouble. When she confronts the fairy who gave her the gift, she is told she must find the strength within herself if she wishes to break the spell.

When diabolical people attempt to use this gift against Ella, forcing her to harm others, she is finally faced with the depth of her inner strength. After many years of unquestioned obedience, Ella finds herself at a crossroads: will she continue to obey, or will she resist and break free from this horrible bondage that has dictated her life for so many years? It isn't easy, but with sweat filled brow, Ella fights with her very being and breaks the wretched curse.

We are a lot like Ella. Sometimes our hormones rage so strongly that we seem bent on destruction. That feeling wells up inside of us (you know what I am talking about), and it is almost uncontrollable. We are at the point of destruction, and it seems impossible to fight. But the God who created us has not left us without the power to overcome. We have the supernatural power of God Himself through the Holy Spirit. The fight may be emotionally draining, but perseverance is assured, for "we can do all things through Christ which strengtheneth us."

TODAY'S HOT FLASH:

We can't overcome in our strength alone; our flesh is weak, but through Christ, we have the power of Almighty God at our disposal. Failure isn't an option.

PRAYER:

Lord, when I am overwhelmed and losing control, remind me to call on Your mighty power. Through You, I know I will persevere. You are all I need. Amen.

MARCH 16
READ: ISAIAH 1:16–21

DEPRESSION OF FLAWS

Come now, let us reason together, says the Lord. Though your sins are like scarlet, they shall be as white as snow.

~ Isaiah 1:18a

Teenagers are experts at inflaming our otherwise mild temperaments. Just today I lost my temper at my very docile and compliant daughter. I can't even remember what it was about—no doubt, something insignificant. When I become irritated and lose my temper at the ones I love most, I feel terrible.

The song "Will You Love Me Tomorrow" plays in my head as I continuously fail and give myself over to my flesh and the wiles of my hormones. "What about tomorrow, Lord?" When I alienate my dearest ones, when I can't bear to minister to another person, when I mumble and complain and find fault in the very essence of life, will you still love me tomorrow?

When the bleakness of life surrounds me and I feel I am going to explode, I am confronted with the weakness of my faith. Still, the Lord spares me from the depths of despair, when in the silence of my heart, in His quiet way, He reassures me. "Come now, let us reason together," He whispers to my soul. "Though your sins are like scarlet they shall be white as snow." What precious words for women who need this ever-present assurance that they are loved and forgiven. I am one of these women; are you?

TODAY'S HOT FLASH:

God will love us tomorrow, and the next day, and the next. He will love us until forever and a day. This knowledge should carry us through the worst of times.

PRAYER:

Ever forgiving Father, thank You that You will love me tomorrow, no matter my mess-ups for today. Help me never to forget this truth. Amen.

MARCH 17

READ: 1 JOHN 4:11–21

GOD'S LOVE MACHINES

No man hath seen God at any time. If we love one another, God dwelleth in us, and his love is perfected in us.

~ 1 John 4:12

As mature women, we have a unique opportunity. We've experienced many years of life filled with joys and heart-wrenching horrors. Our daughters, granddaughters, and many other women we rub shoulders with glean tidbits from our lives for future reference.

We have all the qualifications needed to become God's great love machines. Through us, those we mentor will learn the beauty of such a privilege and practice the art of imitation. We cannot introduce Jesus to the lost in His physical form, since "no man hath seen God at any time." But we can introduce them to Him through our unconditional love. "God dwelleth in us and his love is perfected in us." When others are around us, Jesus' love in us should radiate through us.

When we pour out Christ's love, our children, friends, and loved ones also learn to show His love. Show them, so they can show others and so on and so on. What a difference it would make in this world full of love-starved souls.

TODAY'S HOT FLASH:

You and I are called to be mighty love machines for the Savior. If His love is perfected in you, shine brightly for everyone to see.

PRAYER:

Lord, I want to be Your love machine here on earth. Let Your love flow through and touch the hearts of every person You bring my way. Amen.

MARCH 18
READ: ACTS 25:23; 26:13-32

DON'T LET YOUR GUARD DOWN

Then Agrippa said unto Paul, Almost thou persuadest me to be a Christian. And Paul said, I would to God, that not only thou, but also all that hear me this day, were both almost, and altogether such as I am, except these bonds.
~ Acts 26:28-29

Bernice was the sister of King Agrippa. It was she who sat with Agrippa while Paul pled his case for Jesus, the resurrected one. Born a Jew, Bernice at one time lived out her faith with zeal. As she grew older, she became bored and discontented. Rejecting her faith, she delved into a life of immorality.

Agrippa listened to Paul's story of his Damascus conversion and was touched by his words. "Almost thou persuadest me to be a Christian," he said. Bernice's reaction is not told. We only know that they left the room and went to discuss Paul. God was giving Bernice a chance to repent. Instead, she chose to reject Jesus, and her life fell into a pit of degradation.

If we are not careful, we can fall into that same deadly pit. As we age, we tend to cling to things that make us feel young. For Bernice, it was the constant love and attention that her immoral lifestyle provided. If we let our guard down, we will fall into the same deceptive lie as Bernice. Don't be fooled by the world's view of significance. Our worth comes from God alone.

TODAY'S HOT FLASH:

No fleshly pleasure is worth losing the peace that comes from walking with God daily. Don't sell out for momentary pleasure. It will soon pass. Then what will you have?

PRAYER:

Father, help me keep my eyes on You. Forgive me when I measure myself to the world's standards. Help me to remember it is only Your truth that counts. Amen.

MARCH 19

READ: 2 CORINTHIANS 11:7–15

A BEAUTIFUL LIFE

And no marvel, for Satan himself is transformed into an angel of light.

~ 2 Corinthians 11:14

As little girls, our hearts are filled with dreams of the handsome prince whisking us away into happily ever after, bubble gum trees, mommies and daddies who always stay together, and having ten children who love us and never get dirty or do anything bad.

By the time we are grown, we have experienced numerous shattered dreams. There are no bubble gum trees, and little children are loud, dirty, and often disobedient.

Still, we cling to hope that our husbands can change, children are trainable, and that beautiful ocean front property is still a possibility. Then we turn forty. We evaluate our past, the here and now, and our perception of the future. During the evaluation process, we become vulnerable to Satan, the world, and our own fleshly desires. Many women leave husbands of twenty years, disregard their children's feelings, and trash what *is* for the hope of what can be.

We are told that "Satan himself is transformed into an angel of light." He deceives us into believing that that which is evil is good and that which is good is evil. He is an expert at it.

Don't be fooled by the greatest trickster of all. Life will become a torment, and you will never forgive yourself. Cling to the true Light of the LORD, Jesus Christ. He will make your life beautiful if you only let Him.

TODAY'S HOT FLASH:

Satan is an expert at making sin look pleasurable. But this pleasure is short-lived and fills us with debilitating guilt. Stay true to what is right. You will never regret it.

PRAYER:

Heavenly Father, forgive my moaning and pining for the pleasures of the world. Help me to see the beauty in what You have given me. Amen.

MARCH 20
READ: PSALM 118:1–10

ACCEPTING ME FOR WHO I AM

It is better to trust in the Lord than to put confidence in man.

~ Psalm 118:8

Depending on how far we are willing to go, we can change anything physical about ourselves. If the nose is too wide, it can be reconstructed. If the lips are too thin, a shot of Botox will fatten them up. Facelifts and gastric bypasses are highly in demand.

People from all stations succumb to the surgeon's knife, hoping for greater success and happiness. Satisfaction is fleeting, and they go back every time life gets bad. Personally, other than dying my hair and losing a few pounds, I choose not to succumb to the world's fight against aging. It only takes one disastrous facelift to realize that "It is better to trust in the Lord than to put confidence in man." God created me this way for His purpose, and I will trust in Him. What does a facelift really change? If I was disorganized before, I will be disorganized afterward. If I didn't like the smell of coffee before my nose was reconstructed, I won't after. Why? Because no matter how hard I try to change who I am, I cannot. I am created by God in the image of God to be exactly who He created me to be. Maybe in the second half of my life, I will stop trying to change who God made me to be and start accepting myself as His child, loved, cared for, and beautiful in His eyes.

TODAY'S HOT FLASH:

God is the Creator; in man's eyes you may be flawed and in need of improvement, but in God's, you are His perfectly designed bride. He doesn't make mistakes.

PRAYER:

Father, Creator, Help me to be satisfied with Your handiwork completed in me. Forgive me when I compare myself to the world's standards. I know I am beautiful in Your eyes. Amen.

MARCH 21

READ: ROMANS 7:15-25

WRETCHED CONFUSION

For that which I do I allow not: for what I would, that do I not: but what I hate, that do I. If then I do that which I would not, I consent unto the law that it is good.

~ Romans 7:15-16

If you are anything like me, you find these verses confusing. At the same time, you understand it completely. Why do we do the things we do that we know we shouldn't? Some days I can feel that hormonal splurge working its way up through my throat and out my mouth before I can stop it.

Take today, for example. It happened while homeschooling my grandchildren. My grandson couldn't get a word right in his reading. He knew the words but gave them all the wrong sounds, turned his b's into d's, and whimpered at my constant correction. Finally I had enough, and I slammed the pop bottle I had in my hands against the table in my frustration. The top was off, and it was full. The soda splashed everywhere. It covered my glasses, soiled all the school books, and spilled to the floor. My grandson stared at me, mouth wide open. He didn't know whether to laugh or cringe.

Why do I react to my inner emotional surges this way? I hate myself when I do. Paul said, "For what I would, that do I not, but what I hate, that do I." That's me! How about you? Can you find yourself in this picture anywhere?

TODAY'S HOT FLASH:

Where would we be without God's continuous forgiving nature? Even though we fail him time and time again, He never turns His back on us. His forgiveness is sure.

PRAYER:

Lord, give me Your supernatural strength to fight these emotional uproars. In Your power I know I can keep them at bay. Help me, God! Amen.

MARCH 22
READ: ACTS 10:34-43

NO RESPECTER OF PERSONS

Then Peter opened his mouth, and said, Of a truth I perceive that God is no respecter of persons.

~ Acts 10:34

I will never run the Boston marathon, sing an aria at the Met, or win a million bucks playing the lottery. It is unlikely that I will ever reign supreme as a CEO of a grandiose business or win first place racing in a NASCAR event. I will never be a queen or one of those beautiful, stick-thin super models. I probably won't own a Porsche or bump shoulders with the richest man in the world. My name isn't Oprah Winfrey, Bill Gates, Queen Elizabeth, Donald Trump, or George Bush. The beautiful truth of all this is—that's okay.

I can strive for worldly acceptance and recognition, or I can give God everything I've got where I am planted today. You see, I am an average woman, with the average family, living in an average house, with average children, trying to touch the lives of average people.

There is satisfaction in who I am when I realize that in God's eyes I am a V.I.P. I am His child, and He loves me. When I stand before the judgment seat of Christ, I won't be judged by how spectacular my accomplishments are, but by how faithful I was to my calling. God is no respecter of persons. He doesn't see money flashing before His eyes; He sees the intents of the heart.

TODAY'S HOT FLASH:

I am a V.I.P. in God's eyes. He loves me, He created me, and nothing can take that away.

PRAYER:

Thank You, Lord, for loving and accepting me without the frills of popularity and wealth. May I remain faithful to You wherever You choose to plant me. Amen.

FOR SANITY'S SAKE

MARCH 23

READ: 2 PETER 1:15-21

SOMEDAY MY PRINCE WILL COME

For we have not been telling you fairy tales when we explained to you the power of our Lord Jesus Christ and his coming again. My own eyes have seen his splendor and his glory.

~ 2 Peter 1:16

What woman hasn't sighed as she listened to Snow White's "Someday My Prince Will Come" or been caught up in the fantasy of "Beauty and the Beast"? Each of the heroines in these movies (Snow White and Belle) had visions of the perfect prince whisking her off her feet into the world of happily ever after.

Once we hit midlife, we have a tendency to pine for something different. For that someone we've always dreamed of but have never found. It is in the danger of this thought pattern that many women leave their not-so-charming prince and seek out perfection. Alas, it is never found; flawed humanity gets in the way.

I have good news. We have the perfect Prince Charming in Jesus Christ. He knows our deepest longings, and in His loving arms, He embraces us. He waits for the day, just as we do, when He will come sweep us away in raptured bliss. Someday our Prince will come, and He will take us into a world of fairy tale happily ever after. Hold fast and don't get discouraged. The perfect Bridegroom is out there—He will come—life will never again be the same.

TODAY'S HOT FLASH:

Give your husband a break. He can't be more than his humanity allows. Look to your true Prince Charming, Jesus Christ—your Bridegroom—your perfect spouse.

PRAYER:

Forgive me, Father, when I hold others to the expectations that only Jesus can meet. I yearn for that wedding day when I will spend eternity in those heavenly places with Him. Amen.

MARCH 24
READ: PSALM 100

SHOUT FOR JOY

Shout for joy to the Lord, all the earth. Worship the Lord with gladness; come before him with joyful songs.

~ Psalm 100:1–2

What a horribly emotional week. My anxieties hide any real faith I know I have. My mind tells me one thing, but my emotions! Wow! Talk about out of control! I hate it when I am this way, but for the life of me, I can't seem to get my act together. Why do I disappoint God and my family so much? You would think my love for them would suppress these uprisings of hormonal calamity. There is a remedy. It is by saturating myself in His Word and praising Him in the storm. Only then will I experience that calming joy.

If overcoming is my goal, I must learn to "shout for joy to the Lord." Sometimes I shout loudly as I attempt to convince myself of this joy. Gradually, the calming presence of the Lord satisfies my deeper longing and instead of forced participation, I am worshipping "the Lord with gladness." My obedience in coming to Him is always answered with a changed heart. I often start my praise with something melancholy such as "Just as I am," but before I am through, I am bellowing out "Heaven Came Down and Glory Filled My Soul."

TODAY'S HOT FLASH:

You can attack those hormonal negatives with the power of the Holy Spirit through the power of praise and shouting joyful songs to the Lord.

PRAYER:

Lord, help me fight off the attacks of the flesh in these strong hormonal times. Amen.

MARCH 25
READING: PSALM 99

EXALT YE THE LORD

Exalt ye the LORD our God, and worship at his footstool; for he is holy.

~ Psalm 99:5

These verses in Psalm 99 confront me with God's holiness and my lack of holiness.

How can a holy, righteous God love me? I am selfish; I lose my temper, get lazy, and often murmur and complain. These are only a few of my lesser crimes.

How can this great and holy God leave His throne of glory and become like me? Why would He do that? Why would He allow Himself to be tortured and hated for my sins? In our humanity, we hurt those we love; we let them down and often betray them. In our humanity we often betray Jesus.

I don't fully comprehend this love for me, but I will exalt the Lord. As faulty as my attempts are, His love is so perfect that He will never toss them aside. Through His Spirit, He will glean the imperfections from my life and accept my offerings to Him as pure and holy. I don't understand why He loves me, but I will cling to that love with everything that is in me.

TODAY'S HOT FLASH:

Stop trying to figure out *why* He loves you. Accept it without question. Exalt Him! Love Him! Thank Him! That's all you need to do.

PRAYER:

I can't understand why You love me, Lord, but help me to accept it fully. I exalt You for Who You are. You are holy, May I be holy too. Amen.

MARCH 26

READ: TITUS 2

THERE'S SOMETHING TO BE SAID FOR AGE

The aged women likewise, that they be in behaviour as becometh holiness, not false accusers, not given to much wine, teachers of good things.

~ Titus 2:3

Shelley sees her children only once a week, and then only if I am willing to supervise. She is twenty-six years old. Ending the visit is always painful. How did she get to this place in life, where even her children are taken from her? Life for her is already one miserable succession of disappointments.

I remember when I was twenty-three, a single woman with two children. My future looked bleak. Now that I have made it through those tough times, I can reflect rationally on my pain. I can glean from the truths I have learned and teach this young woman about Jesus' love. If she would turn her eyes to Him and make Him her number one priority, He will see her through.

We can't afford to mess up. Our behavior is to be "as becometh holiness." We have a message of hope for the next generation. We dare not live in defeat.

TODAY'S HOT FLASH:

You have a message of hope and victory to share. Don't let your hormonal struggles keep you from doing God's work.

PRAYER:

Lord, help me to stay holy as I minister to young women. Fill me with Your message of hope for their lives. Open their ears to hear. Amen.

FOR SANITY'S SAKE

MARCH 27

READ: 1 CORINTHIANS 8

STUMBLING BLOCK

But take heed lest by any means this liberty of yours become a stumbling block to them that are weak.

~ 1 Corinthians 8:9

I love the freedom my maturity brings, but I must never forget my calling. If in my Christian liberty I cause a weaker sister to stumble, then I have sinned before my Holy God.

Yes, I have the liberty to celebrate with a glass of champagne, but if it damages my testimony, I am required, out of true Christian love, to refrain from it. Alcohol is only one of the many vices we brazenly flaunt as Christian liberty. You put your weakness in its place. "Take heed" is what Paul admonishes. This implies there is a chastisement waiting for all who ignore this warning.

How often do you claim Christian liberty as you participate in activities of questionable merit? Who's watching you? Someone will notice and use it as ammunition to accuse and as an excuse to sin themselves. God forbid!

TODAY'S HOT FLASH:

When in doubt, stay far away. Someone IS watching and will use your example as an excuse to stray.

PRAYER:

Forgive me, Lord, if I have been a stumbling block to anyone. Keep me focused on the cross and what You have done for me. I don't need anything but You. Amen.

MARCH 28
READ: LEVITICUS 20:1-8

BE YE HOLY

Sanctify yourselves therefore, and be ye holy: for I am the Lord your God.
~ Leviticus 20:7

We spend hours enthralled by the gory graphic details of someone's murder. Our children revel in decapitating, stabbing, shooting, and mutilating opponents in video games. Movies and television have led the way to demoralizing our nation, children, and us.

In a world so obsessed with death, life has been devalued. The very thing God gave us as a gift, we intently watch others annihilate in vivid detail. Watching so much blood, gore, hatred, and anger is detrimental to the already over anxious mind. Don't you think it's time to fill our thoughts with the beauty of life rather than the horrific details of death?

God tells us to "be holy." If we must watch TV or go to the movies, let's choose shows that encourage us, illuminate good moral values, and honor God. They are out there. Isn't there enough anxiety in life without purposely adding to it?

TODAY'S HOT FLASH

It is impossible to "be holy" and fill our minds with the filth of today's media. What is offensive to God should be offensive to us as well.

PRAYER:

Oh, Lord, keep me from the temptation of watching shows that do not glorify You. I want to please You. Let me glorify you in all of my life. Amen.

GREATER IS HE

Ye are of God, little children, and have overcome them: because greater is he that is in you, than he that is in the world.

~ 1 John 4:4

I love pumpkin pie piled high with whipped cream, and chocolate chip mint ice cream three scoops deep on a sugar cone. But as much as I love them, I have removed them from my life. I can't eat them anymore without acquiring unwanted baggage. My thighs, stomach, and buttocks form great friendships with these delightfully deceiving culprits. Keeping weight off was never so difficult. I cut calories and cut some more; still it seems I fight a losing battle.

It is impossible for me to control my eating habits in my strength. The aroma of a hot apple pie wafting in the air draws me nigh. I can't control myself by myself. The flesh and Satan throw temptations by the dozens my way on a regular basis. Thank God for His wonderful truth, that "greater is he that is in me, than he that is in the world." I can and I will win this battle through the power of the Holy Spirit, and so can you.

TODAY'S HOT FLASH:

In the power of the Holy Spirit, you do not have to let the temptation to overeat rule you. He is greater than any temptation.

PRAYER:

Sweet, precious Father, fill me with the fruit of the Spirit of self-control. I need an added measure of Your grace in this area. Amen.

MARCH 30
READ: DEUTERONOMY 32:1–9

REMEMBER

Remember the days of old, consider the years of many generations, ask thy father, and he will shew thee; thy elders, and they will tell thee.

~ Deuteronomy 32:7

Remember the work God accomplished in you when He called you to Himself. Remember the beauty of a firstborn child. Remember that beloved wedding day, your first date, first prom, and first grandchild.

Memories are the jewels of time gone by. Our hearts are warmed, and we sigh as we dwell on them. Go ahead, remember, but don't stay there. If we remain in our memories, God's divine plan for us is stifled. To stay in the past is to hinder the future. Old memories are sweet, but fresh memories are far sweeter. It is time to move on.

Build memories with the people who need you today. Build them with young ladies who will someday be where you are. When they look on the sweet memories they created with you, they will be ready to begin new memories with those who come after them.

TODAY'S HOT FLASH:

Don't forget to remember to spend time building new memories with your next generation, so when it is their turn, they can build memories with theirs.

PRAYER:

Oh, Father, thank You for my memories, but help me not to be stuck in them. Teach me to build fresh memories with the people You have placed in my life. Amen.

FOR SANITY'S SAKE

MARCH 31

READ: MARK 6:1-6

IS HE AMAZED BY YOU?

He could not do any miracles there, except lay his hands on a few sick people and heal them. And he was amazed at their lack of faith.

~ Mark 5:5-6a

When Jesus returned to Nazareth and began to teach in the temple, the people were offended by Him. "And he was amazed at their lack of faith."

They witnessed His miracles, experienced His compassion, and heard His words, but they didn't believe. How often do we amaze Christ with our unbelief? He says, "Be not afraid." Still we fear. He commands us to forgive, but we insist on carrying a root of bitterness instead of love; still we carry hatred in our heart.

Do you amaze Jesus with your unbelief? Are your emotions and hormones too much for Him to control? Do you question His decision to allow you to suffer from irritating hot flashes and mood swings?

Sister, you should be amazed with Jesus, but He should never be amazed with you because of your unbelief.

TODAY'S HOT FLASH:

How long are you going to continue to amaze God with your unbelief? Try something new; amaze Him with your obedience instead.

PRAYER:

Ever forgiving Father, forgive me for the many times I amaze You in my unbelief. I want to believe always, Lord. Help me. Amen.

APRIL

APRIL 1

READ: GENESIS 2:4-25

FORMED BY HIM

And the Lord God formed man of the dust of the ground, and breathed into his nostrils the breath of life; and man became a living soul.

~ Genesis 2:7

What do you see when you look in the mirror? A slightly disfigured person, far from perfect? When you evaluate your talents and gifts, do you see a sorely lacking individual? When you look into your heart, do you see someone with characteristics that turn into flaws way too quickly? Be encouraged; when God looks at you, He sees only beauty.

As sure as God's divine hands formed Adam from the dust of the earth, so has He formed you in your mother's womb. He sculpted you with depth and insight. He created your personhood—that part that makes you, you. He has placed within you very carefully chosen traits and characteristics that are unique to you alone. That person you can't stand to look at is the perfectly clad bride of the divine Bridegroom. Exalt Him for who you are: His precious child, formed by His divine hands.

TODAY'S HOT FLASH:

You are God's perfectly sculpted masterpiece. The Bridegroom believes His bride is beautiful. It's time you started believing it as well.

PRAYER:

Precious Father, help me to see myself as Your beautiful bride, fashioned by Your hands. Thank you for Your continual love. Amen.

APRIL 2
READ: 1 PETER 4:7–15

TIME OF TESTING

Beloved, think it not strange concerning the fiery trial which is to try you, as though some strange thing happened unto you.

~ 1 Peter 4:12

My son lost his job—again. The third one this year. Not for doing wrong but for taking a stand for right. It wouldn't be so devastating if he didn't have a family of nine to feed. Talk about a time of testing! It wasn't too long ago he bowed under pressure and gave in, but he is different now. Praise the Lord, my son's faithfulness has been rewarded with a new and better job ministering to children with autism. He stood firm in his trial, and God blessed his obedience.

The menopausal woman faces her own fiery trial. What is menopause if not a battle between the flesh and the Spirit? Hormones are ignited by our sin-cursed flesh. It is the mature woman's time of testing. How will I react when my hormones encourage me to blow up? Will I wallow in self-pity, or will I remember James' admonition to "think it not strange concerning the fiery trial which is to test you." It is in the trials our faith is perfected.

TODAY'S HOT FLASH:

Trials will come; life guarantees it. Our reaction is the true test of who or what is in control—the Holy Spirit or our own sin-cursed flesh. It's our choice.

PRAYER:

Lord, help me to abandon myself in the Holy Spirit's control. In my own strength, I will fail the test every time. Amen.

APRIL 3

READ: 1 CORINTHIANS 10:24-33

EXPECTATIONS

Give none offence [...] Even as I please all men in all things, not seeking mine own profit, but the profit of many, that they may be saved.

~ 1 Corinthians 10:32a-33

My foster son spends his hard-earned money on frivolities and doesn't mop the way I think he should or take the garbage out often enough. I blow up at him for not doing things my way. I attack him for being different.

Shamefully, instead of being a servant to my foster son, I become a dictator, an unmerciful ruler. With this attitude, I alienate rather than draw in.

Paul says, "Give none offense . . . Even as I please all men in all things, not seeking mine own profit, but the profit of many, that they may be saved." With my control issues, I have offended and pushed away. Age is never an excuse for offending. Shame on me! Shame on you if you are doing it as well!

TODAY'S HOT FLASH:

Each person is unique. We are as different as our DNA. God designed it that way. Embrace the difference, don't resent it.

PRAYER:

Forgive me, Father, for my badgering and complaining. Teach me to look to Your Word for Your standards, not my own opinion. Amen.

APRIL 4

READ: MATTHEW 21:1-11

IF JESUS CAN USE A DONKEY . . .

Saying unto them, Go into the village over against you, and straightway ye shall find an ass tied, and a colt with her: loose them, and bring them unto me.

~ Matthew 21:2

My husband and I owned a horse ranch. From time to time we ended up with a few donkeys in the herd. We decided to add one to our pony ring. Big mistake! When Mr. Donkey copped an attitude and stopped moving, the entire pony ring stopped. We didn't use him again.

How interesting that the Lord used a donkey—an animal known for his stubborn rebellion—to make his entry into Jerusalem. From the moment Jesus said, "Loose them, and bring them unto me." The donkey complied. Even he knew Jesus was God!

As mature women, we often become stubborn and unyielding in our thoughts and actions. Rigid and unbendable. We refuse to trust, believe, or admit our error. Isn't it great that our wonderful Lord can break through that wall and use us in spite of ourselves?

TODAY'S HOT FLASH:

Don't be a donkey. Break yourself of stubborn attitudes before God has to.

PRAYER:

Lord, make me willing and ready every time You call. Forgive my unyielding spirit. Let me be as willing as that donkey was. Amen.

APRIL 5

READ: DANIEL 3:8-18

WE'RE NOT GONNA BOW

If it be so, our God whom we serve is able to deliver us from the burning fiery furnace and he will deliver us out of thine hand, O king. But if not, be it known unto thee, O king, that we will not serve thy gods, nor worship the golden image which thou hast set up.

~ Daniel 3:17-18

At the threat of horrible death, Shadrach, Meshach, and Abednego refused to bow to the golden image. To succumb to their natural instinct of self-preservation was to deny the very God they claimed to worship.

In a different way we face a fiery furnace every day. The overwhelming desire to toss aside right actions for hormonally charged bad behavior constantly entices. If we lose control and fall to the temptation to react, we deny this Jesus we claim to serve.

God is able to deliver us from the fiery furnace of our hormones, but even if he doesn't, let us stand firm and proclaim, "We are not going to bow!"

TODAY'S HOT FLASH:

Hormonal fluctuations are unavoidable, but our bad reactions are absolutely controllable. Stay focused on Christ and victory is certain.

PRAYER:

Lord, don't let me bow to the whims of my hormones. It is a much easier route, but one I don't want to take. In Your strength, keep me strong. Amen.

APRIL 6
READ: JONAH 1:1–4

UNCLE!

But Jonah rose up to flee unto Tarshish from the presence of the Lord.
~ Jonah 1:3a

During a time of play, my husband captured my three-year-old grandson, Mason, between his legs. "Say *uncle*," he said. I knew we were in for a battle of the wills.

"No," replied Mason. For five minutes Mason screamed and thrashed viciously. In all this, he would not say the magic word. Grandpa finally let him go and refused to play with him unless he said "Uncle."

Devastated, Mason jumped into his lap and said, "Uncle, uncle, uncle." Now we can't get him to shut up! He and grandpa have been best of buddies ever since.

Jonah found himself in the grip of God's mighty will, and he too refused to say "Uncle!" Instead, he fled from God. After a severe storm, being thrown overboard and swallowed by an enormous fish, Jonah finally cried, "Uncle!" When he finally bowed to the Lord's will, relief and renewed relationship ensued.

Mason and Jonah created their distress by not bowing to the will of the loving one who held them. How much easier life is when we cry "Uncle!" immediately.

TODAY'S HOT FLASH:

What are you butting heads with the Lord over? What more do you have to go through before you cry "Uncle"?

PRAYER:

Father, I can be stubborn and often want my way. Forgive me when I am like this. I cry "Uncle!" in every area of my life. Amen.

FOR SANITY'S SAKE

APRIL 7

READ: DEUTERONOMY 32:1–9

SHOWERS ON THE GRASS

My doctrine shall drop as the rain, my speech shall distil as the dew, as the small rain upon the tender herb, and as the showers upon the grass.

~ Deuteronomy 32:2

Moses, more than anyone, understood what it meant for God to step in and make something beautiful out of the mess His people often made messes of their lives because of their unbelief. In Deuteronomy 32, Moses is preparing to die and is delivering a song of warning and remembrance to his people. Based on their past record, he knows it won't take long for their faith to weaken and murmuring to begin. To the Israelites, rain and clouds signified dark and dreary days. They couldn't see past the moment. Moses saw the roses for the rain.

Are we any different from the disbelieving Israelites? These aggravating menopausal discomforts will cease, and the mature butterfly (you) will burst from its confining cocoon, perfectly timed and uniquely defined. We can praise God for the showers on our grass; the green newness of what is, that will turn into the blessed maturity of what will be after the rain.

TODAY'S HOT FLASH:

Rain must come into our lives so that the beauty of transition and renewal can blossom forth into a bouquet of vibrant colors.

PRAYER:

Lord, help me to remember that the showers of life come to renew, not destroy. Help me look to the future; keep me focused on the beauty of what is to come. Amen.

APRIL 8

READ: DEUTERONOMY 32:26–37

WHERE ARE THEIR GODS?

And he shall say, Where are their gods, their rock in whom they trusted?
~ Deuteronomy 32:37

What is it that you have placed your trust in? Moisturizing creams? Aerobics class? Low carb, low cholesterol eating? Maybe you visited the fashion police and learned to dress and look years younger. Your vitamin stack reaches the ceiling, and your most plenteous makeup on your shelf is the cover-up. Every day you seek new ways to look and feel younger, all the while fretting over every new wrinkle.

When you're lying on your death bed, your gods of beauty won't come to your rescue. Those trusted remedies of youth will fade away into nothingness, and the time wasted pursuing the impossible will haunt you. Don't fight your age, embrace it. It is the life you live now that matters. How many wrinkles you have make no difference. How many heads you can turn with your beauty helps no one. Focus on the important things in life. You are a mature woman; use those extra wrinkles as a launching pad to make a difference in the world. There's no better time than now.

TODAY'S HOT FLASH:

There's no better time than the present to make a difference for the future. You have experience and wisdom; use these to do great things for God.

PRAYER:

Lord, how much I love You. Thank You for the wisdom and experience You have blessed me with. Teach me where You want me to use them for Your glory. Amen.

APRIL 9

READ: HEBREWS 10:19–25

CLEAR AND PRESENT DANGER

Let us hold fast the profession of our faith without wavering; (for he is faithful that promised).

~ Hebrews 10:23

In the movie "Clear and Present Danger," starring Harrison Ford, the Colombian drug cartel presents a safety threat to the people of the United States. It is only one of thousands of movies that base their storyline on the evils of this world. But who needs fictional media? We only have to watch the news or read the newspapers to know that we live in a dangerous world. Some of us have faced its reality personally.

There is, for the Christian, a more subtle danger lurking, and it is much more devastating to us spiritually. That is the danger of complacency, the feeling that we've done our part and now it's time to pass the torch.

The author of Hebrews posts a warning for all to heed: "hold fast the profession of our faith without wavering." Rather than slowing down, a sense of urgency should take hold. There is so much to do and so little time to do it.

TODAY'S HOT FLASH:

Old age isn't a time for retiring from God's work; it is a time to speed it up. We have less time to accomplish all God wants us to do. Rest comes later.

PRAYER:

Father of all strength, I move a little slower and have much work left to do. Give me the ability to keep on keeping on; don't let me waste a minute. Amen.

APRIL 10
READ: JOHN 21:15–19

FEED MY SHEEP

He saith to him again the second time, Simon, son of Jonas, lovest thou me? He saith unto him, Yea, Lord; thou knowest that I love thee. He saith unto him, Feed my sheep.

~ John 21:16

I live and breathe grandchildren and foster kids. I stumble over them when I wake in the morning and sing them to sleep at night. I love each and every one of them, but if I am not careful, I could get bitter and frustrated at my lack of personal time. It is in my frustration that I am reminded of what our beloved Savior asked Peter, "Lovest thou me more than these?"

"Of course, Lord, you know I do."

"Then feed my sheep."

I don't want Him to have to tell me three times, as he did Peter. Every minute I spend with these precious loved ones gives me opportunity to obey.

Through my love, time, and wisdom, I am feeding His sheep. Someday, I hope to see them doing the same.

TODAY'S HOT FLASH:

Now is the time to feed His sheep. Don't resent it or shove it onto someone else's shoulders. Take every opportunity to teach these children of Jesus.

PRAYER:

Father, thank You for all the precious little sheep You have brought my way. May I be faithful to feed them to overflowing with Your words and Your love. Amen.

APRIL 11

READ: ACTS 10:1-12

A TEACHER'S ATTITUDE

And upon the first day of the week, when the disciples came together to break bread, Paul preached unto them, ready to depart on the morrow; continued his speech until midnight.

~ Acts 20:7

Mature women of the world, awake! Our younger generation is floundering, and they are in danger of sinking without rescue. Now is not the time to stubbornly hoard the wisdom and experiences God has placed in your hands. Who will throw these young ladies a lifeline of truth? Paul did; he realized his knowledge was a gift and spent every opportunity passing it on. He strove to share the Good News because he knew his time was short. He didn't waste a minute.

What good is experience if it isn't used to help someone? What good is knowledge if it is shut up like a hermit in his private cave? Was your pain really for naught? With age comes vast knowledge. With this knowledge comes the responsibility to teach. What you do with what you know will make the difference in the amount of impact you have.

TODAY'S HOT FLASH:

Don't forget where you have been. Share your failures with others and use your experiences for the greater good. That greater good is Jesus Christ.

PRAYER:

Father, everything I know and live is from You. Teach me to share what You've given me with love and humility. And like Paul, continuously. Amen.

APRIL 12
READ: ACTS 20:22–32

THE FINAL COURSE

But none of these things move me, neither count I my life dear unto myself, so that I might finish my course with joy, and the ministry, which I have received of the Lord Jesus, to testify the gospel of the grace of God.
~ Acts 20:24

My knees creak and my hips refuse to bend at times. I lose hair by the handfuls and . . . can we be real here? My butt sags an extra two inches. I exercise, do bun crunches, and it never seems to lift. Brown spots on my face increase in size by the day. I have tried everything advertised—nothing works!

If allowed to fester, these ailments would consume me, and I could spend my remaining years trying to stay young. If serving God is my goal, I can't be controlled by the physical: "neither count I my life dear unto myself." I need to take the time spent seeking the fountain of youth and refocus it on "finishing my course with joy." With God's help, I will fix my eyes on the blessed prize because nothing in this world can compare to what God has in store for me.

TODAY'S HOT FLASH:

True beauty comes from the heart of a woman who is madly in love with the Lord.

PRAYER:

Father, teach me not to focus on what once was but can never be again. Help me to focus on what is to come—eternity with Your Son. That's all that matters. Amen.

APRIL 13

READ: COLOSSIANS 1:9-14

NEW ADVENTURES

Strengthened with all might, according to his glorious power, unto all patience and longsuffering with joyfulness.

~ Colossians 1:11

I recently became the proud foster mother of a newborn. Am I up to the task? All night vigils, dirty laundry, unfinished dishes. Do I have the stamina it takes to supply this little boy with the love he needs? Can I let go when the time comes?

Twenty years ago, I wouldn't have been able to love someone else's child so thoroughly, and I definitely would not have been able to let go had I allowed myself to love so deeply. I do not relish the thought of letting go, but when the time comes, I am sure my maturity and common sense will allow me to cut the ties.

I will not fear my emotions, because God gives me unconditional strength to live and love adventurously and without reserve. When this calling is complete, another will be waiting. Just as hard, just as emotional, and once again I will pass the test. Because I am a mature woman, equipped by God to do all he has for me to do.

TODAY'S HOT FLASH:

A risk-free life is lifeless living. Heartbreak opens us up to a new depth of understanding and a greater adventure.

PRAYER:

Lord, help me not to hold back my love because I fear the pain of hurt. Help me love fully, live fully, grieve fully, and then love again. Amen.

APRIL 14

READ: MATTHEW 5:1–12

ARE YOU A SNOWPLOW?

Blessed are the meek: for they shall inherit the earth.

~ Matthew 5:5

I am woman; hear me roar, and nag, and complain; watch me walk all over everybody. I am older and wiser, so what I have to say is more important.

Have you ever been blasted with such arrogant retorts? Worse yet, have any of these statements flown from your lips?

For years, many of us have spent our lives as dirty doormats, allowing the whole world to wipe their feet on us as we smile and take it with calm reserve. Something happens at about forty. We discover ourselves for the first time, and in extreme retaliation, we give it back full force. We become snowplows. When obstacles block us, we push them out of the way as if they were of no consequence. When someone offends us, we snowplow them into the nearest corner, and boy does it feel good—for a while.

Until we turn around and realize we are bitter and in a very lonely place. Don't let this happen to you. It's okay to exert your womanly strong points, but only for the betterment of others. To snowplow others is to push away those you need the most.

TODAY'S HOT FLASH:

Snowplows often pile snow so deep that you must go around them. Do people have to go around you in order to keep from being plowed over?

PRAYER:

Oh, Lord, forgive any aggressiveness in me that has caused me to plow over people just because I can. Give me a loving, humble heart. Amen.

APRIL 15

READ: PROVERBS 3:19–26

THE TITANIC: "A SHIP EVEN GOD COULDN'T SINK"

For the Lord shall be your confidence, and shall keep thy foot from being taken.

~ Proverbs 3:26

The Titanic was the greatest ship of its time. Every person, from steerage to the first class elite, was excited to be part of its maiden voyage. Some unsuspecting and irreverent soul was heard to have said, "Even God Himself couldn't sink this ship." Call it coincidence or divine justice, but the fact is that on April 15, 1912 at 2:30 a.m., the Titanic plunged to the bottom of the ocean. More than 1,200 souls were lost that day.

Did God cause the disaster? I don't think so; He knows full well the foolishness of men. But could it be that in their complete confidence of a man-made structure, they forgot to acknowledge the Great Protector? Rather than lifting prayers to the Father, they were heralding accolades to the ship and its human builders.

Where does your confidence lie? In a job? A spouse? A monthly check? A degree? Jobs are lost, spouses fail, and self-made success can disappear tomorrow. Only God never fails. He alone should be the only One we place full confidence in.

TODAY'S HOT FLASH:

My confidence lies in the great hands of the Master Creator. He alone can keep me from sinking when the icebergs of this world try to drag me down.

PRAYER:

Father, never allow me to get to a point where I place my confidence in something of this world. You alone are trustworthy and foolproof. Amen.

APRIL 16
READ: MALACHI 2:1–9

DO RIGHT ANYWAY

The law of truth was in his mouth, and iniquity was not found in his lips: he walked with me in peace and equity, and did turn many away from iniquity.

~ Malachi 2:6

My husband went to breakfast without me this morning. I cried. I looked around my house at the overwhelming mess. I cried. My daughter called and told me my grandson was sick. Guess what. I cried. I'm just a little hormonal today.

There are times when my perception of the way things are supposed to be is altered, and I throw myself a little fit. Afterwards, I am consumed with guilt and spend the rest of the day moping because I'm such a horrible Christian.

Reacting negatively comes so easily, but God is never glorified when I allow the flesh to take over in this manner. I am so thankful that, most of the time, the Holy Spirit gently reminds me that God's truth is to generate from my mouth, no iniquity should pour from my lips, and peace is to be my underlying characteristic. Though I often fail, there are more times than not that the Holy Spirit keeps me strong. The more I listen to His still small voice, the more victory I have in my hormonal struggles.

TODAY'S HOT FLASH:

When we stop to listen to the Holy Spirit's prodding, He will keep us from saying and doing things we will regret.

PRAYER:

Father, I have promised to serve You no matter where my emotions lead. Keep me strong today; give me strength to overcome the power of the flesh. May Your Spirit reign. Amen.

APRIL 17

READ: GENESIS 21:1-21

LET GO AND TRUST GOD

And God said unto Abraham, Let it not be grievous in thy sight because of the lad [...] and God was with the lad; and he grew.

~ Genesis 21:12a, 20a

The time draws near. Little Jonny, my three-month-old foster son, leaves soon. I am the only mother he has ever known. But only by association, not by birth. Soon his biological mother will regain the privilege of loving him.

I wondered if I had the patience to take care of a newborn at my age. But between the two of us, we worked it out. It's not that I don't want to give him to his mother, it is his rightful place, but we have formed a bond. I love him.

As God was with Ishmael when heartbroken Abraham had to let him go, so He will be with Jonny. I can hear the silent whisper, "Let it not be grievous in thy sight because of the lad," and I cling to God's promise of protection for Him.

What is it you have to let go of? A person? A job? Painful memories? Give them to God, He knows best.

TODAY'S HOT FLASH:

Abraham had to let go of Ishmael, and there are things He asks us to let go of as well. What are you clinging to?

PRAYER:

Lord, my heart breaks over my loss. What can I do but trust in You? What can I do but cling to Your promises? What can I do but love You no matter what? Amen.

APRIL 18
READ: EPHESIANS 2:14-22

CHIEF CORNERSTONE

*And are built upon the foundation of the apostles and prophets,
Jesus Christ himself being the chief corner stone.*

~ Ephesians 2:20

What is life but a series of challenges and curves? Daily, sometimes hourly, change gushes through our tranquil circumstances and alters everything. Our expectations diminish as we realize our inability to control. Our dreams crash as life swerves in the opposite direction, and we are helpless to intervene.

Where would our peace of mind and mental stability be if Christ was not the chief cornerstone of everything we hold dear? As long as He remains in the picture, the most traumatic experiences cannot drive us to the point of insanity. Even more comforting, in the midst of intense stress, he is growing us into "a holy temple in the Lord."

If it weren't for the trials, how would we know the surety of our Lord's faithfulness? Every incident in life is divinely designed to create within you a spirit that is absolutely and positively dependent on Jesus.

TODAY'S HOT FLASH:

Are you struggling with the curves and challenges life throws at you? Cling to Jesus. His strength will not crumble when yours does.

PRAYER:

Thank You, Father, for Jesus, our chief cornerstone. I give You praise for the assurance that I can endure anything through His strength. Amen.

APRIL 19

READ: PSALM 139

GOD ALREADY KNOWS

Whither shall I go from thy spirit? Or whither shall I flee from thy presence?

~ Psalm 139:7

What is it that keeps you from claiming God's best? Some secret sin? Indecisiveness in your spiritual life? Can you hide anything from God? Are your hormonal surges flaring up as depression? Did you react in a wrong way, leaving you ashamed to go before the most Holy God? My friend, God already knows.

He knows your every intimate secret. Maybe it's a thought or deed that overtakes you in the night hours. God knows. An illegal dealing, immoral action, or something that would cause you or people you love disgrace. God knows.

For years I held back my innermost thoughts from God. I was too ashamed to tell Him about them. Suddenly it occurred to me: God already knows! Scripture says, "Whither shall I go from thy spirit? Or whither shall I flee from thy presence?" Peel away the last of your shell and become completely naked spiritually and emotionally with the One who sees your innermost being and loves you anyway.

TODAY'S HOT FLASH:

Open up and let the words flow freely to the only One willing to wrap you in His forgiveness and bring you into a right relationship with Himself.

PRAYER:

Father, peel away my walls and help me confess those things I have fooled myself into believing are hidden. Amen.

APRIL 20
READ: LUKE 6:28-35

DO UNTO OTHERS

And as ye would that men should do to you, do ye also to them likewise.
~ Luke 6:31

How do you feel when someone yells at you? When was the last time you yelled at someone? What emotions flow through your veins when you are at the receiving end of criticism? When is the last time you criticized someone? Does anything irritate you more than the selfish acts of other Christians? When is the last time you were selfish? With your time, your possessions, your encouragement?

As hormones rage, we find ourselves out of control in many of these areas. At the same time, we are overly sensitive to anyone who mistreats us. Is it possible that the negativity you are receiving is a direct reaction to the negativity you've been giving? A person will only take so much abuse before snapping. Scripture says that "as ye would that men should do to you, do ye also to them likewise." If you don't want to be yelled at, don't yell. Remember how it makes you feel and keep yourself under control. You have the power of the Holy Spirit to help you. Now use it!

TODAY'S HOT FLASH:

In order to receive respectful treatment, you must treat others respectfully. Remember when you taught your children this?

PRAYER:

Forgiving Father, I have not treated others properly. I have allowed my emotions to control me. Forgive me. I want to love, not push away. Amen.

APRIL 21

READ: PHILIPPIANS 2:12-16

HAPPY BIRTHDAY TO ME

Holding forth the word of life, that I may rejoice in the day of Christ, that I have not run in vain, neither labored in vain.

~ Philippians 2:16

I recently celebrated a birthday. I turned 50! I received oodles and oodles of cards from friends, family, and acquaintances. Even though many of my loved ones have a great sense of humor, not one of them, with the exception of my husband, bought me a humorous card making fun of my age. They were all sensitive to my sensitivity on the subject. Truthfully, I didn't really care.

After the fact, my children revealed to me that they wanted to throw me a big party but decided I might be offended, so they decided to ignore it for the most part. WHAT??? I think I've earned a great big bash after 50 years—I've never had a party thrown for me. I would have thought this would have been the perfect time. A rite of passage, so to speak, from what was to what will be, from the pains of the past to the glorious times of my future, from an immature girl to a mature woman. I've just hit the age where people might start believing I know what I am talking about. And they wanted to cover it up? No way! In my next 50 years, I plan on tripling my efforts for God and having a great adventure in the process!

TODAY'S HOT FLASH:

Where are you heading in your next 50, 40, or 30 years? Or whatever time God has allotted you? Meet the challenges head on and "Go, Girl —for God!"

PRAYER:

Father, help me to keep my eyes on the cross so that they do not stray to the left or the right but remain focused on running and finishing this race for Your glory. Amen.

APRIL 22

READ: ECCLESIASTES 3:1–10

GOD'S TIMING

To every thing there is a season, and a time to every purpose under the heaven.

~ Ecclesiastes 3:1

Cindy is a friend of mine and an active member of our church. For longer than I've known her, she has been praying for her husband's salvation. Time has become her nemesis. With each passing year, her faith that God will answer this prayer wanes. She struggles to remain strong. Her mind knows God is in control, but her humanly flawed heart questions it.

Universally, we are all alike. We want what we want, and we want it now. As we age we seem to develop a sense of urgency that we didn't have before. We know time is running out.

The wisest man in the world, King Solomon, knew how futile our worrying is. His advice remains as true today as it was then. "To **everything** there is a season and a time to **every** purpose under the heaven." God is always on time.

TODAY'S HOT FLASH:

What part of "every" don't you understand? Nothing is exempt. Are you waiting for an answer from God? Everything, everything, everything in His time.

PRAYER:

Oh, Lord, I know Your timing is perfect, and for everything there is a purpose. Help me not to question You but to trust You implicitly. Amen.

APRIL 23

READ: JOSHUA 24:14–21

WHOM DO YOU SERVE?

And if it seem evil unto you to serve the Lord, choose you this day whom ye will serve ... but as for me and my house, we will serve the Lord.

~ Joshua 24:15

Every time I ignore the still small voice prodding me to do what's right and choose the easier or more comfortable way, I choose to serve self. Every time I sleep in on Sunday morning, or stay home and watch a movie on Wednesday evening, I become the idol God warns me about in His Word.

Without a second thought, we put things and people above God. Whenever we don't answer the phone or the doorbell, whenever we refuse to take a stand for right, whenever we don't walk out the door and take some food to those we know are in need, we serve self. In the flesh it is easy to forget why God created us, and we easily become consumed with our own needs. As we learn to recognize the nudging of the Holy Spirit, this innate selfishness should gradually dissipate, illuminating Jesus above our own selfish desires.

TODAY'S HOT FLASH:

Don't you think it's time to "choose you this day whom ye will serve"? God first, others second, and me last. That is what I call true service.

PRAYER:

Forgiving Father, daily I fail You in this area. Forgive me. Teach me to put You above all my personal conveniences. Amen.

APRIL 24
READ: 1 CORINTHIANS 9:7-12

CHRISTIAN RIGHTS

But suffer all things, lest we should hinder the gospel of Christ.
~ 1 Corinthians 9:12b

With age often comes boldness. We are more apt to stand up for our "rights" without shame or concern for others. In our adult Sunday school class, we are developing a Christian Bill of Rights. What an eye-opening experience!

Eating steak, speaking my mind, owning a new car, retirement, vacation, my time, and so many more were reluctantly replaced with the following:

The right to serve our Lord as slaves

The right to tell others about Jesus

The right to stand against sin

The right to put others before myself

The right to give God His ten percent

The right to pray

If people are going to be offended, let it be at the Word of God. Never let it be because of my selfish actions for the sake of "my rights."

TODAY'S HOT FLASH:

The older we get, the more set in our ways we become. Never get set in your ways; set yourself in God's ways and His alone.

PRAYER:

So often, Lord, I rudely offend by claiming my fleshly rights. Forgive me. Take my life, and truly let it be consecrated, Lord, to thee and thee alone. Amen.

APRIL 25

READ: LUKE 10:38-42

ENCUMBERED BY THE CARES OF THIS WORLD

But one thing is needful: and Mary hath chosen that good part which shall not be taken away from her.

~ Luke 10:42

My frenzied days often consume my energy, leaving little time for emotional and spiritual nourishment. The "to-do list" in my brain tends to override even my personal devotions. It is a constant struggle to stay focused on Jesus, and guilt is ever present.

Martha was a lot like me. She so wanted to please Jesus that her mind became engrossed in the "to-do's" rather than the person. So much so that her jealousy of Mary's time with the Savior prompted her to complain. What was Christ's reply? "Mary hath chosen that good part which shall not be taken away from her."

Oh, to be like Mary, to be able to forget the rest of the world and solely focus on the Words of the Master. Was Martha's desire to please Jesus wrong? No. The problem developed when her desire to please (impress) Him overpowered her desire to be with Him. Are you encumbered by the cares of the day? Desperately trying to impress God with your busyness rather than enjoying His presence?

TODAY'S HOT FLASH:

God finds pleasure in you. He wants to spend time with you. You don't need to impress Him; nothing you do can make Him love you more.

PRAYER:

Father, I spend so much time trying to impress You. No matter how hard I try, I never feel I've done enough. Forgive my vain efforts. Teach me to bask in Your presence, just You and me, oblivious to the cares of the world. Amen.

APRIL 26

READ: LUKE 2:15-19

PONDER, DON'T POUR

But Mary kept all these things and pondered them in her heart.

~ Luke 2:19

I don't know how it happened, but somewhere, somehow, I turned from a mousy, skittish woman into an overbearing, over-opinionated person who doesn't know when to keep her mouth shut.

What I'd give to be able to be able to zip these lips and do as Mary did, "ponder" in my heart rather than pour out to the nth degree. I pray, "Lord, I am not going to say a word," but two seconds later I am voicing my opinion—loudly! Like that makes it right, or important.

When confronted with the greatest event in her life, Mary didn't pour out; she "kept all these things and pondered them in her heart."

Jesus said, "Every idle word that men shall speak, they shall give account thereof in the day of judgment" (Matthew 12:36). With that in mind, I think it best to say as little as possible. How about you?

TODAY'S HOT FLASH:

God never allows us the luxury of telling others "how it is" unless the "how it is" is the way God says it is.

PRAYER:

Merciful Father, I have a problem. I can't seem to keep my mouth shut. Forgive me. Help me to be a ponderer rather than a pourer. Amen.

FOR SANITY'S SAKE

APRIL 27

READ: MARK 6:32-44

INTRUSIONS

And the people saw them departing, and many knew him, and ran afoot thither out of all cities, and outwent them, and came together unto him.

~ Mark 6:33

My large family is very cliquish. We spend more time together than with anyone else. There are a few outsiders but not many, and we are comfortable with it that way. The problem is that exclusivity does not coincide with ministry. Unfortunately, it has passed on to all my children. Although I understand it, I try to set the example by opening my home to anyone God brings my way.

Many times in Scripture we see Jesus departing from the people. It isn't long before they start following. He always stops to meet their needs. Unlike my family, He does not see them as an intrusion. He recognizes their great need and stops to minister.

If you believe God is totally in control, intrusions don't exist. Stop trying to shut them out and start welcoming them with open arms. How else are we supposed to introduce Jesus to them?

TODAY'S HOT FLASH:

There are no elite cliques in God's kingdom. Everyone is equal, and greater still, everyone is welcome.

PRAYER:

Father, give me unconditional love and acceptance for others, just like Jesus had when He walked on this earth. Amen.

APRIL 28
READ: 1 PETER 5

SATAN'S DECEPTION

Be sober, be vigilant; because your adversary the devil, as a roaring lion, walketh about, seeking whom he may devour.

~ 1 Peter 5:8

A lion doesn't roar while stalking its prey. The roaring comes from its counterparts on the sidelines deceiving the hunted, effectively tricking the prey into believing the danger lies in another direction. When least expected, the hunter strikes. Caught unawares, the victim is nabbed and unable to resist. So it is with Satan; he makes noise in one direction, and we shield ourselves from the onslaught. And then out of the blue, we are slapped in the face with the reality that he has nabbed us. In proving our spiritual strength in one area, we blatantly fell in another. Pride engulfed us, and Satan won after all.

Often I prepare myself to face the day in many different ways. I take my medicines, do my devotions, situate my day to involve the least amount of irritations as possible, and puff up in pride because I have it all under control. Then wham! I've been hit broadside with some unexpected event—little or big—and I crumble like dried mud. I have forgotten the most important thing—Jesus. It's not my day, it's His. Instead of surrendering it to Him, I take control. And that's when I fall.

TODAY'S HOT FLASH:

Are you deceived by the roaring lion? Lulled into believing everything is under control? Beware! The strike will come when you least expect it.

PRAYER:

Oh, Lord, I've done it again. Tricked myself into believing I have it all under control. Forgive me. Take control. Amen.

LIVE!

It is a good thing to give thanks unto the Lord, and to sing praises unto thy name, O Most High.

~ Psalm 92:1

My 57-year-old Baptist preacher husband bought a Harley. I had a choice: refuse to accept it or conform to his newfound love. So I, a conservative pastor's wife, bought a helmet, riding boots, and a leather jacket that says "lady rider."

We women aren't the only ones who experience change as we get older. Aging is universal, and the proverbial time clock clicks for everyone. Why not try new things? Why not step out and take risks? We can either sit on the porch and rock our way to eternity or we can LIVE! I choose to live. God doesn't have a problem with us enjoying life; He has a problem when we don't keep Him in the center of everything we do. I have to admit that I look pretty good in my Harley get up, and I am having a wonderful time. Praise God from whom ALL blessings flow!

TODAY'S HOT FLASH:

Don't be a stooge. Get up and start enjoying life. You may have a day, or you may have thirty years; only God knows. Don't waste a minute!

PRAYER:

Well, I'm off, Lord, to live life another day. May I be full of zest and put my whole heart in whatever it is You have for me to do, whether riding a Harley or watching a dozen kids. And may You, Lord, receive all the glory. Amen.

APRIL 30
READ: PSALM 104

HIS MAJESTY

The glory of the Lord shall endure forever: the Lord shall rejoice in his works.
~ Psalm 104:31

I am amazed at the beauty in this fallen world. Among all the ugly, God has graciously surrounded us with reminders of His majesty. These are some of the things that calm my soul: the roaring awesomeness of Niagara Falls, the brilliance of a sparkling rainbow, the unbelievable calm as one looks out across the vast ocean, the eagle majestically soaring through the sky, the cry of a newborn baby, a drive through the country in the fall, the old white-washed church sitting on a hill in the middle of nowhere. As I am captured by the overwhelming beauty in what I see, I yearn for the most spectacular of all—standing face-to-face with Christ my Savior.

What calms your soul? What turns your thoughts to heaven? These things are precious gifts to the aging soul! It is only as we grow older that we realize how much we've missed by zooming through life instead of stopping and smelling the roses.

TODAY'S HOT FLASH:

Take time to smell the roses, listen to the songbirds, and study the intricacy of a spider's web. Worship God for His magnificent reminders of His majesty.

PRAYER:

O Lord, how manifold are Your works! In wisdom You have made them: all the earth is full of Your riches. You are a mighty and great God, and I will praise Your name. Amen.

MAY

MAY 1

READ: EPHESIANS 2:1–10

TRASH TO TREASURE

For we are his workmanship, created in Christ Jesus unto good works, which God hath before ordained that we should walk in them.

~ Ephesians 2:10

Looking through my craft books, I came across one titled "Trash for Treasure." The author used discarded tin cans, pop bottles, paper bags, and even boxes to make beautifully crafted items. The first words in the book are "Making something from nothing." I couldn't help but draw a parallel.

Isn't that exactly what God does? He takes our messed up lives and turns us into beautiful treasures. He calls us "his workmanship, created in Christ Jesus." It matters not what we look like, how old we are, or where we come from; it doesn't even matter what the rest of the world thinks. If you belong to Jesus, you are His treasure and no one can take that away. He has taken your nothingness and turned it into something wonderful. Maybe you don't believe it now, but someday, after you've breathed your last breath, there won't be a doubt in your mind. You will be like Jesus, perfect in every way. Oh glorious day!

TODAY'S HOT FLASH:

We all feel like trash sometimes, but feelings are deceiving. God calls us His workmanship. And, friend, God don't make no junk!

PRAYER:

Father, so many times I feel useless and like discarded trash. Help me to remember that I am Your treasure and You love me unconditionally. Amen.

MAY 2

READ: NUMBERS 16:1–11

ARE YOU TOO GOOD TO SERVE?

Seemeth it but a small thing unto you, that the God of Israel hath separated you from the congregation of Israel, to bring you near to himself to do the service of the tabernacle of the Lord?

~ Numbers 16:9

The Kohathites, a tribe of the Levite family, were not satisfied with their assignment from God. They asked Moses, "Wherefore then lift ye up yourselves above the congregation of the Lord?" Moses "fell on his face" (vs. 4).

Moses' reply? "Seemeth it a small thing unto you, that the God of Israel hath separated you from the congregation of Israel to bring you near to himself to do the service of the tabernacle of the Lord?

God's reaction? "And the earth opened her mouth, and swallowed them up and their houses" (16:32).

Praise God that we live in a time of grace. Would we have disappeared into the great crevice because of our murmuring and complaining over the "unimportant" jobs of service, while envying those we deemed "important" in the ministry?

TODAY'S HOT FLASH:

There are no unimportant jobs of service. God looks only at the heart. Do we gladly serve in obedience or obediently serve in discontent?

PRAYER:

Forgive me, Lord, for all those times I murmur and complain. May I serve You with a generous and content heart from this day forward. Amen.

MAY 3

READ: ISAIAH 29:9–16

HOW WOULD I KNOW?

Wherefore, the Lord said, forasmuch as this people draw near me with their mouth, and with their lips do honor me, but have removed their heart far from me...

~ Isaiah 29:13

I am a preacher's wife who has taught Sunday school, led women's groups, spoken at seminars, homeschooled my children, published three devotionals, and more. I tell you this, not to boast, but to come humbly before you in admittance that for many years, my words, actions, and deeds were no better than the Israelites when God said, they "draw near me with their mouth, and with their lips do honor me, but have removed their heart far from me." My lips praised the Lord, but my heart was far from Him.

I never would have known the condition of my heart had God not revealed it to me in a very drastic and heart-wrenching way. In a moment of temptation, I succumbed, and my sinful heart was revealed in vivid detail.

As painful as it was, I am grateful for His intervention. In my sorrow and shame, I had to admit that much of my life was as the Israelites. I was putting on a façade. It was in the darkest time of my life that I truly came to Jesus.

How would I have known where my heart was had God not shown me?

TODAY'S HOT FLASH:

How will you know where your heart is until you have been tested? Don't wait for God to reveal it to you. Get it right with Him before He has to.

PRAYER:

Change my heart, O God, make it ever true. Change my heart, O God, may I be like You. Humble me when I need it. I love you so much. Amen.

MAY 4

READ: PROVERBS 31:10-31

FUTURE BENEFITS

Who can find a virtuous woman? For her price is far above rubies.

~ Proverbs 31:10

My husband's grandmother went home to be with the Lord at the age of 94. Married to a Baptist minister, mother of ten children, and widowed early in life, she lived a hard but godly life. The world would say she was a nobody. She didn't make a name for herself, write a book, or become a famous actress. But God saw her differently. He saw a faithful servant who raised her children to serve Him. Three of her sons became Baptist preachers, and numerous grandsons as well. Her influence will thrive for hundreds of years to come.

My husband didn't spend a lot of time with his grandma. But there is one thing he remembers most of all; she was the very first person to ever talk to him about Jesus.

Do you feel your life is wasted? You haven't done anything grandiose. When you die, only a few people will know who you were. That's okay. Invest your life in your children, grandchildren, and loved ones. Make sure you talk about Jesus to each one of them. Your influence will make a difference for eternity.

TODAY'S HOT FLASH:

Just imagine—praising the Lord in heaven, while still collecting rewards for souls here on earth. There's nothing more rewarding than that. Let it be so, Lord.

PRAYER:

Father, may I boldly speak of You to those who are most important to me. May my faithfulness make a difference hundreds of years to come. Amen.

MAY 5

READ: PROVERBS 29:20-27

BABY STEPS

The fear of man bringeth a snare: but whoso putteth his trust in the Lord shall be safe.

~ Proverbs 29:25

My one-year-old grandson is learning to walk. He pulls himself up and just stands there. He looks all around, sees all the things he'd like to do, all the places he'd like to go, and then drops on his knees and crawls. He lacks the courage of his convictions. In truth, he is ready to zoom on his two feet, but his mind and his feet are not yet synchronized.

Isn't that like so many of us? Whether we are 15 or 50, we have things in our lives we know we need to do, yet, for some reason we can't synchronize our thoughts and actions. It could be a sin we've used as a crutch for years. It could be a ministry we know God has called us to, or a person we need to forgive. Up until now, we have been unable to. The underlying factor is fear: fear of failure or rejection. It's just as Solomon said, "The fear of man bringeth a snare." We are caught between action and fear, just like my grandson. Solomon doesn't stop there; he goes on to say, "But whoso putteth his trust in the Lord shall be safe." Now there's a comforting promise.

TODAY'S HOT FLASH:

Fear is not of God. Take baby steps if you must, but take them. Once you free yourself from that snare, you will never want to go back.

PRAYER:

Father, I've held back for so long out of fear and rejection. Remove this hindrance to my spiritual growth and help me step out in faith. Amen.

MAY 6

READ: JOHN 14:1–6

THAT'S ALL THAT MATTERS TO ME

In my Father's house are many mansions: if it were not so, I would have told you. I go to prepare a place for you.

~ John 14:2

I love to travel the countryside viewing mansions of unbelievable beauty. I good-heartedly try to imagine what it would be like to live in such extravagance. Don't get me wrong; I am content where I am. I am not jealous, for I know someday my mansion will outshine any I've seen.

Jesus has gone to prepare a place for me. It will be a beautiful place, and rewards will abound, but those are not the things my heart craves for. I crave to see my Savior face-to-face. I crave those longed-for words of "well done, good and faithful servant." I crave to place those precious rewards at his feet, giving back, if only a little, for what He has done for me. My heart just swells with anticipation when I think of what is to come. Yes, mansions and streets of gold are nice, but, nothing compares to Jesus. That's all that matters to me.

TODAY'S HOT FLASH:

What fills your mind when you think of eternity? The materialistic benefits never realized here on earth? Or finally face-to-face with Jesus your Savior?

PRAYER:

Father, my heart yearns for You. My heart yearns to finally be with your Son Jesus. And my heart yearns to hear "Well done, good and faithful servant." That's all that matters to me. Amen.

MAY 7

READ: ROMANS 8:14-17

ABBA FATHER

For we have not received the Spirit of bondage again to fear; but ye have received the Spirit of adoption, whereby we cry, Abba Father.

~ Romans 8:15

Two days ago I revealed that my grandson was learning to walk. What I didn't mention was that little Jayden did not join our family until he was four months old. He is adopted. To watch him with his parents, you would never know. They love him explicitly, and so do we. In some ways Jayden and I are alike, for I am adopted as well—by God. He is my Father and I am His child, a "joint heir with Christ." I belong, and belonging is a great feeling.

Many people wander aimlessly from one thing to the next, searching for a place to belong. The great thing about God is that He has opened the door for anyone to enter his family through adoption. That adoption door comes through Jesus Christ.

Are you searching for a place to belong? Come to Jesus! Through Him you have the right to cry, "Abba Father." He is the perfect Father.

TODAY'S HOT FLASH:

Are you part of God's adopted family? Only those who are, have the right to cry, "Abba Father," when in need. What are you waiting for? God loves big families. There's always room for one more.

PRAYER:

Abba Father, thank You for choosing me as your own. You could have looked inside my heart, seen the dirty stains of sin, and turned away, but You didn't. I am forever grateful. Amen.

MAY 8
READ: 2 CORINTHIANS 5:1–10

REACTIONS

For we must all appear before the judgment seat of Christ; that every one may receive the things done in his body, according to that he hath done, whether it be good or bad.

~ 2 Corinthians 5:10

My adult son cleared every rock from his yard and then bought a new lawn mower. As soon as he returned home, he fired it up and began mowing. Little did he know that while he was gone, his four-year-old son returned the rocks to their "proper" places.

When the blade hit rock . . . well, let's say, Dad was NOT happy. Little Johnny was in BIG trouble. His daddy was so mad that he banned Johnny from everything he could think of. Then he headed my way, and I heard it too. Well, you know I had to have my say, and it wasn't against my grandson. For in truth, did this action really require such wrath? What's he going to say to Christ when he is asked about his reaction? It may seem like a small thing, but Scripture says, "We must all appear before the judgment seat of Christ . . . according to that he hath done, whether it be good or bad."

It's not what happens in life that counts; it is our reaction to what happens. Are we reacting in the flesh (spurred on by hormones) or allowing the Spirit to control us in every circumstance? The little things determine how we will react in the big things.

TODAY'S HOT FLASH:

How do you react when angered? I already have too many reactions to answer for when I face Christ; I don't want to add any more. How about You?

PRAYER:

Lord, shamefully I know where my son learned to react. Help me to set a better example for those around me. Amen.

MAY 9
READ: 1 JOHN 2

DRAMA QUEEN

My little children, these things write I unto you, that ye sin not.

~ 1 John 2:1a

My foster daughter, Charity (not her real name), is a drama queen. When she is angry, she stomps, screams, slams things, and even hisses on occasion. When she is happy, she bounces like a kangaroo while giggling and making strange gleeful noises. Obviously, her reactions are designed to get as much attention as possible.

Over the years, I have thrown a few tantrums myself. Yes, I must admit, I have played the drama queen. Nothing brings it out more than menopause. My poor husband! I don't know how he lives with it.

John begins chapter two of his letter with the words, "little children," followed by "sin not." I am struck with the realization that at times, I act no better than my four-year-old. Hmmm... was John being a little sarcastic in his loving reprimand?

Too often I return to childish behavior that should have disappeared years ago. That is why the second part of this verse is such a life saver, "And if any man sin, we have an advocate with the Father, Jesus Christ the righteous."

TODAY'S HOT FLASH:

Drama queens love attention. Let's stop the acting and bring attention and glory to the One who deserves it—Jesus Christ!

PRAYER:

Lord, I act childish at times and say and do stupid things. Thank You for Jesus, who bridges the gulf that would otherwise separate You from me. Amen.

MAY 10
READ: JOHN 3:5–16

BORN AGAIN AND AGAIN

Marvel not that I say unto thee, Ye must be born again.
~ John 3:7

In some ways menopause is like being born again. The old me disappears with my changing emotional and physical status. What comes out at the end will be a new and better me, but the process of getting there is long and tedious. I call this my "little" born again experience because truly I am different, yet still me.

Nothing changes me like my original born again experience. This comes only through Jesus Christ. And much like menopause, yet much more, when Jesus enters into our lives, we begin to change. This change, as well, is long and sometimes tedious. We aren't who we used to be; we are different. At the same time, we aren't who we are going to be either. We grow, and grow, and grow some more, until the day we go home to glory. This is called progressive sanctification.

Are you continuously growing in your Christian faith? Just like a baby is born and must grow, so must we. If the baby stops growing, there is a physical problem. If a Christian stops growing, there is a spiritual problem. Are you on the road to progressive sanctification, or are you stagnant and unchanging?

TODAY'S HOT FLASH:

Progressive sanctification is the telltale sign of a true born again experience. If you are not growing, your rebirth experience is questionable.

PRAYER:

Father, thank You for Jesus; help me to continually grow in my faith. To be like Jesus, that is my heartfelt desire. Amen.

LOW DEGREE, HIGHLY EXALTED

Let the brother of low degree rejoice, in that he is exalted.

~ James 1:9

Like most of God's children, I have what I need, pay my bills, and even have a few frivolous items. I am not rich, but God provides. But I have to admit, I've had my share of dreams and desires. Things I imagined owning, places I've imagined going, activities I've imagined doing. I still have these dreams even though I know, realistically speaking, I will never see them fulfilled this side of heaven.

I find it entertaining to dream big dreams, but I don't allow these dreams to consume me. Someday I will have a mansion. Someday I will see the whole world. Someday, diamonds will seem like coal when compared to the treasures waiting for me in glory.

For now I will take comfort in God's promise: "Let the brother of low degree rejoice, in that he is exalted." Fame and wealth are nice dreams but probably not my reality. But I can rejoice, for in my lowliness, I have learned to depend on my gracious Father.

TODAY'S HOT FLASH:

Don't waste your time pining over unfulfilled dreams. Someday your riches will far exceed even the richest of the rich. That's worth waiting for.

PRAYER:

Father, teach me to be satisfied in my lowly estate. Thank You for giving me everything I need. Help me to be content in that. Amen.

MAY 12
READ: JOHN 2:23-25

SECRETS

But Jesus did not commit himself unto them, because he knew all men.
~ John 2:24

Do you have secrets? I mean dark, shameful secrets nobody but you and maybe a very select few know about? I do. No, I am not going to reveal them; I probably never will.

Almost everyone has deep dark secrets, things from their past that deeply shame them. For some, these secrets become debilitating, causing many to hide within themselves and away from others, lest they be found out. Often times the secret-bearers find it hard to open their hearts to God. They live in constant fear of rejection.

My heart breaks for those stuck in their hurt and pain of the past. If only they could grasp the reality of Jesus. He knows every dirty little detail and every unholy, shameful secret that is in me and in them. Scripture tells us "he **knew** all men." There is nothing about us he does not know. More remarkably we are told that "while we were yet sinners, Christ died for us" (Romans 5:8). We don't have to carry the burden of hiding our wretchedness from God. He knows—and He loves us anyway.

TODAY'S HOT FLASH:

Don't let your past haunt you. Lay your secrets at the feet of Jesus and leave them there. He is strong enough to carry your burden so you don't have to.

PRAYER:

Father, my past haunts me. I can't seem to let go of my pain. Please, take these burdens from me. I place them at the feet of Jesus. Help me to leave them there. Amen.

FOR SANITY'S SAKE

MAY 13

READ: NUMBERS 9:15–23

HOVERING CLOUD

And so it was, when the cloud abode from even unto the morning [. . .] or whether it be two days, or a month, or a year . . . "

~ Numbers 9:21–22

When the cloud tarried over the tabernacle, the Israelites knew to stay put; when it was taken up, they journeyed. Sometimes the cloud remained for a day, sometimes a month, and sometimes a year or more. Without a doubt, they always knew when it was God's will to move on.

We may not have a hovering cloud revealing to us God's will, but we have two things with the same clarity and preciseness as the cloud: the Holy Spirit and God's Holy Word.

The Israelites had the hovering cloud to guide them; we have the Bible. It is in His Word that we are told how to walk in His will.

Micah 6:8 says, "He has shown thee, O man, what is good; and what doth the Lord require of thee, but to do justly, and to love mercy, and to walk humbly with thy God." I think this is a good place to start; how about you?

TODAY'S HOT FLASH:

God promises to show us His will for today. Not tomorrow, or the next day or the next. Walk in His Word and you will walk in His Will.

PRAYER:

Father, it's hard to walk in the moment—in just today when tomorrow is right around the corner. Help me to be content knowing Your will one day at a time. Amen.

MAY 14

READ: MATTHEW 5:13-16

PEOPLE NEED THE LORD

Ye are the light of the world. A city that is set on a hill cannot be hid.
~ Matthew 5:14

Out in the hills of Pennsylvania, not far from where I live, a 91-year-old woman was playing hostess to her dead husband and her twin sister. A relative discovered the grisly truth and reported her to authorities. When asked why, she simply said, "I miss them." She talked to them, covered their legs when it got chilly, and combed her sister's hair to keep her presentable.

The outpouring of sympathy and support for this woman has been unbelievable. Many people can relate to her feeling of lonely desperation. The sad truth is that she is only one of millions desperately clinging to anyone or anything they can, lest the loneliness and hopelessness of life consume them.

We see them every day, pass them on the street, work with them, and shop in the same stores—lonely people, lost people, people who need the Lord. We are the light of the world. Are you letting your light so shine before all the lonely and hurting people? They need you to show them Jesus. What are you waiting for?

TODAY'S HOT FLASH:

Some people go to extreme measures to fight loneliness. We must go to extreme measures to bring them hope through Jesus Christ.

PRAYER:

Lord, I know I've let You down. I've walked by sad and lonely people without a second glance. Open my heart to their loneliness; use me to draw them to You. Amen.

MAY 15

READ: EPHESIANS 5:1–5

AM I OLD YET?

And walk in love, as Christ also hath loved us, and hath given himself for us an offering and a sacrifice to God for a sweet-smelling savour.

~ Ephesians 5:2

It boggles my mind that I am writing devotions for menopausal women. I mean, I can't be that old yet, can I? Bernard Baruch's quote, "To me old age is always fifteen years older than I am," fits me to a tee. After all, when I was a teenager, twenty was old; when I was twenty, thirty was old; now that I am fifty, seventy is old. My husband tells me I am in denial.

I am often humbled and reminded that I am not twenty anymore when, in the midst of my hormonal surges, I let go of any pretense of godliness and toss out my nasty remarks like never before. Too often my offering to God is a rotten odor rather than a sweet-smelling savor.

I pray a lot, confess a lot, and hope that just maybe I am winning the war on my hormonal outbursts. Some days I am sure of it, others—well, I fail miserably. When I do, I pick myself back up and start again. There will come a time when I can kiss these fleshly hormonal fits goodbye. Until that day, I'll keep trying and give thanks for every offering of sweet-smelling savor I manage to produce.

TODAY'S HOT FLASH:

Failure isn't final; it is a starting place for future victories. Pick yourself up and continue toward the finish line. The prize is well worth the struggle.

PRAYER:

I did it again, Lord, blew a gasket over something stupid. Forgive me and give me the strength to overcome the flesh in my time of struggle. Amen.

MAY 16
READ: ACTS 2:1–13

WAITING ON GOD

And suddenly there came a sound from heaven as of a rushing mighty wind and it filled all the house where they were sitting.

~ Acts 2:2

On the Day of Pentecost, the disciples were likely waiting in the very same upper room used for the last supper. For three years they followed Jesus. Then He was arrested, convicted in a bogus trial, and quickly crucified. They were devastated. Three days later, Christ arose and revealed Himself to the heartbroken group. For forty days, he taught and ministered to them. But once again, he would leave them. This time, they watched as He ascended on a cloud, delivering his final commands.

First, they were to wait —again! For the Comforter, and wait they did. They had no clue who or what the Comforter was or what to expect. Still they waited. Finally, He came. With a sound as a rushing mighty wind filling all the house, and if that isn't spectacular enough, cloven tongues like fire appeared and sat upon each of them. I think we can safely say that the result was well worth the wait. It was far beyond anything they expected.

I've waited on God many times. When His answer came, there was no doubt it was from Him. God has a way of wowing us even in the smallest of things.

TODAY'S HOT FLASH:

No matter how long you wait, remember this one thing: God is on time—every time. Without exception!

PRAYER:

Father, help me not to doubt You when my prayers remain unanswered. You see the big picture, and I do not. I put my trust in You. Amen.

BM'S AND OBITUARIES

O death, where is thy sting? O grave, where is thy victory?

~ 1 Corinthians 15:55

Now don't laugh, but the older a person becomes, the more they have two things on their mind: death and bowel movements. I worked in a nursing home for many years, and these were the two things the elderly worried about constantly. Patrick Moore once said, "At my age I do what Mark Twain did. I get my daily paper, look at the obituary page, and if I'm not there I carry on as usual." We laugh, but isn't it true that we are a little more interested in the obituaries than ever before?

Lord, take me home quickly if bowel movements become my constant obsession. As far as death is concerned, I refuse to dwell on something I cannot control. Of course, we all think about it, and we hope it comes quickly, painlessly, and many years in the future.

If I am obsessed, let it be with how little time I have left to tell the world about Jesus. If I am obsessed, let it be that my loved ones don't know the Lord. If I am obsessed, let it be for service to my King. As far as death is concerned, I will leave that to God.

TODAY'S HOT FLASH:

Don't dwell on useless things. Dwell on things that make a difference for the kingdom. That will keep your mind busy enough.

PRAYER:

Father, don't let my mind linger on useless things. May I stay focused on my reason for being: worshipping and serving You. Amen.

MAY 18

READ: 2 TIMOTHY 2:11–18

EXERCISING THE MIND

Study to shew thyself approved unto God, a workman that needeth not to be ashamed, rightly dividing the word of truth.

~ 2 Timothy 2:15

John Quincy Adams once said, "Old minds are like old horses; you must exercise them if you wish to keep them in working order." Unchallenged minds become dull and susceptible to deterioration. I believe an unused mind is a sad waste of a vital organ, and if it is a waste, could it possibly be considered sin?

Old age should not be synonymous with depleted brain. I want to continuously grow in my knowledge and wisdom of the Bible, of life, and of God's beautiful creation. Scripture encourages us in this endeavor. Paul tells Timothy to "study to shew thyself approved of God." First and foremost, it's talking about God's Word. We are told to always be ready with an answer when asked a spiritual question. This requires a never-ending study of the Bible. But don't stop there. When you stop learning, life becomes dull and monotonous. Keep learning and keep living.

TODAY'S HOT FLASH:

Romance novels may help you escape, but they do nothing for your mind. Toss the romance and pick up something that will expand your intelligence.

PRAYER:

Father, forgive me for wasting my mind and time on frivolous, foolish things. I want to learn more about Your world and Your people so I can serve You better. Amen.

MAY 19

READ: LUKE 12:15-21

TOMORROW IS NOT PROMISED

A man's life consisteth not in the abundance of the things which he possesseth.

~ Luke 12:15b

I get so caught up in my plans and my purposes that I forget about God's. Even now I have tomorrow planned. From morning to night, I know where I'll be and what I'll be doing. There is a problem with my plans; tomorrow is not promised to me.

The rich fool in Luke chapter 12 thought his life was peachy. He proudly boasted of his excess and decided on a life of ease. God was not impressed. He said to the braggart, "Thou fool, this night thou soul shall be required of thee, then whose shall those things be?" (vs. 20).

One of the benefits of old age is relaxing in our well-earned comfort. We pay off our mortgage, buy nice cars, and begin to believe our work is done.

There is no retirement from Christian service. In fact, as our time dwindles, our service should take on urgency. So little time, so many lost souls, so few people sharing the good news. Don't take the easy way out; it's time to get busy.

TODAY'S HOT FLASH:

Lost souls surround us. If you won't rescue them, who will? Our time of rest comes later; for now, let's get up and at 'em for the kingdom's sake.

PRAYER:

Dear Heavenly Father, only You know my length of days on this earth. May I use them wisely, and may all that I have and do glorify You rather than me. Amen.

MAY 20
READ: GALATIANS 6:7-13

EXHAUSTION AND BAD MANNERS

And be not weary in well doing: for in due season we shall reap, if we faint not.
~ Galatians 6:9

Allow me to confess a very annoying fault of mine. I am a bear when I am over tired. I growl, snap, bare my teeth, and have grizzly fits, and all the while deep inside I chastise myself for behaving so badly. To top it off, when I get this way, my husband, not recognizing it for what it is, says, "You're hormonal" or "take a pill." Oooh, that irks me all the more. My family thinks I am funny; my worst moods are a source of never-ending humor to them.

I don't find it humorous. I am deeply ashamed of my ungodly reaction to my human state of being. I know my actions are not abnormal, and you can probably empathize, having been there and done that yourself.

Paul suffered from ungodly reactions at times, and I am sure it was as much a reminder to him as an admonishment to us when he stated, "be not weary in well doing." Tired or not, I am never given allowance to become a grizzly. Someday maybe I will get it right, but I have a long way to go. How about you?

TODAY'S HOT FLASH:

Defeat comes through discouragement. That's Satan's goal. Spiritual growth through failures is God's. Victory is just around the corner!

PRAYER:

Oh Father, I am so tired of failing. I want to be like Your Son and to please You, but I fail so often. Take my failures and turn them into successes for Your glory. Amen.

MAY 21

READ: NUMBERS 14:11-20

PLEAD FOR THEIR SOULS

Pardon, I beseech thee, the iniquity of this people according unto the greatness of thy mercy, and as thou hast forgiven this people, from Egypt even unto now.

~ Numbers 14:19

In Numbers chapter 14, we find God ready to destroy the rebellious Israelites. Moses, for all he's had to put up with, begs for their lives. For seven verses he pleads their cause, reminding God of His merciful and forgiving ways. He beseeches Him to "pardon the sins of the people."

God replies, "I have pardoned according to thy word" (vs. 20). We tend to think that God answered this prayer because the super saint Moses prayed it. No, God answered the prayer because we are told that "the effectual fervent prayer of a righteous man availeth much" (James 5:16).

Moses' fervent prayer stayed the hand of God, bringing mercy rather than destruction. God granted pardon. If we have a right relationship with God, our prayers can have the same effect.

Do you have loved ones "walking on thin ice" where God is concerned? Do you fear for their souls? Plead your cause before your gracious Holy God who delights in giving you the desires of your heart.

TODAY'S HOT FLASH:

Stand in the gap for your lost and wayward loved ones. You may be the only thing standing between them and destruction.

PRAYER:

Merciful Father, I fear for the souls of my loved ones. I stand in the gap for them; bring them to Your Son before it is too late. Amen.

MAY 22
READ: NUMBERS 13:1–3, 26–33

THROWING AWAY BLESSINGS

But the men that went up with him said, We be not able to go up against the people; for they are stronger than we are.

~ Numbers 13:31

When Moses sent the Israelite leaders to spy on Canaan, they were on the threshold of a new beginning. They were literally standing on the border of the Promised Land. They witnessed the ten plagues, crossed in the midst of the Red Sea, and watched while God annihilated the entire Egyptian army. After all they'd seen, their faith turned to shambles in one moment of selfish fear. Their disobedience initiated a trek of forty years that should have taken only a few weeks. What should have been a great blessing turned to disastrous consequence because of their refusal to follow God.

I can't help but wonder how many blessings I've thrown to the wind because of my refusal to obey God. Even more thought-provoking, how many negatives in my life and in the lives of others are consequences of my selfish behavior?

For one bad decision, countless Israelites died in the wilderness. Would they have obeyed had they seen the consequence beforehand? I think so. I don't want to see the domino effect my disobedience has set in motion. From now on, I am saying yes to God. I'm tired of throwing my blessings away.

TODAY'S HOT FLASH:

How many lost blessings have you piled in God's unused blessing closet? Keep your heart open to God's calling and say yes regardless the cost.

PRAYER:

Lord, I shudder to think of the consequences I've set in motion and for those lives affected by my selfishness. May I be your Yes woman from now on. Amen.

FOR SANITY'S SAKE

MAY 23

READ: NUMBERS 14:1-4

CAREFUL WHAT YOU PRAY FOR

And all the children of Israel murmured against Moses and against Aaron: and the whole congregation said unto them, Would God that we had died in the land of Egypt! Or would God we had died in this wilderness.

~ Numbers 14:2

Can you believe it? Four hundred years of captivity and torturous hard labor, yet when asked to fight for the Promised Land, the children of Israel cried out, "Would we had died in this wilderness." Because of their fear and lack of trust, they refused to go.

There are some days when my hormones get the best of me, and I become the ultimate whiner. It doesn't matter how good things are; I can't see the roses for the thorns. That's when I begin murmuring unworthy prayers of complaint to the Father. Once I prayed that God would allow me some peace from my family; I was exhausted and felt I needed some rest. He did just that. For weeks no one visited me, and I regretted my prayer. I sought them out because I missed them so. I learned a valuable lesson.

The Israelites lived to regret their words. God answered their request. Everyone who murmured and complained died there. I bet they wished they could eat those words.

TODAY'S HOT FLASH:

Don't complain to God; He may give you your requests, and then what will you do? Like the Israelites, the results could be devastating.

PRAYER:

Father, thank You for your patience with me. Guide my tongue and prick my spirit every time I start to complain. Protect me from myself. I really need it. Amen.

MAY 24

READ: NUMBERS 14:7-10

DOES GOD DELIGHT IN YOU?

If the Lord delight in us, then he will bring us into this land and give it to us, a land which floweth with milk and honey.

~ Numbers 14:8

Moses, Aaron, Joshua, and Caleb—the faithful four—were excited about the Promised Land. They were ready and willing to obey God.

The Israelite congregation consisted of more than two million souls. Needless to say, they were far from excited. They refused to go. They didn't have a fear problem; they had a love problem. As far as they were concerned, God couldn't do enough to keep them happy.

God desires His people to love Him and to serve Him with a glad heart and to remember His past faithfulness. The Israelites had short memories. God's anger was kindled—again.

The faithful four sought to please God. They'd experienced the blessings awarded to those who were faithful. They fully trusted God.

My greatest desire is for the Lord to delight in me. Not for the blessings, but because I love Him. When you love someone, you want to please them, with or without reward.

TODAY'S HOT FLASH:

Do you find it hard to remain obedient to the will of God? If you do, you have a love problem. True love desires to please the one loved.

PRAYER:

My gracious Father, I so want to please You. May I fail less and obey more so my love is obvious. To serve You more, to love You more, this is my desire. Amen.

FOR SANITY'S SAKE

MAY 25

READ: PSALM 86

OUR ONE CONSTANT

For thou, Lord, art good, and ready to forgive; and plenteous in mercy unto all them that call upon thee.

~ Psalm 86:5

Here I am, sitting at my desk again and writing my devotional, and I am drawing a blank. I've been thinking about it all day. Still nothing. Unfortunately, my occasional foggy brain is one of my annoying symptoms of menopause. It doesn't happen often, but when it does, I can't read, think, or talk straight; just call me Mrs. Zombie. I'm amazed that I accomplish anything when I am like this—miraculously, I do.

Even my prayers become choppy, but I refuse to give in to discouragement. That is what Satan desires. If he can get me to pity myself and blame God for my situation, then he has won.

I am so thankful for a God who knows me through and through. I am also thankful for the Holy Spirit who delivers my message perfectly to the Father even when I can't get the words out. And most of all, I am so grateful that God our Father is the One constant in my life. When everything goes wrong, when things change faster than I can keep up, He never does.

TODAY'S HOT FLASH:

God never reneges on a promise. He is the one constant in this world of broken promises. Let there be no doubt; if He said it, He will do it.

PRAYER:

Merciful, forgiving Father, You know my mind today. I trust You will clear my mind in Your time, but until then, wrap Your arms around me and never let me go. I need You. Amen.

MAY 26

READ: NUMBERS 14:20–38

LONG-TERM CONSEQUENCES

Surely they shall not see the land which I sware unto their fathers, neither shall any of them that provoked me see it.

~ Numbers 14:23

If you've lived a half century or more, you are probably experiencing some long-term consequences from bad choices you've made earlier in life. These consequences not only affect us but also manifest themselves in and through our children as well. We often are responsible for emotional, mental, physical, and/or spiritual dysfunction in the lives of our loved ones, and we are consumed with regret over our past foolishness. We hope our children will learn from our mistakes, but that isn't always the case.

The children of Israel rebelled against God over and over again. He pardoned their sin every time, but even in His forgiveness, He pronounced a long-term consequence. Sin always pays a price.

Because of their rebellion, they were denied entrance into the Promised Land. They were denied the greatest blessing of all. Because of our sin and rebellion over the years, we experience wayward and lost children, physical and emotional pain, and mental instability.

We can't change the past. What's done is done. What we can do is learn from our past and look forward to a better future. We still have time to pass on blessings rather than consequences.

TODAY'S HOT FLASH:

Make all your decisions with God's Word at the forefront. It will never lead you astray, and it will keep you from adding new consequences atop the old.

PRAYER:

Father, I've seen my family suffer because of my rebellion. I've selfishly followed my own desires, and I am ashamed. I never want to cause them harm again. Amen.

MAY 27

READ: PROVERBS 21:21-31

JUST FOR TODAY, LORD

Whoso keepeth his mouth and his tongue keepeth his soul from troubles.

~ Proverbs 21:23

Just for today, Lord, may I keep my tongue under control. May I not criticize, lie, or scream like a banshee.

Just for today, Lord, may I speak pleasantries rather than complaints, praises rather than discouragements. May my lips smile rather than frown, and may they brighten the day of a disheartened soul.

Just for today, Lord, help me to keep my mouth shut if I don't have anything nice to say, if it's not my business, or if I haven't been asked. Help me to realize I don't have to voice my opinion just because I can.

And just for today, Lord, (this is a hard one), may I humbly submit to my husband without mouthy retorts. If he grumbles, help me to smile; if he annoys, help me to ignore; and if he gets bossy, may I perform my duties without bitterness or retribution.

Just for today, Lord, I want to please You with my words as well as my lack of words. I desire to listen rather than speak. Close my mouth, Lord, that the world may know You still perform miracles. Just for today.

TODAY'S HOT FLASH:

"A word fitly spoken is like apples of gold in pictures of silver" (Proverbs 25:11).

PRAYER:

Dear Lord, keep me from sinning with my words. I want to bless others with my mouth. I know this is possible through the power of Your Holy Spirit. I am asking just for today. Amen.

MAY 28

READ: ROMANS 15:1-6

ARE YOU A GOOD NEIGHBOR?

Let everyone of us please his neighbor for his good to edification.
~ Romans 15:2

Are you a good neighbor? Scripture indicates that a good neighbor is a person who goes the extra mile for someone in need.

When we are in our twenties, we rarely give thought to being a "good neighbor." We are too busy living life to its fullest. In our thirties, we are settled in our homes and raising our children. Pleasing and edifying others outside our family rarely crosses our minds. By the time we are in our late forties or older, life begins to slow down, children are grown, and we find time to focus on our long-term dreams.

As good as it sounds; this is not God's plan. Although God does allow us to live some of our dreams, He never expects us to do it at the expense of others. First, we are to "please our neighbor for his good to edification." In other words, meet their needs, show them you care, and always seek their betterment before your own. This is a hard and selfless thing to do. It is also the right thing to do. There is no better time to be a good neighbor, not only to those near you, but to those farther than walking distance as well.

TODAY'S HOT FLASH:

Personal fulfillment may slip away as we become a good neighbor to others. Lift your eyes to the ultimate prize; someday it will be worth it all.

PRAYER:

Precious Father, some days I don't want to help others. I want to do what I want to do. Forgive my selfish attitude. Teach me to be a good neighbor, no matter how I feel. Amen.

MAY 29

READ: NUMBERS 17

AND THE LORD SPOKE

And the Lord spoke unto Moses, saying . . . "

~ Numbers 17:1

Wow, what a relationship! The Almighty Creator of the Universe initiated conversation with His servant Moses on a regular basis. Sometimes God was instructing him, other times venting his anger, and still other times validating his calling.

Moses conversed just as familiarly. He pleaded for His people, sought guidance, vented his anger, and worshipped God's greatness. There was nothing left unsaid between the two.

I want to know my Lord intimately like Moses did. And I can! Every time I read my Bible, I can imagine the words, "And the Lord spoke to Lisa, saying . . ." Every chapter, every verse, every line is there for my benefit. It teaches, encourages, inspires, comforts, commands, and chastises me. His very heart is laid before us in His precious Word.

If my relationship with my Father suffers, then I've moved from His presence, not the other way around.

TODAY'S HOT FLASH:

"Draw near to God, and he will draw near to you" (James 4:8a). That's a promise!

PRAYER:

Father, to intimately know You, that is my desire. To draw near to You, where nothing interferes or draws me away, this too is my desire. Amen.

MAY 30

READ: JOHN 16:29-33

I HAVE OVERCOME THE WORLD

These things I have spoken unto you, that in me ye might have peace. In the world ye shall have tribulation: but be of good cheer; I have overcome the world.

~ John 16:33

When we first receive Christ into our lives, we plunge into the "honeymoon period." We believe our problems are over, God will provide for us financially, and keep strife at bay. It isn't long before we realize that the honeymoon's over, and our expectations are thrown to the wind.

This conversion bliss, experienced upon rebirth, turns into a questioning of our faith. Thus begins our first crisis of belief. We thought this great God would protect us from the bad of this world, but we quickly learn we were wrong.

As we mature in our faith, we learn a profound truth; God never promises us a trouble-free life; He promises help in time of trouble. He doesn't make it go away; He gives us the strength to endure. With each struggle endured, greater strength for the next is given.

I still fight God sometimes, but the battles are quickly over as He reminds me of His faithfulness. When I pass to glory, may I boldly proclaim: I have failed, I have learned, I have trusted the Savior and finally—I have overcome the World!

TODAY'S HOT FLASH:

"God does not give us overcoming Life: He gives us life as we overcome."

~ Oswald Chambers

PRAYER:

Gracious Father, In Your strength I can overcome the evils of this world. It won't be easy, but You've never let me down, and I know You never will. Amen.

MAY 31

READ: 2 CORINTHIANS 5:11–21

IDENTITY CRISIS

Therefore if any man be in Christ, he is a new creature: old things are passed away; behold, all things are become new.

~ 2 Corinthians 5:17

When I was little, I had beautiful, long, silky hair. When I entered kindergarten, my mother decided to cut it. As my hair fell to the ground, tears flowed down my cheeks. Nobody was going to love me anymore. My hair was me, and without it I was nobody. This was my first major identity crisis.

Ironically, my hair became a part of who I am as an adult. People would say, "I remember you; you're the lady with the big beautiful hair." Secretly, I was proud; at least I had a redeeming physical quality. Then menopause struck!

My hair began falling out by the handfuls (luckily it was very thick), and all my fancy curls went limp. Now my daughters are the ladies with the big beautiful hair.

What do you find your identity in? Your looks? Your emotional stability? Material wealth? How much simpler life becomes when we learn to find our identity in the person of Jesus Christ. Nothing can change who I am in Christ. God says I am "His workmanship, created in Christ Jesus" (Ephesians 2:10). He IS our identity! Nothing else matters.

TODAY'S HOT FLASH:

Don't look to the world to decide who you are; look to Jesus. Through Him, our identity becomes like Him.

PRAYER:

Wonderful Father, I want to find my identity in Jesus. Mold me into the image of Your Son. Amen.

JUNE

JUNE 1

READ: NUMBERS 20:2-6

GOD'S REPRESENTATIVES

And the people strove with Moses, and spake, saying, Would God that we had died when our brethren died before the Lord!

~ Numbers 20:3

I am flabbergasted, again, at the children of Israel's insolence. They entered the Desert of Zin, where there was no visible water. It doesn't occur to them to pray before attacking Moses and Aaron, just like before. For the umpteenth time, Moses and Aaron fall on their faces before God for the people. I wonder if they were ever tempted to let God strike the people down and get it over with.

As a pastor's wife, I've had to endure unfair and hateful attacks against my husband. It is always a challenge for me not to take up his defense. To make things worse, if my hormones are reeling, my first reaction is to attack back.

Have you or someone you love ever experienced verbal attacks for your faith? What was your first reaction? Did you attack back? Whine? Clam up? Don't stop standing strong for the Lord. Most people attack God's representatives because it is safer than hurling insults at God. It's hard not to take offense, but when we realize it is not about us, walking away will become easier.

TODAY'S HOT FLASH:

Put on your shield of righteousness. It will protect you against the fiery darts of Satan. He will use anyone he can to throw them.

PRAYER:

Remind me, Lord, that I don't fight against people, but against powers and principalities and rulers of darkness. If I remember this, I won't take offense at anyone, no matter the offense. Amen.

JUNE 2
READ: NUMBERS 20:7-13

ANGER'S CONSEQUENCE

And the Lord spoke unto Moses and Aaron, Because ye believed me not . . . ye shall not bring this congregation into the land which I have given them.

~ Numbers 20:12

I struggle with God's judgment on Moses and Aaron. Up until this point, Moses' faithfulness has been exemplary. Then comes the rock. After the Israelites' complaint of no water, God sends Moses to speak to the rock so water would flow forth. After months of rebellious verbal attacks and exhaustion, Moses has had enough, and he strikes the rock twice. This one act of disobedience set in motion dire consequences for Aaron and himself. Just one rash angry behavior changed the course of his life. God forbade them to lead the people into the Promised Land.

This seems harsh to me, knowing all my times of irrational outbursts. Goose bumps line my flesh when I realize how lightly I take my behavior and how severely God takes anger. God has not changed; He hates unrighteous anger as much today as He did those thousands of years ago.

Praise God in His mercy and grace that He will never reject us. He didn't reject Moses, but there were consequences to pay. We too must suffer the consequences of our behavior. The hard truth remains; we will always reap what we sow.

TODAY'S HOT FLASH:

Begin today to remove the anger that so easily controls you. With every outburst there is a consequence, whether you realize it or not.

PRAYER:

Lord, I have an anger problem; it's hard to admit. Calm my spirit; help me to view everything in the light of Your Word. Be glorified in my life today. Amen.

JUNE 3

READ: NUMBERS 22:9-34

THROWING CONVICTIONS TO THE WIND

And God said to Balaam, Thou shalt not go with them; thou shalt not curse the people: for they are blessed.

~ Numbers 22:12

Balak decided to war against the Israelites, so he asked the prophet Balaam to go with them. He sought God's guidance and was warned not to go. Balaam denied Balak's request. Undaunted, Balak persisted. He offered Balaam greatness. At first he resisted, but the temptation was too great. Again Balaam petitioned God; in truth, he really wanted what Balak was offering. God, knowing Balaam's heart, said, "Go if you must go, but remember my previous warnings." In his hard-heartedness, Balaam perceived this as a go-ahead and merrily set on his way. God was mad!

Three times God used the Angel of the Lord and Balaam's donkey to block his way. Three times Balaam refused to get the hint.

How many times have we been convicted in our hearts not to do something? We knew God was warning us, but with just a little prodding from outside forces, we threw our convictions to the wind and off we went. When we squelch the Holy Spirit, choosing to love the world rather than God, that must break God's heart.

TODAY'S HOT FLASH:

Take a risk! Become an experiment in obedience. Learn to obey the proddings of the Holy Spirit every time and prove your love for the Savior.

PRAYER:

Father, so many times I've quenched Your Spirit and loved the world more than You. Forgive me. May my life be an experiment in obedience from this day forward. Amen.

JUNE 4
READ: PSALM 42

THIRSTING FOR GOD

As the hart panteth after the water brooks, so panteth my soul after thee, O God. My soul thirsteth for God, for the living God.

~ Psalm 42:1–2

We've all had them, and most of us still do. Desires, dreams, great expectations for what could or should be. It is in this area where I can say my heart changes the most as I grow older. I like nice things, traveling to great places, meeting new people, but I don't feel I need them. With each passing year, I find my soul connecting more and more with the great psalmist as he poured his heart out to God. The following verses echo my growing desire for my Lord. It is my prayer that these verses serenade your thirsting soul as well.

O God, thou art my God, early will I seek thee; my soul thirsteth for thee, my flesh longeth for thee in a dry and thirsty land, where no water is (Psalm 63:1).

My soul longeth, even fainteth for the courts of the Lord: my heart and my flesh crieth out for the living God (Psalm 84:2).

My soul breaketh for the longing it hath unto thy judgments at all times (Psalm 119:20).

I opened my eyes and panted: for I longed for thy commandments (Psalm 119:131).

TODAY'S HOT FLASH:

Age has a way of revealing to us what's important and what's trivial. God is important! Showing our loved ones God is important. That's all that really matters.

PRAYER:

I thirst for You, Lord, more than ever before. Fill my cup with Your soothing presence and calming Spirit. Fill me with You and only You. Amen.

JUNE 5

READ: LUKE 11:5–10

SEEK GOD

For everyone that asketh receiveth; and he that seeketh findeth; and to him that knocketh it shall be opened.

~ Luke 11:10

I wasn't expecting menopause so early. My hormones went cuckoo in a matter of months, and my insecurities flared. Still, there are areas of spiritual growth that may never have matured had I not experienced it during this time of my life.

In my despair and unrest, I was forced to seek God. I needed to know how to fight off the attacks of Satan. If you are struggling with menopause or any other life-changing issue, I encourage you to dig into the Word of God.

And I say unto you, Ask, and it shall be given you; seek, and ye shall find; knock, and it shall be opened unto you (Luke 11:9).

If ye then be risen with Christ, seek those things which are above, where Christ sitteth on the right hand of God (Colossians 3:1).

I love them that love me; and those that seek me early shall find me (Proverbs 8:17).

I am still maturing, but I've learned to grasp these truths full throttle just to survive, and God has worked miracles in my life.

TODAY'S HOT FLASH:

If you need answers and life seems too hard to bear, seek God and you will find Him. He has all your answers in His precious Word. He will lead you to them.

PRAYER:

Father, thank You for bringing me to a point where I must seek You. It changed my life. May I always seek You in good and bad times. Amen.

JUNE 6
READ: PROVERBS 3:1–13

TRUST GOD

Trust in the Lord with all thine heart and lean not unto thine own understanding.

~ Proverbs 3:5

Seeking God is the easy part. Trusting that He will do what He says is much harder. That's why the above verse is so important. Paraphrased, it says, "No matter what happens, no matter how bad things seem, no matter the impossibility of the situation—trust God—and don't doubt or fear. With everything that is in you—trust Him!"

This is easier said than done. Today, when facing trials, don't say, "I can't do it, or "I can't make it through." Say, "Yes I can, if I only trust God."

Verses for your journey:

Though he slay me, (though terrible things happen to me); yet will I trust in him (Job 13:15).

Trust in him at ALL times; ye people, pour out your heart before him: God is a refuge for us (Psalm 62:8).

My goodness, and my fortress; my high tower, and my deliverer; my shield, and he in whom I trust, who subdueth my people under me (In my case: He who subdues my hormones that try to control me) (Psalm 144:2).

TODAY'S HOT FLASH:

First seek God; He is waiting for you. Then, trust what He says; don't question whether it is possible—everything is possible with God!

PRAYER:

So often I waver in my trust. Father, forgive me. Teach me to trust You with my whole heart and not rely on my misleading emotions. Amen.

JUNE 7

READ: PHILIPPIANS 4:1–9

THINK GOD

Whatsoever things are true, honest, just, pure, lovely, of good report, if there be any virtue, and if there be any praise, think on these things.

~ Philippians 4:8, paraphrased

My greatest challenge in my daily walk is keeping my thoughts righteous. They often stray from where they should be to places taboo. Satan and his minions have the ability to whisper in our ears, and when they do, it doesn't take much convincing for us to throw our beliefs to the wind and believe their lies. Hopefully these verses will help you take control of your thought life. The secret is to memorize them and throw them at Satan every time he attempts to deceive you.

Thou wilt keep him in perfect peace, whose mind is stayed on thee (Isaiah 26:3).

Casting down imaginations, and every high thing that exalteth itself against the knowledge of God, and bringing into captivity every though to the obedience of Christ (2 Corinthians 10:5).

Therefore, take no thought (don't worry), saying, What shall we eat, or what shall we drink? Or, Wherewithal shall we be clothed? But seek ye first the kingdom of God . . . and all these shall be added unto you (Matthew 6:31, 33).

TODAY'S HOT FLASH:

If Satan can get into your thoughts, you've already lost. Take precautions; fill your mind with God's Word so you can ward off the attacks of the devil.

PRAYER:

Father, so many times I've allowed Satan in my thoughts. Help me to keep my mind on You so that I might have Your perfect peace. Amen.

JUNE 8
READ: EPHESIANS 5:18–21

THANK GOD

Giving thanks always for all things unto God and the Father in the name of our Lord Jesus Christ.

~ Ephesians 5:20

We seek God, we learn to trust God, and now—even harder yet—we thank God *for everything*. Some people have told me that I am too literal, and it isn't always possible to have a thankful spirit. As much as it feels like that is true, it is not. What part of "giving thanks for all things" don't we understand? We can't pick and choose where to aim our gratitude. In good times and bad, depression, joy, health, or sickness—give thanks. Try it! When you start to thank God for everything, your attitude will change.

Here are some verses for your journey:

In everything give thanks: for this is the will of God in Christ Jesus concerning you (1 Thessalonians 5:18).

Let us come before his throne with thanksgiving (Psalm 95:2a).

Be anxious for nothing; but in every thing by prayer and supplication with thanksgiving, let your requests be made known to God (Philippians 4:6).

TODAY'S HOT FLASH:

Nobody wants to thank God in the midst of trial. We must get past the feelings and live in obedience; only then will we overcome. Make a list of thirty things you are thankful for—then, start praying!

PRAYER:

I am so thankful for Your faithfulness, Father, and for Your Son who died for me even though I didn't deserve it. May I never forget how much You love me. Amen.

JUNE 9

READ: PSALM 113

PRAISE GOD

Praise ye the Lord. Praise, O ye servants of the Lord, praise the name of the Lord.

~ Psalm 113:1

We seek God, trust God, thank God, think God, and now we must praise God, for He is great and greatly to be praised. For this wonderful Father, Creator of the Universe, allowed us to exist and claimed us as His own. In the midst of life's hardships, He is always there. He doesn't always take those hardships away, but we are never alone. Praising God coincides with thinking about God, which coincides with thanking God, which coincides with trusting God, which coincides with seeking God.

Each one is connected to the other, and as we focus on God, our troubles seem to diminish. It isn't an easy task to keep our mind stayed on God; we need all the help we can get. Maybe these verses will make it a little easier for you:

Make a joyful noise unto God, all ye lands: sing forth the honour of his name: make his praise glorious (Psalm 66:1-2).

The living, the living, he shall praise thee, as I do this day: the father to the children shall make known thy truth (Isaiah 38:19).

TODAY'S HOT FLASH:

Psalm 150 is six great verses of glorious praise. Take time to read this small but great chapter every morning before the cares of this world surround you.

PRAYER:

I praise You, Lord. You are great and worthy of all praise. I will sing unto You a song of praise. I will let the whole world know You are my God. Amen.

JUNE 10
READ: JOHN 14:15-21

OBEY GOD

If ye love me, keep my commandments.

~ John 14:15

It's not the hardest, it's possible without desire, but it is the one thing we stiff-necked human beings hate to do most. OBEY! Ask me politely and I may think about it; tell me to do it and you've got a rebellion on your hands. Herein lies the problem. Even if it means peace of mind, happiness, or the absence of problems, we don't like bowing to another's will, and that includes God's.

If you find it hard to obey God, you have a love problem — a kink in your relationship. Take time to ponder this verse and re-evaluate your personal commitment with the Savior.

And hereby we do know that we know him, if we keep his commandments. He that saith, I know him, and keepeth not his commandments, is a liar, and the truth is not in him. But whoso keepeth his word, in him verily is the love of God perfected: hereby know we that we are in him. He that saith he abideth in him ought himself also so to walk, even as he walked (1 John 2:3-6).

TODAY'S HOT FLASH:

Whether you feel like it or not, obey. Right feelings will bring right actions.

When you love yourself more than God, you have become your own idol. This is idolatry.

PRAYER:

Father, forgive me when I put myself first. I want to love You with my entire being. Bring me to the point where obeying You is my greatest desire. Amen.

JUNE 11
READ: JOSHUA 24:14-28

SERVE GOD

Now therefore fear the Lord, and serve him in sincerity and in truth [. . .] And if it seem evil unto you to serve the Lord, choose you this day whom ye will serve [. . .] but as for me and my house, we will serve the Lord.

~ Joshua 24:14-15

Service is the natural progression of a heart fully given to the Lord. After we've accomplished all the previous steps, the only thing left to do is serve. To serve God is to serve others. This includes family and church members, neighbors, friends, acquaintances, the elderly, the handicapped, the lonely, the prickly pears—anyone who crosses our path is a possible recipient of our service. Jesus set the example, and our number one goal in life is to imitate Him.

If any man serve me, let him follow me; and where I am, there shall also my servant be: if any man serve me, him will my Father honour (John 12:26).

I have shewed you all things, how that so labouring ye ought to support the weak, and to remember the words of the Lord Jesus, how he said, It is more blessed to give than to receive (Acts 20:35).

TODAY'S HOT FLASH:

Jesus gave to His very last breath. He didn't stop serving others when inconvenience reared its ugly head. We are to do the same, regardless the cost.

PRAYER:

Lord, help me to serve others as Jesus did. Don't let me linger too long on my issues; I give them fully to You for Your keeping. Amen.

JUNE 12
READ: GENESIS 4:19-23

ADAH'S CONTRIBUTION

And his brother's name was Jubal: he was the father of all such as handle the harp and organ.

~ Genesis 4:21

Adah was one of the wives of the first ever polygamist, Lamech. We don't know a lot about her, other than the fact that she was the mother of Jubal. From Jubal, the world was introduced to the beauty of music, and things were never the same again.

God, in His wisdom and grace, can bring forth great things from questionable circumstances. Jubal, a descendant of Cain with a polygamist father, was created with a melody in his heart.

As a mother, this passage gives me hope. I've rebelled against God many times, yet in my children I witness the merciful hand of a loving God. Yes, they've rebelled, they've done stupid things (who hasn't?), but ever so slowly I see them returning to the Lord and accomplishing great things. I expect their spiritual journey will take them to places I can only dream of. To know my children have accomplished their purpose for the Savior—what more can a mother ask for?

TODAY'S HOT FLASH:

Hope—God's gift to us. Without it, we have nothing—with it, we can believe that God will use our children for great things. I choose hope.

PRAYER:

Father, I cry for my children. I cry for my stupidity that hurt their lives. I know You can turn discarded trash into sweet treasure. I hold onto the hope of Your redemptive power. Do marvelous things through my children. Amen.

FOR SANITY'S SAKE

JUNE 13

READ: LUKE 18:1-8

IT'S OKAY TO NAG GOD

And he spake a parable unto them to this end, that men ought always to pray, and not to faint.

~ Luke 18:1

In this parable of Jesus, we meet an ungodly judge and a nagging widow. This widow wanted the judge to take vengeance on her adversary, but the judge didn't care enough to bother. But that darned widow kept coming back and demanding. Finally, he'd had enough and for no other reason but to get her off his back, he granted the widow's request.

Now, I don't know about you, but I admit I can be a nag at times. I really don't want to be, but once I get something on my mind . . . " Having said this, I also have to admit that I am opposite in my prayers. If I don't receive immediate answers, I often stop with that particular request for a while.

With this parable, Jesus is giving us permission to nag Him. He says, "Men ought always to pray, and not to faint." Continue on. Don't stop. Ask again and again and again. Maybe we don't get answers because God doesn't believe it's that important to us. If God's giving me permission to nag, I'm going to take full advantage of it. Let's see—where do I start?

TODAY'S HOT FLASH:

This is the only time you're going to get permission to nag. So go ahead, nag — twenty-four/seven—nag, nag, nag. Maybe God will finally believe you mean it.

PRAYER:

Father, forgive my short-sightedness and my desire for instant answers in my prayers. People need You too much for me to tire of praying. Amen.

JUNE 14

READ: PHILEMON 1-7

APPHIA: THE DEARLY BELOVED

And to our beloved Apphia, and Archippus our fellow soldier, and to the church in thy house . . .

~ Philemon 1:2

Little is known of Apphia. She was a believer, dearly beloved of Paul, and fellow sister in Christ. By her name, which means "that which is fruitful," we have indication that she boldly proclaimed the name of Jesus. When it mattered, she made a difference in the lives around her. When it mattered, she stood up and carried the weight of her faith. Her name goes down in history as one of the faithful. She lived—and died for her Lord.

Tradition has it that she was stoned to death during the reign of Nero. I don't know if she had biological children, but I am confident she bore many spiritual offspring, many of whom were challenged in belief when she chose to take her faith to the extreme and die for her Lord.

She was spoken of once in Scripture, but what an impact she made. The entire world may never know who I am, but may my life become a challenge to follow for generations to come.

TODAY'S HOT FLASH:

How will you be remembered? Will you be a "dearly beloved sister in Christ?" Or will your name be forgotten because of your lack of kingdom work?

PRAYER:

Father, to be found faithful is my desire, not to be known for who I was but for who I became through You. May my life challenge others to live for You. Amen.

JUNE 15

READ: 2 TIMOTHY 1:1-5

A RAISE OF THE HAT

When I call to remembrance the unfeigned faith that is in thee, which dwelt first in thy grandmother Lois, and thy mother Eunice...

~ 2 Timothy 1:5

Scattered throughout Scripture are the lives we are privileged to glimpse, if only for a moment, of many godly mothers. We don't know a lot about most of them, but God saw fit to "raise his hat" to their contributions, and so they live on in history.

Women like Eunice and Lois, grandmother and mother of Timothy, who raised their son in the admonition of the Lord. Azubah, a God-fearing woman of her time, wife of King Asa, mother of Jehoshaphat, the great and godly king (1 Kings 22:42), Salome, wife of Zebedee, mother of James and John. She encouraged her sons to follow the Messiah, remaining an ardent follower herself through Jesus' ministry and death.

How will I be remembered? Did I encourage my children to face challenges and conquer the world? Did I guide them through the Word and by my example to Jesus, making Him their focal point for life? One day my children will stand before the King. When He looks at them, will He see me, imitating Him, displayed through them?

TODAY'S HOT FLASH:

A woman's greatest legacy is her children. What will your children reveal about you when they come face-to-face with the King of Kings?

PRAYER:

Lord, what a privilege to be the mother of my children. Take my feeble efforts of godliness and magnify them in their lives. Do great things through them. Amen.

JUNE 16
READ: DANIEL 5:5–31

WEIGHED IN THE BALANCE AND FOUND WANTING

TEKEL; Thou art weighed in the balances, and art found wanting.
~ Daniel 5:27

King Belshazzar threw a great feast using the gold and silver from God's holy temple. He filled the goblets with wine and praised his heathen gods. Feeling invincible and godlike himself, he blatantly mocked the One True God.

It wasn't long before the famous "handwriting on the wall" appeared, and Daniel was called to interpret. Before his interpretation, Daniel blistered Belshazzar with a myriad of accusations. He reminded the king that his own father was dethroned for his pride and self-worship. It was a dethroning that Belshazzar witnessed and now, even in his knowledge of the truth, with pompous self-righteousness he spit in God's face.

With one slight of the hand, the king was sentenced. *Belshazzar, you've been weighed in the balance and found wanting.* That night his life was required of him.

Maybe you started your Christian walk strong, but over the years God has taken second fiddle. What will anything else matter if, when we face God, we hear, "You've been weighed in the balance and found wanting."

TODAY'S HOT FLASH:

"Holding forth the word of life; that I may rejoice in the day of Christ, that I have not run in vain, neither labored in vain" (Philippians 2:16).

PRAYER:

Father, keep me strong in my race; may You be my sole purpose for existence. To You goes all honor and glory forever and ever. Amen.

JUNE 17

READ: MATTHEW 5:1–12

BLESSED ARE THE POOR IN SPIRIT

Blessed are the poor in spirit, for theirs is the kingdom of heaven.

~ Matthew 5:3

I never understood this verse until I read a quote from Oswald Chamber's "My Utmost for His Highest." He said, "I am blessed in my poverty. If I know I have no strength of will, no nobility of disposition, then Jesus says—blessed are you, because it is through this poverty that I enter his kingdom. I can only enter it as a pauper."

If I am poor in spirit, I am aware of my utter depravity without Jesus' saving grace, I know that on my own there is no good thing in me, and I am fully aware of my need of a Savior.

Never have I been more aware of this need than as I struggle through my menopausal symptoms. I have no doubt of my depraved nature when I throw a fit or kick the wall in my out-of-control anger.

I am a pauper, poverty stricken in my soul, but it is in this depraved state that I call on my loving Father for relief. Immediately, my Daddy opens wide His arms, allowing His needy daughter some time of respite and restoration. Blessed are the poor in spirit—for they know how much they need the Lord!

TODAY'S HOT FLASH:

Until you realize your depravity, you won't understand your need for a Savior. To know you need a Savior is to be "poor in spirit." Blessed are the poor in spirit.

PRAYER:

Loving Father, I am nothing without You. Thank You for loving me and being my ever-present help in my many times of trouble. Amen.

JUNE 18
READ: 1 JOHN 2:1-6

THE ADVOCATE

My little children, these things write I unto you, that ye sin not. And if any man (woman) sin, we have an advocate with the Father, Jesus Christ the righteous.

~ 1 John 2:1

Where would we be without our precious Savior's cross experience? Who would we turn to if He hadn't opened the portal between us and God? While in the midst of my oceans of emotions, Jesus is all I can cling to. He alone is the reason I am not condemned when I fail. Without Him I am helpless, and so are you. Without Him as my advocate, all is hopeless.

Without Him as your advocate, you face the same fate. It is only through His shed blood that we are able to approach the Father and confess our sins. Jesus became the propitiation for my sin and for yours, and not only mine and yours but for the entire world. He opened the portal for anyone to enter in and accept Him as advocate.

When I am angered, when I scowl or criticize, when I am lazy and self-absorbed, I can rest in the Truth. That Truth is Jesus and what He did for me. Because of Him, I am not condemned.

Have you accepted what Jesus did on the cross for you? The knowledge of His selfless actions is our motivation as we struggle to remain holy when everything inside us is screaming rebellion. Through Jesus, it is possible to endure all circumstances, even menopause.

TODAY'S HOT FLASH:

Without Jesus, there is no hope. With Him, there is not only hope but also victory in all circumstances.

PRAYER:

Oh, Father, thank You for Jesus. What a price He paid for such a sinner as I. Please, help me to serve You with a heart full of gratitude. Amen.

JUNE 19

READ: 2 CORINTHIANS 12:8–12

MAKING A DIFFERENCE

And he said unto me, My grace is sufficient for thee: for my strength is made perfect in weakness.

~ 2 Corinthians 12:9a

In a shocking turn of events, the parents of our foster children decided to surrender all rights. We've had many children for a year or more, but all eventually went home or to relatives. We had all but decided that when these children left, we were going to take a sabbatical from foster care; now we have a decision to make.

We raised our five children. They are grown and raising their own families. With our foster children at ages two, four and six, we are talking about a very long-term commitment. The scary part for us is that it isn't our decision to make; it's God's.

Do you know what I hear when I ask God? "My grace is sufficient for thee: for my strength is made perfect in weakness" (2 Corinthians 12:9). You can "do all things through Christ who strengthens" you (Philippians 4:13). "I heard the voice of the Lord, saying, whom shall I send, and who will go for us?" (Isaiah 6:8). What choice do we have? I must answer as Isaiah did, "Here am I, send me."

TODAY'S HOT FLASH:

All I want to do is make a difference for Jesus. That is my prayer, and as long as I am open to whatever God brings my way, that is exactly what I will do.

PRAYER:

Lord, I won't question You; let me make a difference for You in my life. That's my desire, and that's what I live for. Use me for Your glory. Amen.

JUNE 20
READ: MATTHEW 22:1-10

IT GOES DEEPER—MUCH DEEPER

Go ye therefore into the highways, and as many as ye shall find, bid to the marriage.

~ Matthew 22:9

We had a final visit today with our children's parents. Even though I know it's best, my heart breaks for the unfairness of it all. Three little innocents have been thrust aside as if yesterday's trash. But it goes deeper—much deeper.

Beyond my home base—into this great big world—millions of children are unwanted, uncared for, and have no one to tuck them in or feed them a balanced meal. But it goes deeper—much deeper than that. To a world full of children of every age—0 to 99—lost, unloved, uncared for, forgotten. They are born, live hopeless lives, and die alone, never experiencing the love of their heavenly Father. Herein lies my crime. I have failed to take every effort to lead them to their only hope. Again my heart breaks.

It's not too late. Now is a great place to start! Now is the time to make a difference! It is in the now that we can change the world. What are you going to do?

TODAY'S HOT FLASH:

Your mode of calling may be different from mine, but we are all called to lead the hopeless to the great Author of all hope. What are you waiting for?

PRAYER:

Father, my heart breaks for the children, all the lost children, young and old alike. Show me what I can do to make a difference. Amen.

JUNE 21

READ: JOHN 15:1–5

HAVE YOU BEEN PURGED?

Every branch in me that beareth not fruit he taketh away: and every branch that beareth fruit, he purgeth it, that it may bring forth more fruit.

~ John 15:2

I am a branch. If you know Jesus, you are a branch. Jesus said that every branch that bears fruit "He purgeth." What does it mean to purge?

Webster's Dictionary defines it this way: "to clear of sin or guilt; to become free of impurities or excess matter through a cleansing process." Oxford American Thesaurus uses synonyms such as *remove, get rid of, expel, eject, elude, dismiss, sack, oust, eradicate, clear out,* and *weed out.*

I believe that menopause may be God's final purging process. Oh, we still sin, repent, and continue to grow (hopefully), but like never before He is preparing us for entrance into His kingdom. He expects us to be the examples, not the followers. The process is long and often painful, but after we've been weeded, sin eradicated, cleaned, and purified, a new version of us emerges. Beautifully trimmed and ready to complete our journey to the other side of menopause, as well as eternity.

TODAY'S HOT FLASH:

It is no wonder my menopausal experience has been long and tedious. God must have had a lot of weeding out to do. I sure hope He is almost done.

PRAYER:

Thank You, Lord, for purging me and making me into the likeness of Your Son. May I learn my lessons and set a godly example for those around me. Amen.

JUNE 22
READ: JOHN 15:1–14

ARE YOU ABIDING?

Abide in me, and I in you. As the branch cannot bear fruit of itself, except it abide in the vine; no more can ye, except ye abide in me.

~ John 15:4

The word "abide" appears nine times in the first fourteen verses of John 15. Jesus continuously commands us to abide in Him. How do we do that? So many of us are deprived of the desired intimacy with the Savior because we don't have a clue how to abide.

Webster's Dictionary defines *abide* this way: "to remain stable or fixed in a state, to reside or continue in a place, to dwell." The Oxford American Writer's Thesaurus uses these synonyms to describe it: *continue, remain, survive, last, persist, stay* and *live on.*

This should open a whole new world to many of us. There is no trick to abiding. Only through obedience is it possible. If I remain stable in my faith, dwell on Him and in His Word, continue, remain, and persist in my faith, I am abiding.

He is always with me, and I am always with Him. I continue in the things I know to do because I love Him and because He commands me. There is nothing else I can do.

TODAY'S HOT FLASH:

To abide is to stay fixed on the most important person in the world—Jesus Christ—twenty-four/seven, three hundred sixty-five days a year.

PRAYER:

Lord, help me to remain obedient in all things so I can abide in Your love. Fill me with the overflowing joy promised to those who obey. Amen.

JUNE 23

READ: 1 CORINTHIANS 1:1-9

SANCTIFY YOURSELVES

Unto the church of God that is in Corinth, to them that are sanctified in Christ Jesus, called to be saints . . .

~ 1 Corinthians 1:2a

Webster's Dictionary defines *sanctify* this way: "to set apart as sacred, consecrate, make free from sin, purify." The Oxford American Writer's Thesaurus uses synonyms such as *bless, make holy, hallow, make sacred* and *dedicate to God*.

When the younger generation asks why they shouldn't have tattoos, go to bars, or riddle themselves with holes, I introduce them to this great word, *sanctify*. They aren't the only ones who need reminded.

I still cling to my desire of forever young, buying creams and dying my hair. Are they sin in and of themselves? It depends on my motivation. Am I afraid to set myself apart? Look different? Act different? React different? Can the world see Jesus in me at first glance, or do they have to dig deep?

If I look and act like the world, then I have not sanctified myself to Christ. Unlike the world, my actions and sometimes my looks will tell the world where my dedication is.

TODAY'S HOT FLASH:

I am in this world, but not of it. I have to live here, but I do not have to adopt all the newest fads or imitate popular celebrities. If my life parallels those of this world, I have not sanctified myself from the world.

PRAYER:

Father, sometimes it is more comfortable to fit in and to be like everybody else. But You have commanded me to sanctify myself from the world and unto You. Remind me when I start to cross the line. Amen.

JUNE 24
READ: 2 TIMOTHY 2:1-8

DISCIPLEE OR DISCIPLER

And the things that thou hast heard of me among many witnesses, the same commit thou to faithful men, who shall be able to teach others also.

~ 2 Timothy 2:2

Webster's Dictionary defines *disciple* as "a pupil or follower who accepts and helps to spread the teachings of another." The Oxford American Writer's Thesaurus uses such synonyms to describe *disciple: follower, adherent, believer, admirer, pupil, student, learner; upholder,* and *supporter.* When we first come to know Jesus, our Christian immaturity forces us into the role of disciple, one discipled by the more mature and more knowledgeable in Christ. Unfortunately, many of us never take the leap from disciplee to discipler. If we don't share our knowledge, the Word becomes stagnant, and the disciples become few.

We've entered a new stage in our life; we're wiser, more knowledgeable, and more experienced in this life and God. As Paul told his followers to spread what he has taught them, so are we to pass on what we have learned. It is a never-ending cycle, designed to permeate the world with the Good News. Pick up your Bible, find some willing participants, and share what you have learned, so your disciples can share what they have learned and so on and so on.

TODAY'S HOT FLASH:

We were never meant to hoard what we know about God and His Son Jesus. We are to spread it so far and so thin that everyone we come in contact with is touched by our life and words.

PRAYER:

Father, open the doors wide and bring to me people to disciple, people who are hungry for Your Word. May I teach them what I have learned. Amen.

JUNE 25

READ: JAMES 1:1–12

TRIALS AND TRIBULATIONS

My brethren, count it all joy when ye fall into various trials.

~ James 1:2

What is menopause but a trial, a blip (albeit a long one) in the scheme of life? What is life but a series of afflictions, hardships, burdens, and worries as we journey toward our final destination? No one makes it through a lifetime without experiencing the woes of adversity at some point.

We have the comfort of knowing that our trials have a purpose. James spells it out plainly. He says, "Knowing this, that the trying of your faith worketh patience. But let patience have her perfect work (be completed and matured) that ye may be perfect and entire, wanting nothing" (vs. 3–4).

Your ongoing trial is not a futile exercise. It is an allowed time of testing, and its purpose is to grow you into a matured child of God. Without fire there is no refining. Without trial there is no spiritual growth. Without the test, how can we know whether we've reached our goal?

Will we pass the test and go forward in victory or crumple in defeat, thrusting us back to the beginning for a do-over? We can't grow beyond our crisis unless we faithfully stand the trial.

TODAY'S HOT FLASH:

Tests are never easy, but stand fast and hold on tight; God's still working on you, and His refining fire will turn you into a masterpiece designed for His glory.

PRAYER:

Father, sometimes I feel I will never make it through. I know You are faithful and will give me the strength to pass each test as it comes. Thank You. Amen.

JUNE 26
READ: JONAH 3:1-10

NEVER SAY NEVER

And the word of the Lord came unto Jonah the second time, saying.

~ Jonah 3:1

Jonah was a prophet of God. Didn't he know the futility of saying no to the Creator of the Universe? Didn't he desire to see the souls of Nineveh turn from their wicked ways? Didn't he realize how famous he'd become when he sparked a revival that changed the hearts of an entire city?

Yes, he knew, but he didn't care. His hatred for the Ninevites consumed him, causing him to turn his back on the Almighty. Worse yet, he tried to hide. Didn't he know he couldn't hide from God? Of course he did. Did it stop him? No. What was the end result? God had His way—in spite of Jonah's rebellion.

I'm a lot like Jonah. After our last three foster children went home, I vowed never to take a sibling group again. Then the call came. Absolutely not! No way! I can't! I'm too tired! I'm too old! Let someone else! Then, that still small voice said, "Have you asked me what I want?" "No," "Why not?" "Because I know what you will say." I had my answer.

Just like Jonah, I tried to wheedle my way out, but when He asked the second time, I knew I didn't have a choice.

TODAY'S HOT FLASH:

If we don't ask God because we already know what He will say, then we already have our answer. We are just trying to wiggle out of His will.

PRAYER:

Father, forgive me for trying to walk away from Your best for me. Make my heart sensitive to Your leading and numb to my own desires. Amen.

JUNE 27

READ: JAMES 5:7-11

THE GREAT TABOO

Behold we count them happy which endure. Ye have heard of the patience of Job . . . that the Lord is very pitiful, and of tender mercy.

~ James 5:11

In today's culture, it is hip to talk about almost everything and anything in a social setting—except menopause. Try starting a conversation with a group of women that goes something like this, "My doctor says I'm having menopause symptoms." Even middle-aged women don't like to think about it and barely admit to experiencing symptoms. People are uncomfortable with a subject that has been taboo for so long.

There is a preconceived notion that life as we once knew it is over. Grandma turns to Granny, and rocking chairs appear on the front porch. We picture false teeth, muumuus, and short gray hair. Added to all this is the proof that Granny is losing her mind by her periodic mental breakdowns. No woman wants to admit she has reached this stage in her life.

Because we fear it, we don't talk about it. But fear debilitates and turns us into the very thing we dread. We need to embrace this change and stand up and be counted as viable human beings with greatness yet to offer. If we don't make the world notice, who will?

TODAY'S HOT FLASH:

If you are going to stand up and be noticed, make sure it's Christ in you they see. Only through Christ can we make the change without major collateral damage.

PRAYER:

Gracious Father, I want to be an advocate for women who are afraid to talk about menopause. Fill me with Your wisdom as I seek to help others. Amen.

JUNE 28
READ: JOHN 11:1–15

IS CHRIST GLORIFIED?

This sickness is not unto death, but for the glory of God, that the Son of God might be glorified thereby.

~ John 11:4b

Webster's Dictionary defines glorify this way: "To make glorious by bestowing honor, praise, or admiration". Oxford American Writer's Thesaurus uses synonyms such as *praise, extol, exalt, worship, revere, reverence, honor, adore,* and *magnify*.

Today I am challenged by these definitions, having been sick and on a steroid for almost a month. I'm ashamed to confess that Christ was not glorified in my life today. Only my emotions were magnified.

The apostles had to wonder how anything good could come from the death of Lazarus. But that is exactly what happened, and praise be to God when Christ returned to the home of His friends; truly He was exalted as He shouted the words, "Lazarus, come forth."

You may be suffering from sickness or a debilitating disease. You're on medication, and misery seems a constant state of being. It is impossible for us to know what the future holds; what I do know is that I can trust God with every fiber of my being. Therefore, I will glorify His name.

TODAY'S HOT FLASH:

God is God in the bad times as well as the good times. Praise is not determined by our circumstance. Say it with me: Let's just praise the Lord!

PRAYER:

Father, some way, somehow, turn my failures into blessings. I see only failure, but You can turn ashes into beauty. I will praise Your name forever and ever. Amen.

JUNE 29

READ: 2 SAMUEL 23:6–16

POURED OUT

> *And the three mighty men brake through the host of the Philistines, and drew water out of the well . . . and brought it to David: nevertheless he would not drink thereof, but poured it out unto the Lord.*
>
> ~ 2 Samuel 23:16

How does one pour out a drink offering when the once flowing waters are now withered and dry? You've offered all you have and feel like you have nothing left to give.

David was spent and thirsty from fighting the Philistines. His three mighty men broke through enemy lines to bring their king a drink. They risked their very lives. So moved by this action was he, that David couldn't bring himself to drink the hard-earned water. Instead, he "poured it out unto the Lord" for the blessing he received through his devout warriors. They replenished the king's cistern, and in turn David offered the blessing to God.

Is your fountain dried up? Do you feel you have nothing left to offer? Go to the fountain that never runs dry. Drink heartily, and when you have received your blessing, pour it out—a drink offering unto the Lord—the Living Water.

TODAY'S HOT FLASH:

Don't cling to your blessings; offer them back to the Savior. Once you are able to do this, you become a blessing to others, poured out unto the King.

PRAYER:

Father, whatever I receive from You, may I give back: a drink offering, poured out unto You. For You alone are worthy. Amen.

JUNE 30

READ: HEBREWS 12:3–14

REPEAT OFFENDERS

For whom the Lord loveth he chasteneth, and scourgeth every son whom he receiveth.

~ Hebrews 12:6

Everyone knows the rule: Absolutely, positively DO NOT THROW SAND!

So what did I see when I walked into my backyard? My six-year-old and my four-year-old having a full-blown sand fight. For the umpteenth time, I march them to their rooms and ban them from the sand pile. Frustrated, I can't help but wonder how many times I will have to discipline them for the same behavior.

Our heavenly Father must wonder the same thing. Does He get frustrated with His children? We sin, He chastises, we repent, He forgives—then we do it again!

I plunge into the same bad behavior over and over again. I yell, am prone to angry outbursts, and have a tendency to be selfish. My repeat offenses are no different than my children's. I know what God expects from me, but I seem unable to comply.

I discipline my children because I love them and want them to grow up to be godly young men and women. God's motives are the same. He will do whatever it takes, as many times as it takes, to mold me into the image of His Son.

TODAY'S HOT FLASH:

Our Father never tires of molding His children. He loves us, therefore, He chastens us. Just as we do our children.

PRAYER:

Lord, help me to have more patience with my children; after all, they are just acting like their mother. Forgive me when I don't set a godly example. Amen.

JULY

JULY 1

READ: JOHN 17:10-21

PRAYING FOR FUTURE GENERATIONS

Neither pray I for these alone, but for them also which shall believe on me through their word.

~ John 17:20

Prayer is never finished. There is never enough time in a day to pray for everyone and everything. The command to pray without ceasing seems impossible when you realize the extent of prayers needed to cover every lost and hurting soul, those having financial problems, loved ones and acquaintances riddled with sickness, government and others in authority over us, our children, church family, and so on.

In the process of these hundreds of prayers, how many of us think to pray for our future generations? It is safe to assume very few are praying for the conversion and spiritual growth of your unborn grandchildren; great grandchildren; great, great, great grandchildren; or even great nieces and nephews.

Christ prayed for "those who shall be." We can pray that same prayer for our future generations as well. You may be the only one standing in that gap. With your fervent prayers, you can keep the Christian line flowing in your family.

TODAY'S HOT FLASH:

You alone may be the one standing between Christianity and total Christian annihilation in your family line.

PRAYER:

Holy Father, I pray today for my grandchildren for generations to come. I claim them for You. Put a hedge about them and claim them for Yourself. Amen.

JULY 2
READ: JOHN 17:1–10

ARE YOU READY TO MEET THE MASTER?

I have glorified thee on earth: I have finished the work which thou gavest me to do.

~ John 17:4

Are you ready to meet the Master? Have you spent yourself to the very depths of your soul serving Him? What of today? Did you react to every prodding of the Holy Spirit?

"I'll do it tomorrow," you say. But what if tomorrow your number is up? What if a heart attack, accident, natural disaster, or some unsuspecting disease suddenly claims your life? When your life passes before your eyes, what will you see? A fulfillment of the tasks God has entrusted you with? Or a frittering away of your time, pushing off until tomorrow what should have been today?

Jesus knew His time was ending, and He was confident in His completion of the tasks set before Him. "I have glorified thee on earth: I have finished the work which thou gavest me to do."

How about you? Are you ready? Have you glorified the Father? Have you completed the work He called you to do?

TODAY'S HOT FLASH:

We only have today. Tomorrow is not promised. Don't waste another minute. It's time to forget about self and start glorifying the Master.

PRAYER:

Glorious Father, forgive me for wasting precious time. Please, let me have time to glorify You and to complete the work You have called me to do. Amen.

JULY 3

READ: MATTHEW 26:30-38

THE SORROWFUL HEART

Then saith he unto them, My soul is exceeding sorrowful, even unto death: tarry ye here, and watch with me.

~ Matthew 26:38

Karen Carpenter popularized a song that went like this: "Why does the sun go on shining? Why does the sea rush to shore? Why do the birds go on singing? Don't they know it's the end of the world? It ended when you said goodbye." This song touched a nerve with audiences. After all, pain and sorrow are universal. We understand sorrow in the context of grief or break up, but have little patience for those experiencing it from depression or hormones.

Christ experienced a depth of sorrow most of us will never will know. He earned the weight of the whole world on His shoulders. Maybe in our own vulnerable way, we are confronted with the weight of our own fleshly weaknesses and in our heightened emotional state, it seems too much to bear.

In His moment of temptation, He asked His disciples to pray for Him. When we are emotionally weak, we desperately need the prayers of others. Don't be ashamed to recruit your friends and family as prayer warriors; the more the better.

TODAY'S HOT FLASH:

Sorrow is no respecter of persons. Whether from a broken heart, deep-seated depression, or a significant loss, God's Word, the Holy Spirit, and faithful prayer from friends are the keys to survival and recovery.

PRAYER:

Father, truly my flesh is weak. When my heart sorrows, help me to seek out friends to pray for me, and may I do the same for them. Amen.

JULY 4
READ: GALATIANS 2:15–21

DECLARATION OF NON-INDEPENDENCE

I am crucified with Christ: nevertheless I live; yet not I, but Christ liveth in me: and the life which I now live in the flesh I live by the faith of the Son of God, who loved me, and gave himself for me.

~ Galatians 2:20

On July 4, 1776, the Continental Congress officially adopted the Declaration of Independence. It announced the independency of the first thirteen states. They chose to separate themselves from England's rule. This was the beginning of what we now know as the United States of America. Thousands died fighting for this freedom. Even today, men and women die fighting for this same cause. Freedom is worth fighting for!

The Christian, as an individual, is called to a different place. A place of submission, of dying to self, of giving up personal rights for the sole purpose of promoting Jesus. The world can't understand this, and many Christians don't get it either. "I am crucified with Christ," I am dead to self, what I wanted and what I stood for in the past plays no relevance in my life. Why? Because it is not about me anymore. "Yet, not I, but Christ liveth in me." This is my declaration. Not a declaration of independence, but of non-independence.

TODAY'S HOT FLASH:

We menopausal women tend to be a tad bit assertive. We stand up for ourselves quite well, thank you very much. Unfortunately, that's the flesh in us! Total submission to Jesus is imperative. When Christ lives through us, the flesh is defeated.

PRAYER:

Father, I pray that I may be crucified with Christ, bowing to His will alone and none other. Crucify this strong streak of independence, that I may surrender to You in all things. Amen.

JULY 5

READ: GALATIANS 5:1-6

LET FREEDOM RING

Stand fast therefore in the liberty wherewith Christ hath made us free, and be not entangled again with the yoke of bondage.

~ Galatians 5:1

Have you ever been in bondage to something or someone? The feeling it conveys is that of a caged animal that throws itself at the bars and claws at them until it is depleted of energy.

People are no different. Once something gains a stronghold on us, we become powerless to escape. Exhaustion and hopelessness set in, removing the desire to fight. We are like caged animals, albeit, no visible bars; they are there nonetheless.

The good news in all this tragedy is Jesus. He is the bondage breaker, the cage opener, the energy supplier. He renews a desire within us to break free from the bonds that hold us tight.

"Christ has made us free," and if we are free, then the things which once held us captive can no longer ensnare us.

Free from alcohol, drugs, sexual addictions, anger, and bitterness. Free from the binding yoke that held us fast. Free from the entanglement of anything that held us firmly in its grasp. We are free indeed!

TODAY'S HOT FLASH:

To know Jesus is to know freedom. Keep focused on Christ and deny those sins that entangle you. Freedom is yours for the taking.

PRAYER:

Gracious Father, in You I am truly free. Help me keep focused on Jesus so that I may remain free from all the bondage makers always within grasp. Amen.

JULY 6
READ: JOHN 7:37–53

RIVERS OF LIVING WATER

He that believeth on me, as the Scripture hath said, out of the belly shall flow rivers of living water.

~ John 7:38

What did Christ mean by "out of his belly shall flow rivers of living water"? Christ is talking of the Holy Spirit. At the time of His teaching, the Holy Spirit had not yet come. The disciples had not personally met this indwelling and life-changing third person of the Trinity. His teaching caused more questions than gave answers.

This is not the situation for us. If we belong to Jesus, we experience the Holy Spirit's indwelling presence every day. He guides us, encourages us, and continually prods us to righteousness. Because He lives in us, our outward life should exhibit a passionate zeal that ignites a fire within and bubbles outward. Our satisfaction with Christ bleeds over to others, and we become channels of blessings to everyone we cross paths with.

Others are refreshed by the flow of living water that pours from our being when we are in a right relationship with the Savior. When Christ is in us, and we allow Him to flow out from us—lives are changed!

TODAY'S HOT FLASH:

Are you a channel of blessing to every person that you come in contact with? If the Holy Spirit is possessing, you will be doing the blessing.

PRAYER:

Gracious Father, make me a channel of blessing. My life possessing, my service blessing, make me a channel of blessing today. Amen.

JULY 7

READ: ROMANS 4:13-25

WHAT KIND OF FAITH DO YOU POSSESS?

For the promise, that he should be the heir of the world, was not to Abraham, or to his seed, through the law, but through the righteousness of faith.

~ Romans 4:13

Have you been waiting on the Lord for answered prayer? You've remained faithful in your spiritual life, continuous in prayer, and still the answer evades you.

Abraham and Sarah received a promise directly from God. Sarah would bear a son. Year after year they waited with no result. In a moment of weakened faith, they decided to take matters into their own hands. Hagar, Sarah's handmaiden, bore a child in her place. Thus, Ishmael was born, a child of the flesh. God informed Sarah that Ishmael was not the awaited heir.

It wasn't until Sarah was beyond the age of childbearing that God made His move. At the age of eighty-nine, Sarah conceived. God delivered on His promise.

Have you been praying for a lost loved one? Seeking an answer to a life-changing question? Seeking God's will for your life? There is only one thing to do. Remain faithful where you are. Don't fall to the temptation to take matters in your own hands. It always fails.

TODAY'S HOT FLASH:

What kind of faith do you possess? That which Ishmael represents, taking matters into your own hands, or Isaac, trusting God will do what He promises?

PRAYER:

Faithful Father, thank You that You are always faithful. Keep me strong against the temptation to take things into my own hands. Amen.

JULY 8
READ: 2 CORINTHIANS 10:1–10

BEG IF YOU MUST

Now I Paul myself beseech (beg) you by the meekness and gentleness of Christ who in presence am base among you, but being absent am bold toward you.

~ 2 Corinthians 10:1

Paul spent a lot of time begging his spiritual children to live godly lives. He did not cower or hold back for fear of rejection. He didn't worry whether their anger would keep them from coming around. He had a greater motive and saw the bigger picture.

Like most parents, he rebuked, encouraged, and prodded his spiritual offspring to live the life of victory in Jesus. And, like most parents, when they didn't obey, he questioned their love for the Father. He begged them to obey the words of the Lord, to walk the walk and talk the talk. His heart ached over their indifference.

Often we cower from challenging our children, family members, and close friends when we see them straying. We fear their rejection and refuse to confront them in their sin.

Paul cared more for their spiritual welfare and refused to be hindered by fear. Are we so concerned with our loved ones' eternal destination that we refuse to let the possibility of rejection hinder us? Beseech them for the sake of their very souls!

TODAY'S HOT FLASH:

Beg if you must, plead with them to live righteous lives. Even if they don't listen, you won't have to live with the guilt that you did nothing.

PRAYER:

Father, forgive my negligence where my family and friends are concerned. Teach me to speak out boldly—to beg if I must—regardless the results. Amen.

JULY 9

READ: JOHN 13:6-9

HONORING OUR PARENTS, PLEASING OUR LORD

If I then, your Lord and Master, have washed your feet; ye also ought to wash one another's feet.

~ John 13:14

During a Sunday school class, I had my children wash one another's feet. Some refused, and some of their parents were aghast. They'd never do such a thing! This was Peter's attitude when Jesus attempted to wash his feet. "Never!" Peter replied.

Peter learned a valuable lesson that day; Christ-likeness requires uncomfortable and at times unpleasant service. As the Baby Boomer generation ages, so do our parents, and some of us are called to a place where previously we would have stood with Peter and cried, "Never!"

Service to our elderly loved ones can be hard, tedious, and may last for years. We find ourselves in the midst of tasks once thought disgusting. We have entered the realm of true role reversal. It's hard emotionally and also terrifying as we witness in vivid detail our future.

Be encouraged, my friend, that in honoring your parents, you are honoring the Father. He's had to do a lot of clean-up where we're concerned. I'm glad He never thought the job too hard, tedious, or disgusting. He would have given up on me long ago.

TODAY'S HOT FLASH:

Do not begrudge the honor due your parents, even if unearned. By serving them, you are pleasing God. Jesus washed feet; we can do no less.

PRAYER:

Father, may I be a daughter who is well pleasing to You. Teach me to honor my parents in a way that glorifies You. Amen.

JULY 10

READ: JOHN 1:1–10

THIS LITTLE LIGHT OF MINE

He was in the world, and the world was made by him, and the world knew him not.

~ John 1:10

Jesus arrived in a world filled with sin, hatred, and self-righteousness. Blinded eyes refused to recognize Him. "He was in the world [. . .] and the world knew Him not." He was a light shining brightly in a dark place. Most were unable to see, not for lack of light on the outside, but for lack of light in their hearts.

How long have you lived amid this darkness? Does your light blaze through the darkness and shine into the lives of others? For many of us, our spiritual journey began passionately, but over time our zealousness dwindled, turning this great light to a flicker. Disillusionment, rejection, and hardships wear us down, and our testimony becomes dulled. Once we blazed as the light of the world. Now that light is hidden under a bushel of cares and cynicism. Satan has rendered us useless; he has accomplished his goal.

Awake, my friend, to righteousness. Each person is allotted a specific amount of time to shine brightly. What will you have to show for your life?

TODAY'S HOT FLASH:

Is your light hidden under a bushel, or are you letting your little light shine for all the world to see?

PRAYER:

Light of the World, may my light shine for all to see. May I not hide it under a bush, and may the brightness of it be seen throughout the world. Amen.

JULY 11

READ: JOSHUA 1:1-9

UNWAVERING FAITH

But let him ask in faith, nothing wavering. For he that wavereth is like a wave of the sea driven with the wind and tossed.

~ James 1:6

We pray for healing, financial security, wayward children, lost loved ones, or relief, but God is silent. How long can this last? Is God listening? Is there sin I need to confess? We rack our brains in the attempt to determine the cause of God's silence. If we are not careful, frustration and anger set in and we start to question God, our faith, and well-meaning encouragers.

It is easy to praise God in the good times, but when our faith is tested, we falter. Job said it best when he said, "What? Shall we receive good at the hand of God, and shall not receive evil?" (Job 2:10b).

Isaiah 55:8 tells us, "For my thoughts are not your thoughts, neither are your ways my ways, saith the Lord."

Finally, let me conclude with this great verse: "Have I not commanded thee? Be strong and of good courage; be not afraid neither be thou dismayed: for the Lord thy God is with thee whithersoever thou goest" (Joshua 1:9).

TODAY'S HOT FLASH:

Can we say we have faith when we only believe in the good times? God hears and always answers our prayers—in His time, in His way.

PRAYER:

Father, when things get tough and my prayers seem unanswered, help my faith to be strong. Forgive my doubt and complaints. Help me to wait for Your timing. Amen.

JULY 12

READ: ROMANS 8:5-13

FEEDING THE SPIRIT, DENYING THE FLESH

For they that are after the flesh do mind the things of the flesh; but they that are after the Spirit the things of the Spirit.

~ Romans 8:5

Susanna Wesley bore nineteen children, nine of whom died early. She met and married Samuel Wesley, a dissenter who was forced to take a remote, poverty stricken parish where for more than thirty years Susanna raised her children.

She credits her survival to a strict regimen and two hours a day with her Lord. As she aged, she added another hour at midday. Now I don't know this for sure, but having pulled my Bible out more than once during my most hormonal times, I believe she may have been struggling with her own menopausal demons. She was able to stay focused because she refused to feed the flesh, and she spent three hours a day feeding the Spirit. How did she find the time?

If we are to remain godly amid raging hormones and life's never-ending turmoils, we must learn to deny the flesh and feed the Spirit. Spiritual and emotional survival requires time— sometimes a lot of it—alone with our Lord. Only then will we have the fortitude to remain godly in the worst of circumstances.

TODAY'S HOT FLASH:

Susanna set an example of faithfulness rarely seen today. What fleshly pleasures do you need to forsake in order to feed the Spirit and deny the flesh?

PRAYER:

O Lord, I waste so much time doing nothing worthwhile. Forgive me, convict my heart to spend more time with You and less with the things of this world. Amen.

JULY 13

READ: 1 THESSALONIANS 4:7–11

STUDY TO BE QUIET

And that ye study to be quiet, and to do your own business, and to work with your own hands, as we commanded you.

~ 1 Thessalonians 4:11

How do you study to be quiet? Somehow I missed that command. Had I known it earlier in life, I may not have had to struggle so hard. Being so behind in my studies and having an already developed habit (of opening my mouth at all the wrong times), I don't know if I will ever excel in this subject. But that's not all Paul commands us to do.

His second command in this single verse is to "do your own business." In modern-day terms, "mind your own business." He can't expect us to excel in both admonitions, at the same time, can he? For a woman who has spent her entire life putting her foot in her mouth and making sure she knows the latest news in everyone's lives, this could be detrimental. She may burst! Relief doesn't come until she's expelled her opinion.

I try to keep my mouth shut; I even make it for a minute or two, and then—I can't stand it! I must have my say. It's like the world will end or something important will be missed if my words aren't heard. Suddenly, it occurs to me. I must have a high opinion of myself.

TODAY'S HOT FLASH:

Do you think the world will end if your opinion isn't heard? Maybe it's time to spend more time studying how to be quiet and thinking a little less highly of ourselves.

PRAYER:

Father, I know I have a long way to go. Help me to learn to be quiet instead of forcing my opinion on others. Only in Your strength is this possible. Amen.

JULY 14
READ: 1 PETER 1:13-19

CALLED TO HOLINESS

Because it is written, Be ye holy; for I am holy.

~ 1 Peter 1:16

My son has coined a saying that I like to spout and try to live. It goes like this: "We've heard it said that Christians don't have to sin, but probably will; the truth is, Christians can live sinless lives, but probably won't." It is a standard to be met, a goal to strive for, and a commandment to obey.

In our day and culture, we are taught to strive for self-satisfaction and happiness. We are goal-oriented, but we are reaching for the wrong goal. In trying to please the desires of the flesh, we fall short of pleasing the only One worthy of the effort, Jesus Christ.

Oswald Chambers said it best when he said, "The destined end of man is not happiness, nor health, but holiness. God is not an eternal blessing machine for men. He did not come to save men out of pity; He came to save men because He created them to be holy."

TODAY'S HOT FLASH:

Holiness is possible. It's not easy, it defies the flesh, and our minds fight against it, but in the power of the Spirit, and a desire to please God, we can be holy.

PRAYER:

Lord, I want to be holy as You are holy, but my flesh fights against it. Give me the strength to say no to the flesh and yes to living a sinless life. Amen.

JULY 15

READ: 1 CORINTHIANS 10:1–10

THE LITTLE SINS

Now these things were our examples, to the intent we should not lust after evil things, as they also lusted.

~ 1 Corinthians 10:6

I often skim over this verse, assuming it no longer applies to me. After all, I've overcome the big sins; therefore, lust isn't a problem anymore. When I think this way, I am setting myself up for a fall. Scripture says, "Wherefore, let him that thinketh he standeth take heed lest he fall" (1 Cor. 10:12).

It isn't the big things that beset us; it's the everyday temptations we barely notice that we succumb to. The temptation to be lazy when there's work to do; the temptation to scream and holler or lose control; the temptation to rule our husbands rather than submit; the temptation to not answer the phone, to overeat, or to watch an inappropriate television show. These are all small but important sidesteps which can separate us from a right relationship with Christ. Whenever we allow ourselves the luxury of these little sins, we are lusting after evil things.

We must deliberately walk away from anything that causes us to put the flesh above our Savior. It's hard, but anything worthwhile usually is.

TODAY'S HOT FLASH:

Satan lulls us to a place where we think we've got it all together. Beware if you've come to this place. It is where we become the most vulnerable.

PRAYER:

Lord, show me the little sins in my life. I want to get rid of everything in my life that separates me from having a right relationship with You. Amen.

JULY 16

READ: HEBREWS 4:1-7

HARDEN NOT YOUR HEART

Again, he limiteth a certain day, saying in David, To day, after so long a time; as it is said, To day if ye will hear his voice, harden not your hearts.

~ Hebrews 4:7

What have you hardened over your heart? We've all done it. Someone comes to us with loving criticism, and we know they are right. Pride and anger flail up within us, and we refuse to alter our behavior. Maybe someone criticized our children, and we took it as an affront to our parenting skills.

The inner nudgings of the Holy Spirit are the most often felt and also the most often ignored. He nudges, we ignore. We hear, "You know you shouldn't watch that TV program," yet we watch it. Or we hear, "You've already had two pieces of cake," and we grab a third. Every time we ignore those inner proddings, we add another layer of thickness to our already hardening hearts.

If a soft pliable heart is our goal, we must learn to listen and react the first time the Spirit confronts us. If we are not careful, we will stop hearing His voice, and our hearts will turn hard as stone.

TODAY'S HOT FLASH:

How hard is your heart? Have you learned to quench the proddings of the Spirit, or do you react immediately when He pricks your conscience?

PRAYER:

Father, help me to obey the Spirit's nudgings. Keep my heart soft and pliable and willing always to obey. Amen.

JULY 17

READ: 1 CORINTHIANS 13:1–7

LOVE IS LONGSUFFERING

Love suffereth long . . .

~ 1 Corinthians 13:4

Many times throughout our lives, our flesh—controlled by a deceitful heart (see Jeremiah 17:9)—and God's Word disagree. It is vital that we stand strong in our faith, not reacting to any given situation without firm backing from His Word. Following our heart often leads us down the path of destruction. Doing what is right and not what feels right is hard and unpleasant at times. As we learn to do it God's way, we spare ourselves and others the grief caused by rebellion.

Suffering long for the betterment of others—isn't that what our Savior did? Should we do less? It doesn't feel good, but we follow Christ's example because we love Him. It is an act of true longsuffering when we remain steadfast even in the middle of dire circumstances. How do we show love to those around us? By putting all our circumstances and all our loved ones into the hands of the One who out-loves us all. His love is perfect, and He will accomplish His will perfectly. We only have to trust Him.

We can love continuously, regardless the offense, because Christ does the same for us. It doesn't matter how often we fail Him, He never turns His back on us.

TODAY'S HOT FLASH:

By the time we reach our 50s, we should be experts at longsuffering. But many of us haven't had much practice. Start now. Practice makes perfect.

PRAYER:

Father, thank You for being so longsuffering with me. Where would I be if You got fed up with my sin? Help me to be longsuffering to everyone around me. Amen.

JULY 18
READ: 1 CORINTHIANS 13:1-7

LOVE IS KIND

Love suffereth long and is kind...

~ 1 Corinthians 13:4

Is kindness a simple act of helping someone out of a chair, sharing our cookies, or giving a compliment? It can be, but it is much more. Kindness becomes noteworthy when it is bestowed on those who are causing us to "suffer long." Acts of kindness are easy when we give it back to those who give it to us first. What is the reward in that? Where's the test in that? How do we treat others who treat us bad?

Love your enemies, do good to them which hate you, bless them that curse you, and pray for them who despitefully use you. And unto him that smiteth thee on the one cheek offer also the other; (yeah right, how many of us are going to do that?) *and him that taketh away the cloak forbid not to take thy coat also* (Luke 6:27-29).

Only those who are indwelled with the Holy Spirit can truly love their enemies (or those who have betrayed them). When Christ abides in us, His love naturally overflows onto every person He brings our way—friend and foe alike.

Our faith is demonstrated by our actions; our words alone mean nothing. True Christ-like love eagerly provides kind services for those in need.

TODAY'S HOT FLASH:

Christ's love within us shines brightly by the kindness we show to others.

PRAYER:

Father, teach me to have a kind heart, not only to those around me and not only to people I like, but to every person You bring my way. I want to share Jesus' love. Amen.

JULY 19

READ: 1 CORINTHIANS 13:1–7

I WANT THAT! AND THAT AND THAT . . .

Love suffereth long and is kind; love envieth not.

~ 1 Corinthians 13:4a

It doesn't matter how old we get; that green-eyed monster called jealousy seems to follow us wherever we go. We set goals of material gain, reach those goals, and always want more. When is enough enough? Will enough ever be enough? In the flesh, the answer is no.

Envy turns to bitterness, even hatred, when we question why others have more and better than we do. It often ignites unrighteous, passionate acts such as adultery, theft, and murder. We hear it in the news every day: a husband murders his wife's boyfriend; a mother murders a father over a custody dispute. We also experience envy when losing a promotion to someone less experienced or when we feel anger over the prosperity of our neighbor.

There are plenty of things that would be nice to have, but I refuse to allow the flesh to push me to a point of jealousy. Paul's wisdom is unsurpassed in this area. He said, "But godliness with contentment is great gain" (1 Timothy 6:6). He also said, "For I have learned, in whatsoever state I am, therewith to be content" (Philippians 4:11). What a great world it would be if we all developed this attitude.

TODAY'S HOT FLASH:

True love poured out on others does not look inward to what we don't have, but outward to the blessings of others.

PRAYER:

Father, forgive me when my desires of the flesh override my desire for righteousness. Oh, that I may be content in whatsoever state I am. Amen.

JULY 20
READ: 1 CORINTHIANS 13:1–13

PROUD AS A PEACOCK

Love vaunteth not itself, is not puffed up.

~ 1 Corinthians 13:4b

A peacock instinctively knows he is beautiful, especially to his future mate. All he has to do is puff up his chest, flash those colorful feathers, and he's drawn attention to himself. Fortunately for him, God designed him this way; what we see as pride is really survival. Not so with the human race. Why then do we exhibit the same traits?

By the time we've reached midlife, most of us have our share of trophies. Our children, our careers, our homes, our resumes, our knowledge, whatever it is, we hope others recognize our achievements; this makes us feel important.

Every good thing comes from the Father. No matter how brilliant our talents, they are gifts administered to us by the Holy Spirit for the sole purpose of glorifying God. Boasting glorifies self; humility steers all compliments upward. Humility is not easily gained, but God knows what it will take to humble us. He has a way of gradually eking out the tiniest morsel of pride. We don't relinquish it easily. It is hard to let go of self and give God the glory for everything that makes us look good.

TODAY'S HOT FLASH:

Every time peacocks flash those brilliant feathers, God automatically receives the glory. Every time we puff ourselves up, we steal the glory from God and shine it on ourselves.

PRAYER:

Lord, without You, I am capable of nothing worthy of praise. Without You, I am capable of nothing worthwhile. Remind me to always give You all the glory. Amen.

JULY 21
READ: 1 CORINTHIANS 13:1-13

BEHAVE YOURSELF

(Love) doth not behave itself unseemly.

~ 1 Corinthians 13:5a

Are you behaving yourself? What a question to ask an older woman, but . . . it needs asked. So, I ask again, "Are you behaving yourself?" If you were to ask me that question, the answer would differ according to the day.

Have you lost your temper recently? Attacked others through gossip and slander? Spoken foully? Kicked the dog? Do we use the excuse, "I can't help it, it's my hormones"?

Galatians 5:15 warns us against biting and devouring one another. Ephesians 4:31 cautions us against bitterness, wrath, and anger. In 1 Timothy, Paul warns the bishops against drinking, greediness, and brawling. Although directed to bishops, the standard applies to us all.

Do you talk too much? Irritate others? Misuse waitresses or loudly raise your voice when your rights are violated? Do you cut in line? When we behave in this way, we defame the name of Christ. He has set us free from the bondage of sin, yet we coddle and embrace these little, insignificant actions. In doing so, we throw our love for the Savior to the wind and nurture the flesh for our own satisfaction. God forbid.

TODAY'S HOT FLASH:

Behave yourself today! Smile, compliment, encourage, complete unfinished work, and do it all in the name of the One who set you free. Free to be Holy.

PRAYER:

Lord, help me to behave myself. Remind me to say pleasant and kind words and to set a godly example for all who are watching. Amen.

JULY 22
READ: 1 CORINTHIANS 13:1–13

J.O.Y.
(JESUS FIRST, OTHERS SECOND, YOU LAST)

(Love) doth not behave itself unseemly, seeketh not her own, is not easily provoked, thinketh no evil.

~ 1 Corinthians 13:5

We are all guilty of "seeking our own" to some degree. We are fascinated by the things of this world and frivolously spend our money, blinded to the struggles and needs of our neighbors. We shut our doors to visitors, turn off the phones, and ignore our e-mail. It makes us uncomfortable to spend time on others' needs when our flesh craves worldly pleasures. We mean well, and in our time, and in our way, we do our good deeds.

God's timing is not our timing. Do we love Him more than we love ourselves? Are we willing to pour our love out on others when it is inconvenient? God expects us to sacrifice ourselves to meet the needs of others. Our sacrifice proves our faith and our love for the Lord.

For many of us fighting the battle with hormones, the added stress of meeting others' needs when we are barely meeting our own sounds intimidating if not downright impossible. It *is* impossible—in our own strength. Only in the supernatural power of the Holy Spirit can we put others above ourselves.

TODAY'S HOT FLASH:

Don't stop and think about whether you should meet another's needs; just do it. If you think too long, you will talk yourself out of it.

PRAYER:

Ever-caring Father, forgive my selfishness. Many times I have put myself above others. Teach me to put others first, regardless of how I feel. Amen.

JULY 23

READ: 1 CORINTHIANS 13:1-13

ARE YOU EASILY PROVOKED?

(Love) is not easily provoked.

~ 1 Corinthians 13:5b

Do the actions or words of others provoke you to argue or retaliate in some way? Do you blame others for your sinful reactions? We only have to look to the Savior for guidance; He said it best. "You have heard that it was said, eye for eye, and tooth for tooth. But I tell you, do not resist an evil person. If someone strikes you on the right cheek, turn to him the other also. And if someone wants to sue you and take your tunic, let him have your cloak as well. If someone forces you to go one mile, go with him two miles. Give to the one who asks you, and do not turn away from the one who wants to borrow from you" (Matthew 5:38-42).

The Romans attempted to provoke Jesus. They ripped the hair from His precious head, spat on Him, and verbally abused Him. He did not retaliate. Instead, He pleaded to the Father for their forgiveness. What matchless love, this love of the Savior! The offenses against us are nothing compared to those inflicted on Jesus. He repaid good for evil, even praying for the offenders. Love—is not easily provoked. If you are, it is not a hormonal problem; it is a love problem.

TODAY'S HOT FLASH:

True love takes an offense without taking offense. Turn the other cheek, give them your coat, pray for them—but don't strike back.

PRAYER:

Father, help me to love those who deliberately provoke me. I want to show Your love by my lack of reaction. Guide my words at all times. Amen.

JULY 24

READ: 1 CORINTHIANS 7:17–24

SERVE OUT OF LOVE

For he that is called in the Lord, being a servant, is the Lord's freeman: likewise also he that is called, being free, is Christ's servant.

~ 1 Corinthians 7:22

What is service? Back in the good ol' days if you pulled into the gas station, an attendee rushed out ready to offer his services, but for a cost. The pretty, young waitress at the family diner couldn't be friendlier; even her smile comes with a price. Countless people offer their services by ringing the bells every Christmas season for the Salvation Army; they used to do it for free, but many are now paid.

Is this God's perception of service? Does He expect us to look around and serve only those who benefit us? Is it okay to pick and choose the easiest and most beneficial circumstances?

Jesus was a servant extraordinaire, a gracious giver and healer of the helpless. He was a tireless teacher, a seeker of sinners, and a fellow foot-washer. He exemplified the very essence of servanthood. He did this so you and I could reach beyond ourselves to offer others extreme service. We're not spring chickens anymore. Every day gone by is a day wasted if we are not spending it serving out of love for our Savior.

TODAY'S HOT FLASH:

Step out of your comfort zone and serve in a way you've never done before. And while doing it, do it with your entire being. Jesus did.

PRAYER:

O Lord, to serve as Jesus served, that is my desire. May I not waste another moment. Show me whom to serve today. Amen.

JULY 25

READ: ROMANS 8:14-17

SECURITY OF ADOPTION

For ye have not received the spirit of bondage again to fear; but ye have received the Spirit of adoption whereby we cry, Abba, Father.

~ Romans 8:15

When my soon-to-be adopted son came to live with us, his permanency was iffy. He was so damaged that by the middle of the school year, the school kicked him out (he was in kindergarten). Every day I threatened to send him packing. His tantrums and violent behavior wore me down, and when I should have loved him unconditionally, I was campaigning to send him away.

His behavior has not improved drastically, but my reaction to him has. I no longer grab the bags and threaten him with inevitable departure. I have chosen to accept this troubled, hard-to-love child as my own, and he will soon receive our family name.

It works the same way with you and me. We accept Jesus as Lord, and God adopts us into His family. He accepts us regardless of our screw-ups, and if you are anything like me, there's been plenty. We frustrate Him with our constant rebellion, but we are "adopted;" we have His family name. He will never disinherit us.

TODAY'S HOT FLASH:

There is security in knowing that we will never be disowned by our loving, forgiving Father. He may spank us, but He will never cast us aside.

PRAYER:

Thank You, dear Father, for the security I have in You. Thank You for adopting me into Your family. May my gratitude be shown through my actions. Amen.

JULY 26

READ: COLOSSIANS 1:9–14

BEAUTIFUL REDEMPTION

In whom we have redemption through his blood, even the forgiveness of sins.
~ Colossians 1:14

With the exception of the name of Jesus, *redemption* could very well be the sweetest word on earth. There is no greater relief, no greater hope ministered, no greater love experienced than through redemption. The thief on the cross experienced redemption. The woman with the issue of blood experienced redemption. Saul-turned-Paul received redemption on the road to Damascus. Peter, after denying Christ three times, experienced redemption. In each case, lives changed forever. No one was ever the same again.

The thief found joy in the promise of paradise. The woman's touch of faith healed her issue and gave her new life. Paul forsook all for the One he previously defied. Peter became a preaching powerhouse. All experienced the relief of pardoned sin, the hope of eternal life, and the unconditional love of a friend turned Savior.

I will ever be grateful for His redemption poured out on me. As it did with the thief, the healed woman, Paul, and Peter, redemption has changed my life forever. Has it changed yours?

TODAY'S HOT FLASH:

Redemption—something only Christ offers. Without it, life is hopeless, and nothing is worth the effort. With it, all life has purpose, and that purpose is Jesus.

PRAYER:

Thank You, Father, for Your Son, for His redemptive blood. Without it, where would we be? Why would we be? Thank You for giving me purpose. Amen.

JULY 27

READ: MARK 9:14-29

HELP MY UNBELIEF

Lord, I believe; help thou mine unbelief.

~ Mark 9:24b

The desperate father cried out to Jesus. The plight of his son, plagued by an evil spirit since childhood, seemed hopeless. Heartbroken, exhausted, and with no place to turn, he reached out to Jesus. "Lord, I believe; help my unbelief." The long-endured frustration and pain nearly jumps from the page and into our very soul. We feel it because we've all been there.

Your child walked away from his faith, and you pray for his return. A loved one has died, and you wonder if the pain will ever end. You have been praying for the salvation of your spouse for years, but still his heart remains unmoved. Menopause, physical, or mental pain plagues you; will you survive another day? Foreclosure or joblessness threatens your security. Is there a way out?

Jesus said, "If thou canst believe, all things are possible to them that believeth"(Mark 9:23b). He may or may not "fix" the problem as you desire it, but He will carry you through and strengthen you for your journey. In His strength, you will prevail because all things are possible through Jesus if you believe.

TODAY'S HOT FLASH:

Trust God! Believe God! Live God! He never fails. His ways are not our ways, but His ways are always right, even if we don't understand them.

PRAYER:

Lord, I believe; help my unbelief when I waver, worry, or feel like giving up. All things are possible with You. May I never forget that. Amen.

JULY 28

READ: EPHESIANS 5:18–20

PERFECT PRAISE

Speaking to yourselves in psalms and hymns and spiritual songs, singing and making melody in your heart to the Lord.

~ Ephesians 5:19

One day we will offer perfect praise to our King. We will sing with hearts focused on none but Jesus, uniting with the voices of saints and angels.

Perfect praise! Pure worship! Today, when saints of God unite in chorus, we experience only a glimmer of what it will be like as we lift our voices in eternal glory. Wonderful and terrible at the same time, voices raised, magnifying the entire realm of the heavens, pure voices, sinless hearts, and perfect praise. Can you hear it? Come quickly, Lord, that we may offer you perfect praise. Until then, let us never cease to lift up praise to the One who is worthy of all praise.

Don't drink too much wine. That cheapens your life. Drink the Spirit of God, huge draughts of Him. Sing hymns instead of drinking songs! Sing songs from your heart to Christ. Sing praises over everything, any excuse for a song to God the Father in the name of our Master, Jesus Christ (Ephesians 5:18–20, The Message).

TODAY'S HOT FLASH:

Do you want to brighten up your day? Overcome a bad mood? Override the pulls of Satan's interference? Sing songs of praise. It works every time!

PRAYER:

I lift up my voice to You, gracious Father; I will praise You with a song. For You and You alone are worthy of all praise in heaven and on earth. Amen.

JULY 29
READ: GALATIANS 6:6–10

DON'T PLAY THE BLAME GAME

Be not deceived, God is not mocked: for whatsoever a man soweth, that shall he also reap.

~ Galatians 6:7

At seventeen, I found myself pregnant and married. At twenty-one, I was single and on my own with two kids. I had dreamed of wedded bliss, beautiful children, a two-story house, and happily ever after. The whirlwind of flawed humanity clutched its claws into my dream world and ripped it apart piece by piece. *Why doesn't life go the way we plan? Why is there so much suffering? Why do my children have to grow up without the loving embrace and strong guidance of their biological father?* These questions plus a million more flooded my thoughts.

Had I been truthful with myself, I would have admitted my open rebellion against God. I allowed traumatic circumstances outside my control to slowly build a barrier to my heart and my once intimate relationship with God. I turned my back on God long before my disastrous marriage. Deep inside, I knew I was wrong. In order to hide the nagging conviction that plagued me, I filled my life with worldly pleasures. I played the blame game, laying all my woes at the feet of Jesus.

TODAY'S HOT FLASH:

Jesus doesn't cause our problems, we do. Wrong decisions, sinful reactions, and bitterness cause us to blame the only One who is ever faithful.

PRAYER:

Lord, forgive me for blaming You for all my problems. I take responsibility for my wrong decisions. Teach me to stay focused on You so this never happens again. Amen.

JULY 30

READ: 1 CORINTHIANS 1:10–17

ARE YOU PART OF THE PROBLEM?

For it hath been declared unto me of you, my brethren, by them which are of the house of Chloe, that there are contentions among you.

~ 1 Corinthians 1:11

Contentious, according to *Webster*, is defined as "inclined to quarrels and disputes, often over unimportant matters." In our passage, Paul chastised the Corinthian church for their contentious behavior.

Like the petty Corinthians, I have a tendency to waste time arguing over unimportant issues, and my contentious behavior is magnified by my raging hormones. When I allow myself to argue over stupid things, I have become a part of a problem that has plagued Christians (and all people) since the beginning: self-absorption and self-importance. This leads to divisions and disruptions in our Christian walk.

When we feel we must win an argument (whether we are right or not), we have allowed our pride to get in the way of our Christian love. This is never okay. If you notice this happening, and the argument is unimportant—concede. Divisions and hurt feelings are never worth proving you are right.

TODAY'S HOT FLASH:

Do you always feel like you have to have the last word? Practice the opposite today. Let someone else have the final say for once.

PRAYER:

Father, forgive my big mouth. I don't know why I think I have to have the last word all the time. Shut my mouth and help me give others the chance to speak for a change. Amen.

JULY 31

READ: GALATIANS 1:1-9

BEAUTY OR THE EVIL?

Who gave himself for our sins, that he might deliver us from this present evil world, according to the will of God and our Father.

~ Galatians 1:4

As I travel the countryside, I am confronted with the magnificence of God's creation. How can anything so beautiful have evil in it? I can't remain amid the beauty forever but must venture into the dregs of the city where trash, iron bars, and homelessness clash with my previous vision.

If we could remain in the beauty and never experience the evil, what good would we be for Christ? We must journey into the darkness to reach the lost; thank God we now have the ability to see the beauty in spite of the evil.

Jesus alone, through His redemptive work, changes our view. Once we were blind; now we see. Where once our hearts were filled with bitterness and hate, making everything evil, now we are filled with gratitude and hope, and the view changes.

We are the tools God uses to reveal His beauty. We cannot convince others of it; we must show them through our changed lives.

TODAY'S HOT FLASH:

Do you see the world through delivered eyes? Where there is hope, there is beauty. Where there is no hope, evil prevails. We can offer hope through Jesus.

PRAYER:

Father, I want to see only the beauty. Yes, I know there is evil, but because of You, there is hope. That is the most beautiful thing of it all. Amen.

AUGUST

AUGUST 1

READ: PSALM 48

HOW GREAT IS YOUR GOD?

Great is the Lord, and greatly to be praised in the city of our God, in the mountain of our holiness.

~ Psalm 48:1

We sing the song, How Great is Our God" by Chris Tomlin with emotional zeal. But do we believe the words we are singing, or do we walk out the door into our messy lives? Do we trust God is in control? Or do we pick up our petty sins as we exit the church building? What we experienced in "church" mode disappears in the reality of life.

If this is true in your life, then my question is this: how great is your God? Is He only great enough to stand the tide while in worship service surrounded by other worshippers? And if your God is so great, why do you fail to win the victory over the sins that drag you down? How can you sing so ecstatically about that which, where the rubber hits the road, you do not believe?

If we truly believed His greatness, why isn't that greatness powerful enough to strengthen us to overcome our sin? We experience the feeling of it but get stuck in the living of it. Victorious living is determined by how great our God truly is. If He is the "name above all names and worthy of all praise," where is our action that proves our belief?

TODAY'S HOT FLASH:

If you are having difficulty overcoming sin, then it is not the size of the sin that is the problem, but the size of your God.

PRAYER:

Great Father and God, Help me to trust You fully. May my actions portray how great You truly are. You are name above all names and worthy of all praise. Amen.

AUGUST 2

READ: JOHN 10:1–11

JESUS ONLY

I am the door: by me if any man enter in, he shall be saved, and shall go in and out, and find pasture.

~ John 10:9

Never before have we lived in such a religious society. Everyone has a personal idea of what heaven is and how to get there. As well, everyone has a personal idea about sin, Satan, God, Jesus, and hell.

According to Barna statistics, half of all Americans believe that Christianity is only one of many faith options people can choose from. It states that 65% of American Christians believe that many different religions can lead to eternal life.

Where does that leave those of us who know the truth? How can we help close this gap between truth and fallacy? By standing strong in our faith regardless the cost. By knowing what we believe and becoming unwavering in that belief. By always being ready with an answer—God's answer, not our own. Until we go home to glory, we must stand boldly and say, "Jesus is the way, the truth and the life, no man comes to the Father but by Him" (John 14:6). Jesus only is the gateway to heaven.

TODAY'S HOT FLASH:

People choose different beliefs because it makes heaven attainable on their own terms. One day they will get the surprise of their life. And it won't be pleasant.

PRAYER:

Father, may I boldly stand for the truth of Jesus. Guide my words. May I always be ready with Your answer when confronted about my belief. Amen.

AUGUST 3

READ: ACTS 1:8-11

OUT OF SIGHT, OUT OF MIND

And when he had spoken these things, while they beheld, he was taken up, and a cloud received him out of their sight.

~ Acts 1:9

I don't know how many times I've given my children a command and then left the room, only to come back and find it undone. The moment I left the room, their attention reverted back to whatever they were doing. I was out of sight; therefore, I was out of mind.

Jesus gave a command just before He ascended on a cloud. "Ye shall be witnesses unto me both in Jerusalem (your hometown), and in all Judea (your state), and in Samaria (your country), and unto the uttermost parts of the earth (the rest of the world)" (Acts 1:8).

The apostles lived out this command until their dying day, but over the years, out of sight, out of mind became the norm for many others, and although there has always been a remnant of faithful followers, the majority has shrugged off their God-given responsibility.

How about you? Are you reaching others for Christ? Or are you an out of sight, out of mind Christian? Do you focus only on the tangible and the here and now? It's great if you are reaching your family for the Lord, but it shouldn't stop there.

TODAY'S HOT FLASH:

"Be ye witnesses" is not a command solely for the apostles. Everyone who claims Christ carries the responsibility. It starts in our homes but shouldn't stay there.

PRAYER:

Father, show me how I can reach people for You in every area You have commanded. I want to live in obedience to You in all things. Amen.

AUGUST 4

READ: 2 CORINTHIANS 4:11–18

DELIBERATE ACTION

For which cause we faint not; but though our outward man perish, yet the inward man is renewed day by day.

~ 2 Corinthians 4:16

With the onset of menopause, and the added infirmities of aging, comes greater introspection and magnified awareness of our mortality. People tend to react in one of three ways. They may become depressed and self-focused, shutting down and barely functioning. Or, they may become apathetic, choosing to ignore the reality of imminent death, thereby removing personal responsibility that comes with knowledge. The third reaction is a sense of urgency; time is running out, and there is still much to do. This should be the reaction of every Christ follower.

Ignoring a reality never makes a truth disappear. We must face that truth and work for the day is coming. The realization of that truth should spur us to deliberate action.

Whatever your infirmity, never lose sight of the goal, which is to bring glory and honor to the Lord Jesus Christ every day. Paul suffered infirmities, but he kept focused, "For which cause we faint not, but though our outward man perish, yet the inward man is renewed day by day" (2 Corinthians 4:16).

TODAY'S HOT FLASH:

"Our light affliction, which is but for a moment, worketh for us a far more exceeding and eternal weight of glory" (2 Corinthians 4:17). Friends: IT WILL BE WORTH IT ALL!

PRAYER:

Father, I am tired. I look around and see so many who need You. Renew my strength for today, that I might bring glory and honor to You. Amen.

AUGUST 5

READ: JOHN 8:1–11

NO STONE THROWING ALLOWED

He that is without sin among you, let him first cast a stone at her.
~ John 8:7b

The scribes and Pharisees were the "it" crowd of the day. They were pompous and righteous in their own eyes. They followed the law to a tee and therefore thought they were better than everyone else.

In a very uncaring and manipulative manner, these "men of God" entrapped and humiliated a woman caught in adultery with the intent of "tripping up" Jesus. His reply is one of the most eye-opening and self-revealing statements in Scripture. "He that is without sin among you, let him first cast a stone at her" (John 8:7b).

There have been times in my life when I've pointed a self-righteous finger accusingly at others. How much better it would have been to quietly and compassionately say, "He who is without sin cast the first stone." The perfect words for the perfect occasion.

The next time someone comes to you complaining, gossiping, or maliciously slandering another, don't get caught up in the stone throwing. Reply as Jesus replied, and it will stop them in their tracks and put an end to it before it has a chance to fester.

TODAY'S HOT FLASH:

Not one of us can stand the scrutiny of an inner revealing. In the past, we have all been guilty of stone throwing. Let it not be so for our future.

PRAYER:

Merciful Father, forgiver of my sins, I have thrown those stones in the past, and I am sorry. May I lift up and encourage rather than tear down and destroy. Amen.

AUGUST 6
READ: EXODUS 34:10-17

AT WHAT ALTAR ARE YOU WORSHIPPING?

But ye shall destroy their altars, break their images, and cut down their groves: for thou shalt worship no other god: for the Lord . . . is a jealous God.

~ Exodus 34:13-14

Do you have any altars that need to be destroyed? Any images that need to be hewn down? Are there any "gods" that stand between you and the Father? Are there things in your life that make God jealous?

What or who do you worship at the feet of? Is it your time? Is it divided—eight hours work, three hours family, two hours God—each in its allotted spot? What about your home? Is it your personal sanctuary or an avenue of ministry?

What of your hobby? Does it take you from what is most important? Whenever the Israelites pursued their interests above God's, they suffered dire circumstances.

God is to be our hobby, our number one interest, our major goal in life. Beware when you decide you need a break from the Creator and His work. You may open a door wide enough for Satan to squeeze through, and before you know it, you will be worshipping at the feet of a different altar.

TODAY'S HOT FLASH:

Anything we do that does not include God is a bad idea. Make God a part of every area of your life. Don't put Him in a box and set Him aside until His allotted time.

PRAYER:

Father, help me to integrate You in every area of my life. If You can't be part of it, it shouldn't be a part of my life. Keep me focused, Lord. Amen.

AUGUST 7

READ: JAMES 1:1–12

FAITHFUL ALL THE TIME

My brethren, count it all joy when ye fall into divers temptations.

~ James 1:2

My husband and I cut our teeth in the ministry in the suburbs of Chicago. I was young, insecure, and unprepared for what lay ahead. We were called to revitalize a dying church. Our first week there, my husband was handed an itinerary he was required to keep. Each day began at 8 a.m. and ended at 6 p.m. The housing they provided was two hours from the church.

I was given my orders, as well. I was required to lead the women's group, lead a weekly prayer vigil, and partner with my husband in the youth ministry. I was a stranger in a foreign land. It quickly became evident that our desire to serve God translated into the church members' desire to control and manipulate us for their purposes.

Looking back, we both consider this a pivotal time in our Christian walk. We served, regardless the command. We prayed, determined not to leave until God gave the okay, and we trusted that God knew what He was doing.

We learned humility, chain of command, obedience, self-sacrifice, unconditional love, and most importantly, we learned that God is faithful—all the time.

TODAY'S HOT FLASH:

If you are in a tough situation, don't question God's faithfulness. He's preparing you—for what, I don't know. But His purpose will shine through in the end.

PRAYER:

Thank You, Lord, for the hard times. Thank You for Your faithfulness. Help me to remember that You are in control and that everything happens for a reason. Amen.

AUGUST 8
READ: GENESIS 3:1–6

POUNCING ON THE BAIT

And when the woman saw that the tree was good for food [...] and a tree to be desired to make one wise, she took of the fruit...

~ Genesis 3:6

Why did Adam and Eve choose the forbidden fruit over their God? As deceitful as he was, can we place the blame on the serpent? Satan gambled in the garden that day. He knew God gave the man and woman the ability to choose their own fate. Satan may have provided an enticing lure, but Adam and Eve pounced on the bait. They chose to worship themselves instead of God. Ever since that fateful day, man has been lured by his own lusts, pouncing on the bait of this world rather than choosing God's way.

The world says to look after me first, to say what I feel no matter who it hurts, and to blame others for my problems. Sadly, I am often guilty of falling to these temptations. I joke and blame Adam and Eve for this curse of sin, but would I have done any differently?

I am so grateful that, even from the beginning, God had His redemption plan in place. Knowing the evil intents of man's heart, God still chose to love and redeem us. If I were God, I am not sure I would be so generous.

TODAY'S HOT FLASH:

God in His graciousness did not leave Adam and Eve in a state of hopelessness. He provided a way for deliverance, and it stands firm still today.

PRAYER:

Lord, forgive me when I fall to the temptations of this world. Help me to call on the Holy Spirit's power and say no to sin and the lures of Satan. Amen.

AUGUST 9

READ: JAMES 2:14-20

FAITH TAKES A STAND

Even so faith, if it hath not works, is dead, being alone.

~ James 2:17

How do you react when you witness an injustice? When you see a child being bullied, or when your child's (or grandchild's) school decides to discontinue the Pledge of Allegiance? Do you complain without action? When the school chooses to teach elementary children about alternative lifestyles, or a court house opts to remove the Ten Commandments, do you speak out? What do you do when someone greedily takes the last three pieces of chocolate cake, or a church visitor is offended by a member? Do you stand in the gap for someone falsely accused?

Faith always takes a stand! It is not ashamed of the gospel of Christ, but what does this mean? Is it speaking the name of Christ boldly? Yes. Is it sharing your faith? Yes. But it is much more. To stand for Christ is to stand for right, speak against wrong, and take action when necessary, regardless the cost. "Faith, if it hath not works, is dead, being alone." All words and no action is what put this country in its present predicament. Don't you think it's time your faith took a stand?

TODAY'S HOT FLASH:

What have you been burying your head in the sand about? Don't you think it's time to pull it out and take a bold stand? You won't be a lone voice in the wilderness.

PRAYER:

Lord, give me the boldness to take a stand for all that is right, and to speak against all that is wrong. In Your strength I can do this. Amen.

AUGUST 10
READ: MARK 11:20–26

IN SPITE OF OUR DISOBEDIENCE

And when ye stand praying, forgive, if ye have ought against any: that your Father also which is in heaven may forgive you your trespasses.

~ Mark 11:25

When my daughter is struggling in her marriage, she calls me to try to work through it. I have nothing new to say to her. Even so, she needs help, and I am there for her.

The other night as I was counseling her, my grandson bolted through her door, bellowing because his four-wheeler was stuck in the mud. My daughter is a reactor, and her first response is usually anger (she's a redhead). She refused to help, claiming he got himself into this mess and could get himself out of it.

BINGO —teaching moment! I said, "Do you realize what you just did?"

"No."

"You just turned your back on your son in his time of need."

"He disobeyed me. Why should I help him? I've told him over and over again."

"Why should God forgive us over and over again?" I asked.

She thought about that and, in spite of her initial reaction, she helped my grandson out of his self-made predicament.

Does this sound familiar to you? How many times do we do the same thing over and over again? We've promised God we wouldn't, but there we go again, screaming, hollering, smoking, (you put in the deed). And once again we cry to the Father for help out of the mess we have made. The amazing thing is, He never turns His back on us or tells us we are on our own. When we need Him, He is always there.

TODAY'S HOT FLASH:

How many times do we cry out to our ever-present Father, "Help!" We expect Him to be there for us. Should our loved ones expect any less?

PRAYER:

Yet again, Father, I have failed You. You are always there when I call. Help me to do no less for those whom I love. By this I can show Your love. Amen.

AUGUST 11
READ: PSALM 86:6–15

THE COMFORT OF HIS LOVE

But thou, O Lord, art a God full of compassion, and gracious, longsuffering, and plenteous in mercy and truth .

~ Psalm 86:15

Rochelle (not her real name) was hurt and misused as a child. She now struggles to forgive, especially if she feels she's been deliberately mistreated. She carries this attitude over to everyone she meets. She knows she needs to let go of the anger because it is destroying her ability to live a productive, fulfilled life, but she's stuck in the bitterness. Each time we meet, we talk about the same thing. It never changes. Still, when she cries out for help, I am there. Many people have asked me why I'm "wasting my time," and I am disheartened by their lack of understanding.

As parents, friends, spouses, grandparents, and just plain decent human beings, our Christ-like duty is to help whoever is in need, whenever it is needed. Not just once or twice, but every time.

Patiently, God listens to us as we repeat our cries for help over and over again. He's given us the answer, but we are stuck in our pain, so round and round we go. Still, "He is full of compassion, and gracious, longsuffering" and wraps us in the comfort of His love. We are to share that same love to everyone in need, over and over again.

TODAY'S HOT FLASH:

Because Christ shows compassion, mercy, and longsuffering toward us, we are called to do the same for others.

PRAYER:

Merciful Father, may I be quick to forgive, ready to help, slow to judgment, and full of Your love. May I exhibit the compassion of Christ, every time. Amen.

AUGUST 12
READ: 1 CORINTHIANS 4:1-8

MY PLAN VS. GOD'S PLAN

Moreover it is required in stewards, that a man (or woman) be found faithful.

~ 1 Corinthians 4:2

By fifty, I planned on having a nice, remodeled home with beautiful area rugs and new furniture. I also dreamed of long vacations in warm climates. I realize now that these dreams will never come to pass. That's not a complaint, just an observation.

With three troubled children and a new puppy, I can kiss those dreams goodbye. I refuse to dwell on them or lose any sleep over them.

As much as I have my plans, I have learned that more often than not, they are not God's plans. I have learned to cling loosely to my desires and act immediately when I know what God wants me to do. God chooses where He will put me and what I will do. My choice is to obey or rebel. I choose to obey.

God created time. He is outside of time. When He looks at my life, He views it from beginning to end. Doesn't it make sense to submit to the One who sees, knows, and totally controls this entire jigsaw puzzle called life?

TODAY'S HOT FLASH:

All my little insignificant desires cannot compare to my greatest desire of all: to have my Savior say, "Well done, thou good and faithful servant."

PRAYER:

Omniscient Father, Creator of time and all that is in it, may my desires be Your desires, and when my time is done, may You find me faithful. Amen.

AUGUST 13

READ: ROMANS 6:16-23

TOO GOOD TO BE TRUE

For the wages of sin is death; but the gift of God is eternal life through Jesus Christ our Lord.

~ Romans 6:23

Get a free laptop, get a free plasma TV, just fill out the survey. Have you ever seen those ads? Have you ever participated? I have—what a frustrating experience. Their promises are true, but these surveys consist of sponsors who want you to try their products. Before I was halfway through, I'd spent more than fifty dollars and committed to at least three clubs. At that point, it may have behooved me to finish, but I was so disgusted that I quit. I am sure that is their hope; they make money and don't have to give anything away. It was an offer "too good to be true."

Most things in this world that appear "too good to be true," are. But there is one wonderful "too good to be true" offer that is guaranteed, and it can be found in only one person, Jesus Christ. "The gift of God is eternal life through Jesus Christ our Lord" (Romans 6:23), and "If thou shalt confess with thy mouth the Lord Jesus Christ and shalt believe in thine heart, that God hath raised him from the dead, THOU SHALT BE SAVED" (10:9, emphasis mine). No more "too good to be true" offers of the world for me. I'll stick to the one I can be confident in.

TODAY'S HOT FLASH:

Eternal life through Jesus—is it too good to be true? Yes! But true, it is! And it's yours for the asking. What's stopping you?

PRAYING:

Lord, forgive me for wasting time and money on "too good to be true" offers of this world. Thank You for Jesus, the one grand offer that is absolutely true. Amen.

AUGUST 14
READ: ROMANS 8:1-4

CONDITIONS

There is therefore now no condemnation to them which are in Christ Jesus, who walk not after the flesh, but after the Spirit.

~ Romans 8:1

When I was growing up, I learned quickly that blessings came with obedience. If I wanted to stay up late, I had to get up without complaint in the morning. If I wanted a cookie, I had to eat all my dinner. The same principle applies in our Christian walk. Every blessing from God has conditions. And why shouldn't they? Do you give your children blessings when they disrespect or disobey you?

The Christian woman does not experience judgment IF she does not walk after the flesh, but after the Spirit. If we humble ourselves and pray, and seek His face and turn from our wicked ways, then He will heal our land (2 Chronicles 7:14). If you forgive others, God will forgive you (Matthew 6:14). The list goes on and on.

Are you expecting blessings from God without doing your part? God is merciful and full of grace; therefore, we receive more than we deserve, just because. Begin a life of obedience and see the blessings come pouring down.

TODAY'S HOT FLASH:

God is in the blessing business. Obey and live life more abundantly. Rebel and live a life of continual defeat. Sounds like a no-brainer to me.

PRAYER:

Thank You, Lord, for Your many blessings every day. Help me to remain obedient in all things, that I may reap the benefits of Your love. Amen.

AUGUST 15

READ: PROVERBS 17:17–22

GO AHEAD AND LAUGH

A merry heart doeth good like a medicine...

~ Proverbs 17:22

When I was young, I thought forty was ancient. Now that I'm almost fifty, one hundred might be ancient, but I am not even sure about that. Commercials advertise fifty as the new thirty, and to some degree, they are right. Technology, advanced procedures, and obsessiveness all play a part in the older woman's image today. In all this serious concentration, I feel we've lost a vital link to staying young, and that is the ability to laugh. We take ourselves too seriously and view aging as a tragedy. My grandmother looked like a grandmother, but she could laugh. She found humor in her experiences and had a story for every wrinkle.

Proverbs 17:22 tells us that "a merry heart doeth good like a medicine," and I agree. Nothing makes me feel better in a hurry than to have a good laugh. But it doesn't always have to be loud, boisterous laughter; a heart full of joy is just as pleasing and lasts longer than the moment.

What makes you laugh or fills your heart with joy? When is the last time you laughed until you cried? In the seriousness of life, we've forgotten how. Don't you think it's time to focus on the joys of life and leave what we can't control in God's hands?

TODAY'S HOT FLASH:

Laughter is good for the soul. Stop taking life so seriously; it only adds wrinkles. Stop wasting time. As the saying goes, LIVE, LOVE, AND LAUGH!

PRAYER:

Father, help me to find the joy in my life and to see the positive rather than the negative. Sometimes it's hard, but with Your help it is possible. Amen.

AUGUST 16
READ: 1 JOHN 5:9–15

LOOKING FOR LOVE IN ALL THE WRONG PLACES

He that hath the Son hath life; and he that hath not the Son of God hath not life.

~ 1 John 5:12

Elizabeth Taylor was married eight times. Eva Gabor was married five times; her sister Zsa Zsa, nine. The entire Hollywood scene breeds whirlwind marriages and divorces. But Hollywood is not alone in its marital rollercoaster. Many in my church (and probably yours) were married multiple times before salvation.

God created every person with a need for Jesus. He placed a void within them that is only sated through His presence. Many of us attempt to fill that void with other things or people, but it never works. Satisfaction turns to dissatisfaction, and we resume our search. I've been there, and you probably have too. How sad it is that so many refuse to let in the only One who satisfies, and their search continues until death. They don't realize their mistake until it is too late.

Everyone feels the need to fill the void. Everyone feels the need to be important—to have a purpose. Why is Jesus usually the last choice? Why do we have to try everything else before we accept Him? Are you still trying to fill a void? Have you submitted to Christ fully? Don't you think it's time?

TODAY'S HOT FLASH:

If you haven't surrendered all to Jesus, there remains a crack in your void. Fill it the rest of the way; give yourself fully to the service of the Savior, and be satisfied.

PRAYER:

Lord, forgive me for holding back part of myself. Take all that I am and help me to hold nothing back. Fill this void and satisfy my soul with Your presence. Amen.

AUGUST 17

READ: JOHN 21:18-25

IT'S NOT ABOUT SERVICE, IT'S ABOUT THE SAVIOR

And when he had spoken this, he saith unto him, Follow me.

~ John 21:19b

We have a tendency to believe that the most important thing for the Christian to do is to share Jesus, to be missionaries in our own land and abroad. But when our minds think in this manner, we have aligned ourselves with the work and not the Master.

The most important thing for a Christian to do is to obey. To cling to every word our Savior speaks and to follow unconditionally. The greatest commandment Jesus ever gave is not to "go" or to "love" but to "follow me."

This includes going, serving, teaching, forgiving, and everything else associated with Christianity. But, we must be careful lest our devotion to service overrides our relationship to the Savior. He is what it is all about.

This mindset has saved me much grief over the years. When my feelings turn negative toward others, service, life, my husband, and/or marriage, I turn my thoughts toward Jesus. What does He want me to do? What does He say in His Word? How do I stay in a right relationship with my Savior? When we ask these questions, our priorities remain in place.

TODAY'S HOT FLASH:

When we make it about Jesus and not about what we are doing, feelings play no part, and this keeps us from making a lot of stupid mistakes.

PRAYER:

Father, help me to remain focused on Jesus, not on all the things I am doing. May I follow Your leading and not succumb to my own desires. Amen.

AUGUST 18
READ: 2 CORINTHIANS 5:1-10

SORRY TO DISAPPOINT YOU

Therefore we are always confident, knowing that, whilst we are at home in the body, we are absent from the Lord.

~ 2 Corinthians 5:6

I may not be at death's door, but sometimes I feel like it. With a chronic illness, I have to admit my mind has wandered to the heavenly realm a little more often.

Death is not something to be feared, but an anticipated everlasting adventure. Granted, our flesh desires to remain among our loved ones, but "in this tabernacle we do groan, being burdened, not for that we would be unclothed, but clothed upon, that mortality might be swallowed up of life" (vs. 4).

There are many people today who comfort themselves with the belief that their departed loved one is watching over them from heaven. I am sorry to disappoint you, but as for me, I will be fully preoccupied with adoring the Savior. "To be absent from the body is to be present with the Lord." GLORY HALLELUJAH! What a day that will be!

I'll leave the earthly things, including my family, into the caring hands of the Father and His guardian angels. After all, He can do a much better job than I can.

TODAY'S HOT FLASH:

God alone watches over His children. If they are with Him, they are completely focused on Him. Don't begrudge them the greatest pleasure of all.

PRAYER:

Father, what a glorious day it will be to worship at the feet of Jesus and to have Him fully encompass my mind. I wait with anticipation. Amen.

AUGUST 19

READ: LUKE 6:46–49

BUILD A FIRM FOUNDATION

He is like a man which built an house, and digged deep, and laid the foundation on a rock: and when the flood arose, the stream beat vehemently upon that house, and could not shake it: for it was founded upon a rock.

~ Luke 6:48

God did not design women to self-destruct (J. Ron Eaker), and menopause is not a disease needing to be cured. It is a normal transition of life. How we weather this transition is up to us. We stand a better chance of emotional survival if we build a firm foundation. In Luke 6:48, the man dug deep and laid a firm foundation on solid rock before entering into the gigantic task of building his house. Soon after the house was completed, the floods came and battered the structure, but it stood firm. Because he took the time necessary to keep it strong, it remained erect in a time of great turmoil.

Jesus is our solid rock. He is our firm foundation, and as long as we dig deep into His Word and cling to His presence, He will give us the strength to remain erect when we feel like crumbling. We can't let our guard down for a second. Establishing a firm foundation takes time, and the minute we slack, our foundation weakens, opening the door to destruction.

TODAY'S HOT FLASH:

Daily build on the firm foundation of Jesus Christ through His Word and prayer, lest your foundation weaken and you come tumbling down.

PRAYER:

Father, You are my firm foundation, my solid Rock. You alone can keep me standing strong in a time of turmoil. Thank You for keeping me from falling. Amen.

AUGUST 20
READ: JOB 38:1–8

PUT ON YOUR BIG GIRL PANTIES AND DEAL WITH IT

Gird up thy loins like a man; for I will demand of thee, and answer thou me.

~ Job 38:3

Are you a whiner? Do you find yourself moaning and groaning over the little things of life? My husband has often asked me if I want a little cheese to go with my whine. It's not the big things; it's the small things that I find irritating. My chronic health issues, my messy house, and lack of time or energy to do all that I want to do. Sometimes it's the nonstop work of taking care of three small children or the constant influx of family and friends needing a word of encouragement, a babysitter, or help solving a problem. See—I'm whining again.

Instigated by his friends, Job found himself doing a little whining. Then God steps into the picture, and do you know what He says to poor Job? "Gird up thy loins like a man." We often say "suck it up," or "take it like a man."

When I read "Put Your Big Girl Panties On and Deal with It," I laughed hysterically. It was perfect! And that is exactly what I need to do. Do I believe God is in control? Yes. Do I believe everything happens for a reason? Yes. Do I trust God? Yes. Then what's the problem? It's time to "put on my big girl panties and deal with it."

TODAY'S HOT FLASH:

Are you easily irritated? Do little things bother you? Don't you think it's time to "put on your big girl panties and deal with it?" Oh—in a godly way, of course.

PRAYER:

Father, forgive me for whining and complaining about the little things in life. Forgive my critical heart and fill me with a loving spirit. Amen.

AUGUST 21

READ: 1 KINGS 18:20–40

IF THE LORD BE GOD, FOLLOW HIM

And Elijah ... said, How long halt ye between two opinions? If the Lord be God, follow him: but if Baal, then follow him. And the people answered him not a word.

~ 1 Kings 18:21

Elijah was sent by God to challenge the Israelites who were torn between following God or following Baal. When asked who would stand up and proclaim the Lord God, not one person said a word. So Elijah offered a challenge to the prophets of Baal.

He told them to build an altar and place a bullock on it. Then they were to summon their god to consume it with fire. A ridiculous scene followed. They danced and screamed and hopped around and cut themselves with knives, and all the while Elijah is on the sidelines, taunting them. Nothing happened.

Now it was Elijah's turn. He built his altar and doused it with water, and then he prayed. "O God, hear me that this people will know that thou art the Lord God" (vs. 37). And a fire fell from heaven and consumed the bullock, stones, and wood and licked up every last bit of the water. GOD had spoken! When God does a work, he does it in such a way that everyone watching knows He is the one true God.

TODAY'S HOT FLASH:

The challenge is here; the challenge is now. Are you going to stand boldly and proclaim He is God, or will you keep silent as the Israelites did, thus denying Him?

PRAYER:

Almighty God, You will someday soon show the entire world You alone are God. Help me to boldly proclaim You every chance I get. Amen.

AUGUST 22
READ: PSALM 19

I KNOW GOD IS BECAUSE . . .

The heavens declare the glory of God and the firmament sheweth his handywork.

~ Psalm 19:1

I know God is because . . . the heavens declare His glory.

I know God is because . . . the invisible things of Him from the creation of the world are clearly seen (Romans 1:20).

I know God is because . . . He loved me so much that He sent His Son to die for me (John 3:16).

I know God is because . . . I am not who I used to be. I am a new woman in Christ Jesus (Ephesians 4:24).

I know God is because . . . the sin that once controlled me no longer has dominion over me (Romans 6:14).

I know God is, and I know God loves me, and I know that nothing can separate me from the love of God—not "tribulation, or distress, or persecution, or famine, or nakedness, or peril or sword . . . neither death, nor life, nor angels, nor principalities, nor powers, nor things present, nor things to come, nor height, nor depth, nor any other creature, shall be able to separate me from the love of God, which is in Christ Jesus our Lord" (Romans 8:35-39).

TODAY'S HOT FLASH:

God *is*—and I know it—and because God is, I will daily show it. Will you show that God is—every minute, every hour, and every day in your life?

PRAYER:

Omniscient Creator, You are and always will be. You are great and greatly to be praised; I find peace and comfort in Your everlasting love. Amen.

AUGUST 23

READ: PSALM 90

THIRTY DAYS TO LIVE

So teach us to number our days, that we may apply our hearts unto wisdom.

~ Psalm 90:12

Kerry and Chris Shook wrote a book titled *One Month to Live*. In this book, they challenge Christians to live their lives as if they had only thirty days left to live on earth. I have to admit, the challenge is daunting.

If I knew I was dying in thirty days, I would have to get out of my comfort zone and start pounding the pavement. First, I have many loved ones that I have not aggressively pursued for Christ. They know what I believe, I have witnessed, and now I am "leaving it in God's hands." I also have neighbors that I've been kind to; I've invited them to church and taken them gifts at Christmas time; I've even placed gospel tracts at their door, but shamefully, I've failed to personalize my love for Jesus to them. These are only a few of the priority pressures that come to mind.

What if you had only thirty days to live? What comes to mind? Who comes to mind? Are there people you need to reconcile with? Loved ones who don't know Christ? Have you made a lasting kingdom mark on all who know you and even those who don't?

TODAY'S HOT FLASH:

Spend the next thirty days living like they're your last. The truth is that you may have only one day left; only God knows for sure. Leave nothing undone or unsaid.

PRAYER:

Almighty Father, only You know the number of my days. Don't let me waste a moment; don't let me leave a word unsaid or a deed undone. Amen.

AUGUST 24
READ: JOHN 16:29-33

ANOTHER DAY, ANOTHER YAWN

In the world ye shall have tribulation: but be of good cheer; I have overcome the world.

~ John 16:33b

What's on your agenda today? Something new and spectacular, or are you doing the same old same old: getting up, getting dressed, eating your oatmeal with two pieces of peanut butter toast, watching the morning news or reading the morning newspaper, and then gradually doing what must be done. You know what to expect of your day, and you like it that way. Another day, another yawn, but that's okay because you find comfort in the familiar.

Jesus didn't live that way, and neither did His disciples. Their lives were so unpredictable that they never knew what the morning would bring. It could be a demon-possessed boy needing freedom or an angry mob attempting to stone them. There was never a day without disruption. The disciples struggled with this at first. What had they gotten themselves into? But Jesus offered some valuable insight, He said, "In the world ye shall have tribulation: but be of good cheer; I have overcome the world" (John 16:33b). Whatever the ordeal, whatever the challenge, whatever the discomfort, the battle is already won. Faithfulness is the only requirement.

TODAY'S HOT FLASH:

Spice up your life a little. Take risks for Jesus. You will suffer some tribulation, some discomfort. But be of good cheer, Christ has overcome the world.

PRAYER:

Father, forgive my complacency. Spice up my life with Your service. Help me not to shy away because it may cause me discomfort or rejection. Amen.

AUGUST 25
READ: COLOSSIANS 4:1-6

SPIRITUALITY—A HOT TOPIC

Walk in wisdom toward them that are without, redeeming the time.

~ Colossians 4:5

Everywhere you go, you face it. Every time you turn around or turn on the TV, it slaps you in the face. Everyone has an opinion, and everyone is talking. It may not be the right opinion, but they are open to the subject of spirituality. That is our cue.

Just yesterday I filled out a survey on science fiction and fantasy television. Questions frequently asked were: "Do you believe in the supernatural? Do you believe in life after death? Are you a spiritual person?"

If you talk with a nonbeliever for any amount of time, inevitably, a spiritual comment will come up. Once the door is open, it's time to act. God is handing you an opportunity; grab it and run with it. Don't forget to say a quick prayer of guidance before you begin.

"Walk in wisdom toward them that are without, redeeming the time" (Colossians 4:5). It may be your only time with this person; use it wisely. I've faced regret too many times for not speaking out when the subject was introduced. "Let your speech always be with grace, seasoned with salt, that ye may know how ye ought to answer every man."

TODAY'S HOT FLASH:

The world is bombarded with a false type of spirituality. It is our job to make sure they hear the truth. What they do with it is up to them.

PRAYER:

Father, give me wisdom to speak to those You bring my way. Make me sensitive to their comments and aware of the openings You are giving me. Amen.

AUGUST 26
READ: 1 JOHN 3:16

MIRROR, MIRROR ON THE WALL

Hereby perceive we the love of God, because he laid down his life for us: and we ought to lay down our lives for the brethren.

~ 1 John 3:16

Mirror, mirror on the wall, who's that grouchy old woman peering back at me? Okay, it doesn't rhyme, but have you ever asked yourself that question? I vowed never to become one, yet, here I am. It is easier, at times, to be grumpy, mouthy, and critical rather than kind, gentle, and caring. Shouldn't it be easier to be good now? You know, all that Christian maturity and practice makes perfect stuff? Still, I struggle.

Just when we think we have it all together, life throws us a curve ball. It's called menopause. If that weren't enough, our bodies start to break down, and we must fight against the physical as well as the mental. Whatever made me think it was going to be easier?

It would be easier to allow myself to morph into that grouchy old woman, but I will fight it with all that I am. Why? Because, "Hereby we perceive the love of God, because he laid down his life for us . . . "(1 John 3:16). His ultimate sacrifice—for me, overwhelms me. How can I do anything but lay down my life for Him?

TODAY'S HOT FLASH:

To know Him is to love Him. To love Him is to desire to please Him. Will I struggle? Yes! In His strength, I will persevere. What else can I do?

PRAYER:

Father, don't let me become that grouchy woman in the mirror. Morph me into the woman You have made me to be. Thank You for loving me so sacrificially. Amen.

AUGUST 27

READ: MATTHEW 5:13–16

STEP OUTSIDE YOUR INNER CIRCLE

Let your light so shine before men, that they may see your good works, and glorify your Father which is in heaven.

~ Matthew 5:16

I recently decided that I have not been doing enough spontaneous acts of kindness. I meet needs when confronted with them, but for the most part, I've gotten so entangled in my affairs within my inner circle that others' needs pass me by.

With three troubled children, an Internet business, a devotional to write, music and lessons to prepare for church, and babysitting grandchildren, my schedule is full. In all this, I stay pretty close to home and have become oblivious to the needs of others.

Just today I learned of a long-time member who has been struggling with depression. Barely able to get out of bed, she's missed some church—and I didn't even notice. If I can't find time to care about those around me, then I am too busy. I've decided to make a list of at list three people that I can personally reach out to this week. But I have to do more than decide; I have to act. Only by my actions will they really believe I care. Have my good works been causing others to glorify the Father? I am going to make sure of it from now on.

TODAY'S HOT FLASH:

In order for the world to see my shining light, I must be stepping outside my inner circle and entering into the realm of needy people.

PRAYER:

Understanding Father, forgive my nearsightedness. Help me to step outside my comfort zone and start meeting the needs of hurting people around me. Amen.

AUGUST 28
READ: 2 CORINTHIANS 5:11–21

MY GUILTY PLEASURE

And that he died for all, that they which live should not henceforth live unto themselves, but unto him which died for them, and rose again.

~ 2 Corinthians 5:15

Every Tuesday night at eight o'clock sharp, I turn on the TV, situate myself in my comfy chair, and prepare to walk the journey with the contestants of my favorite reality show, *The Biggest Loser*. My motives are pure. I enjoy watching the miraculous transformation that takes place in such a short time. The contestants enter the "Ranch" feeling defeated and hopeless; they leave it filled with hope and expectation for the future. Where once they allowed nothing to come in between themselves and their lust of the flesh, they now choose to live differently. This new mindset opens up a reality they've never experienced before, and life is never the same.

How much more wonderful is the reality of this truth in a spiritual sense. Who we once were in the flesh is replaced with a new reality—Jesus Christ. He offers the greatest life-changing transformation ever presented. Unlike the biggest loser, this transformation is more than physical; it is spiritual, and it is eternal. Weight can be regained. Our old life before Jesus is gone forever. "Behold, I make all things new" (Revelation 21:5b).

TODAY'S HOT FLASH:

We really are the biggest losers. We've lost the old, sinful creature that kept us in bondage and gained a Savior and through Him eternal life in Christ Jesus.

PRAYER:

Father, thank You for the miracle of new life. You have given me more than I could ever ask for. I am ever grateful. Amen.

AUGUST 29

READ: GENESIS 22:1–19

EXTRAORDINARY OBEDIENCE— EXTRAORDINARY BLESSINGS

Because thou hast done this thing, and hast not withheld thy son, thine only son: that in blessing I will bless thee.

~ Genesis 22:16b-17a

Few people reach the point of extraordinary obedience. This is a point when God's command is heeded without complaint or discussion. It is possible, but improbable for most. The act of relinquishing every part of oneself to another is too much for most to give.

Abraham came to this lonesome place of extraordinary obedience. It didn't happen overnight; it only happened after numerous failures. But finally—without question—God called and Abraham answered. "Here am I," was his reply, and he remained steadfast, even after hearing God's request. We have no record of Abraham sharing his burden with others; it was his to bear. God called. Abraham obeyed. Extraordinary obedience! Because of this extraordinary obedience, God lavished Abraham with extraordinary blessings.

"Because thou hast done this thing, and hast not withheld thy son, thine only son: that in blessing I will bless thee . . ." Abraham was an ordinary man with an extraordinary obedience, and God blessed him beyond his wildest imagination.

TODAY'S HOT FLASH:

God has not changed. He desires to reward extraordinary obedience today. But first we must be willing to say, "Here am I, Lord," without question or complaint.

PRAYER:

Father, make me a person of extraordinary obedience. May my faithfulness to You be remembered for years to come, and may You receive all the glory. Amen.

AUGUST 30

READ: ISAIAH 53

WHAT MANNER OF LOVE?

But he was wounded for our transgressions, he was bruised for our iniquities: the chastisement of our peace was upon him; and with his stripes we are healed.

~ Isaiah 53:5

Why would the sinless Creator of the universe desire to take on my burden of sin—or yours, for that matter? There have been uncountable times I've lied and cheated, misused and abused others. So many times I couldn't see the cross for the pride clouding my vision. Still, He chose to forgive my trespasses and take the burden on Himself.

"He was wounded for my transgressions" (Isaiah 53:5). 2 Corinthians 5:21 says, "He was made to be sin for us." "By His stripes we are healed" (Isaiah 53:5). Technically, the word stripes is "stripe." His body was one great big gaping piece of raw flesh. His pain was beyond what anyone has experienced before or since. As horrible as it sounds, I am grateful and humbled by His sacrifice.

The burden of sin on a human soul is heavy. It is impossible to carry on our own. He foresaw this and chose to carry it in our stead. All our dirty, disgusting sins, He carried within His own being, that we might be free. I can't even begin to understand this kind of love, but I am so thankful for it.

TODAY'S HOT FLASH:

What manner of love is this, that He would carry my sin to the cross, removing a burden that would have been too much for me to bear?

PRAYER:

Father, thank You for seeing me outside my sins. By Your stripes I am healed. I can never repay such a debt. Amen.

AUGUST 31

READ: MATTHEW 7:7–14

NOTICE THE INVISIBLE

Therefore all things whatsoever ye would that men should do to you, do ye even so to them: for this is the law and the prophets.

~ Matthew 7:12

Every month our church holds a prayer breakfast at a local restaurant. We enjoy a time of fellowship and good eating. But what has caught our attention is the waitress. To most of the world, she's invisible. To us, she is the epitome of excellence in her field of work.

She's not a Christian, but she has embraced our group and has been our sole waitress for almost a year. With over thirty of us, she has risen to the challenge, memorizing what people like, who gets coffee, and other little details.

We joke with her, inquire about her family, and treat her like one of our own. Because she has been so faithful, we have decided to honor her at our next breakfast by presenting her with a beautifully arrayed, lavishly filled gift basket. It is our hope that God uses this to continue to tear down her wall and open her heart to Him.

She is only one of thousands working quietly without recognition in their field of work. They're doing a great job, but most of us are too busy to notice.

TODAY'S HOT FLASH:

Who are the invisibles that touch your life? Take time to notice someone with an act of kindness. After all, there are no invisibles in God's eyes.

PRAYER:

Father, so many people touch my life, and I have taken them for granted. Forgive me for this and open my eyes to them as individuals, not just a service offered. Amen.

SEPTEMBER

SEPTEMBER 1

READ: ROMANS 6:11-16

CRASH AND BURN

Know ye not, that to whom ye yield yourselves servants to obey, his servants ye are to whom ye obey; whether of sin unto death, or of obedience unto righteousness?

~ Romans 6:16

In any given moment of our lives, we are yielded to one of two spiritual sides: sin and Satan or righteousness and God. Before our feet hit the floor in the morning, it is imperative that we make the choice of whom we will serve.

A plane left on autopilot will never make it to the runway. Without the pilot's guidance, it plummets to the ground. If I begin my day on autopilot, expecting to naturally do what is right, I will always crash and burn. Without going to the Master Pilot, reviewing the instruction manual, and discussing the details of my course, I am doomed to a day of utter failure.

A ship without a helmsman drifts off course and ends up at an unintended destination. We are like this ship. Our intentions are pure, we expect to remain righteous, but in the course of our daily lives, we drift because we have not given over the helm to the great Helmsman. Before we know it, we end up in a place we do not want to be. Lost and confused with nothing left to do, we finally seek the Almighty Deliverer.

TODAY'S HOT FLASH:

Choose the right course today. Seek God's guidance; make a decision to keep Him in the center of your life. You may falter, but you will not crash and burn.

PRAYER:

Father, I hand over the helm to You today. Keep me from drifting off course. Pilot me through my day so that I may not crash and burn when things get tough. Amen.

SEPTEMBER 2

READ: 1 PETER 1:24

THE NOSTALGIA OF THE YESTERYEARS

For all flesh is as grass, and all the glory of man as the flower of grass. The grass withereth, and the flower thereof falleth away.

~ 1 Peter 1:24

There is something unsettling about the comparison of man to dying plants. We know the truth of the statement. Time whips by so fast we barely realize it's gone until one day we stop and say, "WHOA! Where did it go? How did I get so old?" A new sadness emerges, and if we are not careful, it will consume us.

It seems like only yesterday I was the eight-year-old grieving for my little brother; has it really been forty years? It seems only yesterday that I gazed upon my first true love. Has it really been thirty-four years? I find myself captured in the nostalgia of the moment every time I hear a particular song or see a person from my past. If I am not careful, the sadness of the yesteryears will replace tomorrow's reality from my mind.

Paul wisely stated, "Forgetting those things which are behind, and reaching forth unto those things which are before" (Philippians 3:13b). He realized the necessity of the here and now. The time is short. Don't waste precious moments—once gone, you can't get them back.

TODAY'S HOT FLASH:

Time passes quickly. If we spend too much time dwelling on the past, our future will become our past, and we will have nothing to offer our King but regrets.

PRAYER:

Father, it's hard not to dwell on on my past—the good and the bad—but Lord, I don't have time for that. Keep me focused on the here and now so I have no regrets. Amen.

SEPTEMBER 3

READ: ACTS 7:54–60

SACRIFICIAL COMPASSION

And they stoned Stephen, calling upon God, and saying, Lord Jesus, receive my spirit.

~ Acts 7:59

Fanny Crosby was blinded as an infant by a wacko doctor; she spent most of her young life totally dependent on others. But as the world was opened to her, she became unstoppable. It wasn't until she was in her forties that her drive and unique capabilities took her in the direction of kingdom work.

Noted for writing more than 8,000 hymns, Fanny's name is recognized throughout the world. What isn't widely known is that Fanny received a mere pittance for her hymns. Even though Fanny was world-renowned and many would have provided her with much greater means, Fanny refused to accept their offers. She planted herself in the midst of the tenements where she could meet the needs of the poverty stricken around her. Many of her songs were written as a result of their desperation.

I wish I could say I self-sacrifice like Fanny. Unfortunately, I have yet to reach this place. God help me, I have a long way to go. How about you?

TODAY'S HOT FLASH:

Where does your sacrificial compassion take you? Stephen knew he risked stoning as he presented the gospel. He did it anyway. I want to be more like him.

PRAYER:

Father, I want to be more like Fanny and Stephen and so many more of these self-sacrificing individuals. Show me what holds me back so I can go there too. Amen.

SEPTEMBER 4

READ: LUKE 22:28-34

SATAN WANTS TO KNOCK YOU DOWN

And the Lord said, Simon, Simon, behold, Satan hath desired to have you, that he may sift you as wheat: but I have prayed for thee that thy faith fail not.

~ Luke 22:31-32a

Today is D-Day in our household. We've committed ourselves to sixteen more years of child-rearing. Today we will stand before the judge and say, "I do." I promise to love and cherish these children until death do us part, but Satan has other plans. He does not want it to happen.

Our six-year-old son has caused havoc in school this week. He gave one child a goose egg; another, a bloody nose; and kicked a girl three times. He managed to tip over every chair and almost every table in his classroom, causing total disarray.

I believe that God is going to do great things with our hard-to-handle son. So much so, that Satan is doing everything he can to knock him out of the picture. Why else would he pull out all the stops this week? If he succeeded in keeping us from adopting him, he would have removed him from the only Christian home he may have ever had. Satan did not win, and today at 2:30 we will officially accept this boy as our son. I can't wait to see what God is going to do with him.

TODAY'S HOT FLASH:

Are you in a hard spot where someone is concerned? Don't give up! Satan desires to steer you away from God's best. Hold on tight. God has great plans.

PRAYER:

Father, I know You have great plans for this child. Use him mightily in Your kingdom work. Don't let me stand in the way of what he is going to do for You. Amen.

SEPTEMBER 5

READ: 1 JOHN 3:11-18

HOW SWEET IT IS TO BE LOVED BY YOU

> *Hereby perceive we the love of God.*
> ~ 1 John 3:16a

> *For God so loved the world.*
> - John 3:16a

> *Who shall separate us from the love of Christ?*
> ~Romans 8:35a

I love chocolate fudge, cheesecake covered with cherries, and cinnamon roll cookies—anything sweet and soft that melts in my mouth. I like to eat it slowly and savor every bit of the luscious taste. As much as I love these things, I must not enjoy them to excess, lest I suffer the consequences. First, I will get a stomach ache and second, I will gain weight. My love for these items must be limited.

There is one thing that I cannot get too much of. That is the love of Jesus. As sweet as chocolate fudge is, Jesus' love for me is soooooooo much sweeter. I will gladly give up every ounce of sugar to experience His sweet love. There is no mountain high enough, no ocean deep enough, no chocolate sweet enough to keep Jesus' precious love from me.

His all-consuming love carries me when life seems too much to bear. It lifts me when my weary bones can't take another step, and it encourages me when I'm down-hearted. What can separate me from the love of God? Nothing. How sweet it is to be loved by Him.

TODAY'S HOT FLASH:

You can take everything I own, everything I am, throw me in a deep, dark dungeon, but nothing can remove me from the love of God. Praise God, He's all I need.

PRAYER:

Father, I worship You for loving me so much. Your love sacrificed Your Son; I can never repay that debt. Thank You that I don't have to. Amen.

SEPTEMBER 6
READ: 2 SAMUEL 15:7–12

BEFORE YOU ACT

And they went in their simplicity, and they knew not anything.
~ 2 Samuel 15:11b

Have you ever been duped? When it dawned on you that you'd been scammed, you were dumbfounded. This happened to the men of Israel who followed Absalom to Hebron. They were oblivious to his true intentions and followed him blindly. Imagine their surprise and feelings of betrayal as well as fear when they learned the truth.

In our overly emotional state, we tend to do things rashly and without much forethought. This can get us into a lot of trouble. We spend money we shouldn't spend, say things we shouldn't say, and do things we wouldn't normally do.

Now more than ever is the time to hold back, think things through, get godly counsel, and **just listen** carefully to what trusted others have to say. If we don't, we may find ourselves in a very uncomfortable or even dangerous situation, just like David's men did.

I know it is hard, but hold back and don't rush into anything without knowing the who, what, when, where, and why of the situation; and if it defies God's Word in **any way,** stay far, far away.

TODAY'S HOT FLASH:

If you're planning to do something that you are uncomfortable sharing with those closest to you, stop in your tracks and walk away. Doing right never brings shame.

PRAYER:

Father, keep me focused on You and Your Word. Help me to make all my decisions according to Your will and way. Stop me from doing anything stupid. Amen.

SEPTEMBER 7

READ: PROVERBS 21:17-25

ARE YOU FIXED YET?

Whoso keepeth his mouth and his tongue keepeth his soul from troubles.

~ Proverbs 21:23

Every Sunday evening, I teach a women's class on anger. One of the ladies made the comment that the harder she tries not to be angry, the worse things get. I have to agree. When we first address an issue of sanctification, we gain the attention of the spiritual world. Satan and his minions do not want us to "fix" our spiritual imperfections.

When I was younger, I was quite timid, but not so much anymore; my mouth constantly gets me into trouble. I expected to be all fixed by now, but it only seems to get worse.

When we become serious about our faith, the spiritual world takes notice. If they can discourage us and cause us to give up, they have won the battle, and we are stuck in spiritual stagnation.

Perfection comes with obedience, but with obedience comes spiritual warfare. Perfection is something to strive for, and someday we will reach that point. When we do, we will be enjoying the streets of gold and sitting at the feet of Jesus.

TODAY'S HOT FLASH:

Don't become discouraged. If you're catching Satan's attention, you are doing something right. Victory will come, but it never comes easily.

PRAYER:

Father, I try and try, and it seems like I fail and fail. Give me the strength to continue my fight, for the victory is Yours and Yours alone. Amen.

SEPTEMBER 8
READ: 1 CORINTHIANS 10:23-33

SHINING EXAMPLE

Whether therefore ye eat or drink, or whatsoever ye do, do all to the glory of God.
~ 1 Corinthians 10:31

Joni Eareckson Tada is one of my heroes. She was paralyzed from the neck down in a diving accident at seventeen. She is now more than sixty years old. She ministers to the disabled through retreats, wheelchair giveaways, and many other avenues, including books, art, and music.

In 2010, Joni was diagnosed with breast cancer. When she was interviewed, this was her response: "I want to assure you that I am genuinely content to receive from God whatever He deems fit for me, even if it is from His left hand because better something from His left hand than no hand at all."

From the moment she gave her life to the Lord as a young woman, Joni hasn't stopped seeking ways to serve her Savior. She lives the verse "Whether therefore ye eat or drink, or whatsoever ye do, do all to the glory of God" (1 Corinthians 10:31). If she can serve God so fully, in spite her handicap, we have no excuse. God will use you to the full extent you allow Him to. Joni is a shining example of what God can do if you are only willing.

TODAY'S HOT FLASH:

May I serve the Lord with as much enthusiasm as Joni. I am held back only by my own mental limits. With God in control, He will accomplish miracles through me.

PRAYER:

Father, I have no excuse for not serving You to the full extent. Keep me focused on Jesus, that I may serve Him every minute of every day. Amen.

SEPTEMBER 9
READ: GALATIANS 6:1–9

LASTING CONSEQUENCES, PRECIOUS MERCY

For he that soweth to his flesh shall of the flesh reap corruption, but he that soweth to the Spirit shall of the Spirit reap life everlasting.

~ Galatians 6:8

If there is one thing I've learned over the years, it is that my actions often have long-lasting consequences. God isn't punishing me. He's not daily reminding me of how bad I've been. It has nothing to do with God. It has to do with my disobedience. God warns us in His Word what will happen if we do certain things. Why is it we think we can ignore Him and live life unscathed?

In our youth, we tend to have a sense of invincibility. After all, death is for the elderly. We drink, have premarital sex, smoke, do drugs, and take unnecessary chances. Unfortunately, we don't stay young, and our bad choices have a way of catching up to us. Lung cancer, emphysema, regret, guilt, divorce, hurting children, and so much more begin to plague us.

In all this, there is precious hope; it comes in three fantastic words: forgiveness, mercy, and grace. All describe the unfathomable love our Lord has for each one of us.

TODAY'S HOT FLASH:

We cannot outrun the consequences of our past actions. Just as true, nothing we do can thwart God's redeeming plan of forgiveness, mercy, and grace toward us.

PRAYER:

Gracious Father, You have given us the ultimate gifts to be thankful for: forgiveness, mercy, and Your grace toward us. Thank You for these gifts. Amen.

SEPTEMBER 10
READ: PROVERBS 22:1-6

AGONIZING OVER GROWN CHILDREN

Train up a child in the way he should go: and when he is old, he will not depart from it.

~ Proverbs 22:6

When I was a young mother, I wished my kids were older. The waking up two or three times a night, and hiring babysitters I couldn't afford, physically and mentally exhausted me. I couldn't wait for the children to reach a point where I didn't have to worry about them so much or tend to them so often.

Now my children are grown, and I can't help but wish for the time when they were young. I can't help desiring to gather them under my wings so I can control their lives like I used to. It's not that I desire to control them; it is that I desire to keep them from the aches and pains of adulthood. I desire to keep them from life's heartaches. I want to wrap them in my arms and whisper in their ears that everything is going to be okay. But I can't; I have to stand by and watch. I have to fully trust God to watch over them. It's agonizing to watch your children make mistakes that you know will cause them pain. I wonder—is that the way the Father feels about me when I choose the wrong path or walk away from His best for me? Do I cause Him pain?

TODAY'S HOT FLASH:

God our Father must experience the paternal pain of watching a child stray. Still, He steps back and allows us to learn the painful lessons on our own.

PRAYER:

Dear Father, forgive me for the times I've caused You emotional agony. Thank You for allowing me to learn the hard way so I never want to do it again. Amen.

SEPTEMBER 11

READ: 2 KINGS 20:1-7

DEATH: ONLY GOD KNOWS WHEN

Turn again, and tell Hezekiah the captain of my people, Thus saith the Lord, the God of David thy father, I have heard thy prayer, I have seen thy tears: behold, I will heal thee.

~ 2 Kings 20:5a

With age often comes infirmity. We face new physical obstacles with each passing year. Many of us have heard the dreaded words, cancer, diabetes, Alzheimer's, etc.

Hezekiah heard these dreaded words from the prophet: "Set thine house in order, for thou shalt die" (2 Kings 20:1b). He was devastated and, with a broken heart, began to beseech God for his life. God heard his prayer and granted him another fifteen years.

I am not telling you that God is going to grant you or a loved one another fifteen years if you seek him with a broken heart. Only God holds the power of life and death in His hands, and only God knows the plans He has for each of His children. Because this is true, no other human being can place a time limit on my life. Maybe I only have two months, and just maybe God will grant me two years. The question is this: What am I going to do with the time I have left? Brood and feel sorry for myself, or get up and get going for the Lord? Time's a-wastin'!

TODAY'S HOT FLASH:

Mere human beings cannot determine my life span. What I know is that with every breath I take, I will serve my Lord. How long I do it matters not, just that I do it.

PRAYER:

Lord, I can't presume to imagine how long I have left on this earth. May I not take for granted even a minute and serve You with my whole heart all of my days. Amen.

SEPTEMBER 12

READ: 1 CORINTHIANS 14:23-26

ARE YOU A JEALOUS WOMAN?

Let all things be done unto edifying.

~ 1 Corinthians 14:26b

In context, this verse portion is pertaining to the confusion of spiritual gifts in the church. But the concept is true in every area of our lives. When my husband and I first married, I was young, insecure, and threatened by everything that excluded me. I was also threatened by every woman involved in his pre-Lisa life.

As time went on and my relationship with the Lord strengthened, I had to shamefully admit that I was a jealous woman. In the process of my insecurity, I rarely edified others. Everyone was at fault but myself. It took a long time for me to overcome these selfish sins. Past hurts flooded into my memory whenever I thought I was gaining control. But in time, I conquered my jealousy (most of the time). I still am not perfect, and if I stop allowing the Holy Spirit to guide me, I fall back into old habits, but that is rare.

Now when jealousy threatens to invade my thoughts, I focus on Jesus. This perfect God gave up heaven and His security to be born a baby in a sinful world—for me—knowing most would hate Him. Because of this, I can remain righteous for Him.

TODAY'S HOT FLASH:

Are you a jealous woman? Stop trying to control the world around you and bask in the love of a God who left heaven to be born a vulnerable baby—for you.

PRAYER:

Father, forgive me when I attack others because of my jealousy, I am better than I used to be, but not where I should be. Help me to edify and not tear down. Amen.

SEPTEMBER 13

READ: 2 CORINTHIANS 10:8–18

CLINGING TO OUR IMPORTANCE

But he that glorieth, let him glory in the Lord.

~ 2 Corinthians 10:17

Mark Twain was a genius. He made sure he wouldn't be forgotten. Who would have known that one hundred years after his death, his final book would surface and become a bestseller? But to what end? Is there some profound wisdom or last minute insight into who this man was and what he believed? I have to wonder, will this book glorify God in any way?

Mark Twain, (Samuel Clemens), exceptional as he was, was confused and unsure in his spiritual life. He believed in the almighty God but refused to believe in an excruciating place called hell. He also did not believe in the inerrancy of the Holy Scriptures. In his brilliance, he failed to honor the very One who bestowed upon him such a wonderful gift.

In his search for immortality, he found a way to keep himself alive. The publishing of his book, one hundred years after his death. He clung to his importance even unto death.

If we spend our lives clinging to our own importance, death only brings dissatisfaction and confusion. After all, Scripture commands us to glory in the Lord alone. On my death bed, I want to know that I clung to Jesus, not my own significance.

TODAY'S HOT FLASH:

Stop clinging to your own importance. Who we are doesn't matter, except in the light of Christ. If you leave a legacy, leave one that glorifies the King.

PRAYER:

Lord, may I be remembered by my love and faithfulness toward You. Let anything else fade away into oblivion. I choose to cling to the importance of You. Amen.

SEPTEMBER 14
READ: GENESIS 3:14–19

SUBMISSION . . . ME?

And thy desire shall be to thy husband, and he shall rule over thee.

~ Genesis 3:16b

If you want to get a menopausal woman's dander up (which isn't very hard), tell her she must submit to her husband in all things. In my daughter's words, "I don't think so!" Yes, I know this is a rebellious attitude, and I try not to react in this manner, but it is difficult at times. I am very fortunate that my husband doesn't try to boss me around or "lord" anything over me, but if I even get the notion that he is, I get this prickly feeling inside pushing me to rebellion. The hormonally enhanced sin within me is barely contained at times. If I could, I'd shed this sinful shell immediately and be done with my sin.

Jesus, on the other hand, chose to confine Himself to a fleshly shell—sinless, of course, but with the ability to sin and the limitations of all human beings. Why did He do this? To me, this is the ultimate sacrifice. He did it so He could become like us and offer Himself for us. This act of submission to His Father is far greater than any I will ever be asked or able to give.

Submission is often regarded as a dirty word, yet to the Savior it was an absolute necessity. Had He decided we weren't worth the effort, we'd all be doomed.

TODAY'S HOT FLASH:

Jesus exemplified submission. He submitted in ALL things to His Father. Why do we have so much trouble following His example?

PRAYER:

Father, I am weak in this area. Submission is not a word I like to hear. But Lord, if I am going to follow Jesus, I must submit in all things. I need Your help. Amen.

SEPTEMBER 15

READ: PHILIPPIANS 3:10-16

ARE YOU ABOUT GOD?

That I may know him, and the power of his resurrection, and the fellowship of his sufferings, being made conformable unto his death.

~ Philippians 3:10

What part does God play in your daily life? Not God's business or God's ministry, but God Himself. As Beth Moore said in her book *Jesus the One and Only*, "Are you about God?" She states, "When it is all said and done, I would give my life for people to say, 'She was just about God.'"

May anything accomplished in my life shine light on who He is and point away from me. May any remembrance of me be that I lived God in every breath I took. May God's presence override any part of me, and when I go home to glory, may it be said that "she was all about God."

How about you? Do you desire to mesh personalities with God? Do you seek His glory rather than your own? When it is your time to enter those pearly gates, are they going to say, "She was all about God"?

TODAY'S HOT FLASH:

Christ-likeness is our goal. Where are you on a scale from one to ten? If we want to be about God only, then we must first surrender every part of ourselves to Him.

PRAYER:

Gracious Heavenly Father, show me where I need to surrender, that I might begin the process of being all about You and You alone. Amen.

SEPTEMBER 16
READ: LUKE 2: 41–52

NEVER STOP GROWING

And Jesus increased in wisdom and stature, and in favour with God and man.

~ Luke 2:52

How do I want my children and grandchildren to grow? As Jesus did, "in wisdom and stature, and in favor with God and man." The Greek word for wisdom is *sophia*. It applies first to having the skills one needs to survive in life, including practical wisdom and sound judgment. Secondly, in respect to the divine, it means to grow in knowledge and deep understanding.

With the exception of stature, these attributes are continuous. You can never outgrow wisdom. There are always new things to learn and new truths revealed to us through God's Word. With each passing year, our children's wisdom, as well as our own, should increase. If I can teach those around me the importance of wisdom, worldly and spiritual, and the ability to apply it in a way that they grow in favor with God and man, then I have accomplished much.

I've walked this earth for half a century now, and still there is much I do not know. In order to help my children grow, I must continue growing myself. Wisdom is deeper and vaster than the greatest ocean. There is always more to learn.

TODAY'S HOT FLASH:

Never stop seeking wisdom. To stop learning is to stop growing. If we stop growing, we become dull and stagnant. Is that how you really want to be?

PRAYER:

Father, there is so much I don't know. May I continue to grow in wisdom and in favor with God and man. Be glorified in my life. Amen.

SEPTEMBER 17

READ: ISAIAH 53

BEAUTIFUL TO ME

He hath no form nor comeliness; and when we shall see him, there is no beauty that we should desire him.

~ Isaiah 53:2b

When I first met my husband, I thought he was the sweetest man I'd ever met. As he came from a "notorious" family, others attempted to warn me that heartache was just around the corner. I didn't agree, and we have been married more than twenty-five years.

That's why I have a hard time with our verse for today, which says, "he hath no form nor comeliness, and when we shall see him, there is no beauty that we should desire him." Maybe it's romantic thinking, but I can't help but imagine Jesus as the most beautiful person that ever walked this planet. Maybe not His physical beauty, but by the inward beauty of His perfect Spirit radiating from His very being. Even the rough, tough fishermen and tax collectors were drawn to this Man. They noticed it immediately and followed Him.

Jesus still has this appeal today. It is so strong that we either run toward Him or spend our entire lives running from Him. Of one thing, I am sure: His very name illuminates beauty and you will never convince me otherwise.

TODAY'S HOT FLASH:

How do you perceive Jesus? Does thinking on Him bring visions of beauty and peace or fear and trepidation? If it is the latter, you may have a love problem.

PRAYER:

Beautiful, wonderful Savior, You are beautiful to me. I live for the day I will see You face-to-face and truly be mesmerized by Your awesome presence. Amen.

SEPTEMBER 18
READ: PROVERBS 31:10-31

A MOTHER'S INFLUENCE

She looketh well to the ways of her household, and eateth not the bread of idleness.

~ Proverbs 31:27

John Dillinger was one of America's first celebrated criminals. "Every policeman and every school child of the Middle West had Dillinger's facial characteristics graven in his mind. His ability to 'shoot and run away and live to shoot another day' led the public to believe that he was a master mind, a super criminal of brilliant intellect" *(John Dillinger,* by Dary Matera). He was notorious for hundreds of bank robberies and the undisputed leader of many criminal gangs.

When asked why he turned out so bad, he said, "I only wish I had a mother to worry over me, but she died when I was three. I guess this is why I was such a bad boy. No mother to look after me."

Mothers, I don't care how old you are; your influence on your children never wanes. A child, no matter how old, will listen to mother before listening to anybody else. Maybe your child is in his forties or fifties now. It matters not. You remain the most important person in their lives. It's never too late to start setting a godly example for them.

TODAY'S HOT FLASH:

We walk a tightrope with our grown children. We must walk in the Spirit before them without controlling or alienating them. In the end, our influence matters.

PRAYER:

Father, help me to be a godly example to my grown children. May who I am in You make a difference in their lives. Amen.

SEPTEMBER 19

READ: ROMANS 12:1-8

IT AIN'T MUCH, BUT IT'S YOURS, LORD

I beseech you therefore, brethren, by the mercies of God, that ye present your bodies a living sacrifice, holy, acceptable unto God, which is your reasonable service.

~ Romans 12:1

I've always considered myself a healthy person—until the last couple years, that is. Severe asthma, aching joints, and limited functions plague me every day, and I haven't even hit the half century mark. This isn't a complaint. I still get out of bed every morning, take care of my children, accomplish my daily chores, and keep the house in a livable condition.

Paul tells us in Romans to present our bodies a living sacrifice, holy and acceptable unto God, and I gladly do this. It ain't much. I can't run marathons or dream up delicious fanciful meals. I will never win a Nobel Prize, and as hard as I try, a book deal may only be a dream. I am not the best mother, housecleaner, Sunday school teacher, or singer; nonetheless, I offer all these things to my God: my best effort put forth for His service. I'd like to give Him more and better, but that is my flesh talking. My Lord wants only all that I can give, and that I offer to Him gladly. May God be glorified in my meager efforts.

TODAY'S HOT FLASH:

God created you. He doesn't want absolute perfection. He wants only the best you can give where you are today. Go ahead, give your all, and trust it is enough.

PRAYER:

Father, may I serve you today with a glad heart. My efforts are not perfect, but they are the best I can give. Thank You for loving me for being me. Amen.

SEPTEMBER 20
READ: EPHESIANS 3:13-21

START BY DOING WHAT'S NECESSARY

That he would grant you, according to the riches of his glory, to be strengthened with might by his Spirit in the inner man.

~ Ephesians 3:16

St. Francis of Assisi once said, "Start by doing what's necessary, then what's possible, and suddenly you are doing the impossible." The problem most of us run into is obtaining the motivation to do the necessary. We can waste an entire day just trying to accomplish the "must-do's" on our list. Have you ever done that? I am an expert at it.

I'll do a little here and a little there, a little now and a little later, and before you know it, the day is gone and I've accomplished absolutely nothing but puttered with almost everything. Disappointed again, I feel like a failure and a lousy mother and wife. Why do I do it? Why do I take all day to do something that would take only fifteen minutes of concentrated time? The world would say that I have ADD tendencies and need some medical help, but I know the truth.

I have a self-discipline problem; I always have. Am I too old to change? I don't think so. The question is "Do I really want to?" When the will to change is strong enough, the action will always follow.

TODAY'S HOT FLASH:

People rarely change until staying the same becomes too painful to bear. Why wait for the pain? Change before it comes.

PRAYER:

Father, I really do want to change. I want to accomplish the necessary early, so I can move on to the possible and even the impossible. Give me strength of will. Amen.

SEPTEMBER 21

READ GENESIS 37:28-36

LOSS

And Jacob rent his clothes, and put sackcloth upon his loins, and mourned for his son many days.

~ Genesis 37:34

Loss is loss, and it doesn't matter who you are or what station in life you hold, the pain is always great. In our society, we seem to revere the pain, maybe even romanticize it. Thousands of movies and books are produced every year on the theme of heart-wrenching pain.

There was nothing romantic about the pain Jacob felt when he was told Joseph was dead. Can you feel it? He "rent his clothes, and put sackcloth upon his loins, and mourned for his son many days" (Genesis 37:34). He could not be consoled.

As we grow older, we find ourselves attending more and more funerals. Mortality slaps us in the face with ferocity. We can't run and hide. It has found our friends and loved ones; we know it will find us. Instead of living life to the fullest with the time we have left, we pour over the obituaries and pine over the past. When we do this, death has already won.

TODAY'S HOT FLASH:

Don't waste another minute thinking on death. There will be time enough for that later. Live life to the fullest in the here and now. You won't regret it.

PRAYER:

Father, forgive me for dwelling on things I have no control over. Life is a precious gift; remind me to live every minute to its fullest. Amen.

SEPTEMBER 22
READ: ROMANS 8:28-39

GOD KNOWS WHAT HE IS DOING

And we know that all things work together for good to them that love God, to them who are the called according to his purpose.

~ Romans 8:28

My stepson was admitted into the hospital last night. For months now he has been dragging his leg as he walks. He didn't realize it until my husband mentioned it to him. His MRI revealed lesions on his spinal cord and in his neck. The uncertainty of the situation is unsettling at best.

Regardless the diagnosis, God is in control. He has the situation firmly in His grasp. It may be nothing serious, or it may be something extremely serious; nonetheless, God's grace is sufficient to see us through.

His wife and children are concerned, but they have one thing many people do not—faith. It is this faith that will carry them through the hard times.

Maybe you are awaiting some news. Or maybe you already received some, and it has thrown you for a loop. Cling to this promise from God; the circumstance never changes the truth. Trust God—and believe. He knows what He is doing.

TODAY'S HOT FLASH:

Emotional pain is often blinding to those experiencing it. That is why it is imperative that you spend this time believing that what God says is absolutely true!

PRAYER:

Father, You know the circumstances. Help me to cling to Your unchanging truth. You have everything under control, and I will trust in You. Amen.

SEPTEMBER 23

READ: JOHN 12:42-50

IS IT TIME TO PASS THE TORCH?

For they love the praise of men more than the praise of God.

~ John 12:43

Before menopause, my body changed very little. Since menopause, the changes come continuously, and I find it unnerving and frustrating at best.

I love to sing. I have a library of accompaniment tracks for any occasion. But with the onset of asthma and other physical ailments, my singing ability has dwindled to almost nothing. I hold on to the music in hopes that this too shall pass.

Why am I clinging to this part of my life? What I know and lived is changing, and along with that, my self-worth is altered. My children stand before the church with their beautifully gifted voices, and my heart desires to be where they are. Part of me still seeks the personal affirmation that others provided.

I know in my heart what I need to do. It is time to pass the torch and begin my new phase of service. Part of this service is to teach and encourage others to fill the gap. As long as I cling to what used to be, my service is limited. I may not be able to sing like I used to, but I know God has something spectacular in mind for me to do.

TODAY'S HOT FLASH:

In order to fulfill God's destiny for you, you must first let go of what used to be, and open your heart to what will be if you allow God full access to your life.

PRAYER:

Father, I am letting go. I don't need that glory; I don't need to cling to what used to be. I need to serve You in whatever capacity that takes. Help me, Lord. Amen.

SEPTEMBER 24
READ: 1 CORINTHIANS 2:1–8

SOME THINGS NEVER CHANGE

And I, brethren, when I came to you, came not with excellency of speech or of wisdom, declaring unto you the testimony of God.

~ 1 Corinthians 2:1

No matter how many things change, there will always be characteristics I wish would change but never will. For instance, I am a social blunderhead. Put me in a situation where I need to talk to strangers, and I become tongue-tied and confused. I have left more than one party kicking myself because I said something really stupid. This may sound very critical of myself, but it is how I have always been. If I could communicate by writing or teaching only, I'd be fine, but unfortunately, I can't. I am afraid this part of me will never change.

If the redemption of souls were up to me, very few would ever come to the Savior. It's not that I don't speak of Him; it's that my blundering speech makes it hard to understand. I am forever grateful to the Spirit who speaks to the soul in spite of my reckless communication. When someone comes to the Savior because of something I've said, I know it is in spite of me!

As much as I would like this part of me to change, God knows best. He wants everyone, including me, to know that if hearts change, it is because of Him alone.

TODAY'S HOT FLASH:

God made us who we are, and He will use us as we are. Stop trying to change the things you can't and work on those things that keep you from God.

PRAYER:

Lord, I am not an eloquent speaker, and I mess up my words all the time; use them for Your glory in spite of me. I will be satisfied with that. Amen.

FOR SANITY'S SAKE

SEPTEMBER 25

READ: MATTHEW 9: 36-38

WHERE JESUS IS . . .

> *But when he saw the multitudes, he was moved with compassion on them, because they fainted, and were scattered abroad, as sheep having no shepherd.*
>
> ~ Matthew 9:36

Where Jesus is . . . love becomes action. Where Jesus is . . . action becomes self-sacrificing.

Where Jesus is . . . words become compassionate. Where Jesus is . . . compassion becomes tearful interaction.

Where Jesus is . . . lives are changed. Where Jesus is . . . changed lives abound.

Where Jesus is . . . the homeless find shelter. Where Jesus is . . . the sick find relief.

Where Jesus is . . . the weary find rest. Where Jesus is . . . the angry find in their heart to forgive.

Where Jesus is . . . the sinners find forgiveness.

Is Jesus in your life today? Is your love shown by self-sacrificing action? It's not too late to implant Jesus in the center of your universe and turn your life into a living example of . . . where Jesus is.

TODAY'S HOT FLASH:

You're never too old to begin sharing Jesus. It will affect every area of your life and, in turn, affect every life you touch. What are you waiting for? Start now!

PRAYER:

Father, fill my heart with Your love. May my heart fill with compassion for the homeless, sick, and weary. May I be Your agent of grace today. Amen.

SEPTEMBER 26
READ: MARK 9:1–6

WHEN YOU HAVE NOTHING TO SAY . . .

For he wist not what to say ; for they were sore afraid.

~ Mark 9:6

Peter, James, and John were granted a great privilege when Jesus allowed them to witness the transfiguration on the top of a mountain one glorious morning. Shining raiment, white as snow, perfection and beauty beyond compare. Just as astounding were the two companions talking with Jesus.

The three disciples stood there gaping, eyes as big as saucers, until Peter broke the silence with his clumsy blurt: "Hey guys, this is great! Come on over here and we will build three tabernacles, one for each of you." Why'd he say that? He must have felt like a bumbling idiot. He blurted out something ridiculous—because he didn't know what to say (vs. 6).

Have you ever blurted out something ridiculous? There's something about hormones — they turn meek and mild into loud and obnoxious! Since menopause, my mouth has said more stupid things than it has in the past forty years. I can imagine Peter whispering to himself, "Ohhh, why'd I say that? I can't believe I said that. I'm an idiot!" It may be a cliché, but it still rings true: "When you have nothing to say, say nothing at all."

TODAY'S HOT FLASH:

Make it a habit to practice silence. It truly is golden, and you won't kick yourself for the next two days because you said something ridiculous.

PRAYER:

Father, You know how my mouth runs wild. Give me the ability to remain silent when there is nothing to say. May You be glorified in my words today. Amen.

SEPTEMBER 27

READ: JOHN 6:60-67

WILL YOU LEAVE HIM TOO?

From that time many of his disciples went back, and walked no more with him. Then said Jesus unto the twelve, Will ye also go away?

~ John 6:66-67

When Jesus miraculously fed the five thousand with just a few loaves of bread and some fish, the people were amazed. These same people who experienced the miracle were not so impressed by His words. After their bellies were filled, Jesus began to fill them spiritually with mind boggling words. Scripture tells us that they "walked no more with him."

Our small church of seventy or so has baptized and joined into fellowship with hundreds of converts. Most stayed for a while . . . until, that is, they heard some hard truths from the Word that didn't fit with their way of life. Henry Blackaby in his *Experiencing God* series calls this a "crisis of belief." We've all been there. When confronted with an uncomfortable truth about our lives, or with an action God is asking from us, we are forced to make a decision. Will we obey without question, or will we walk away? More have walked away than taken up their cross for the Savior. If you haven't experienced this "crisis of belief" in your life yet, you will. The question is this: will you leave Him too?

TODAY'S HOT FLASH:

Your crisis of belief will be different from mine. You may be asked to do something you know is impossible to do. Will you trust the One who is asking?

PRAYER:

Father, I have wavered a few times in my life when You've asked for more from me than I thought I could give. Forgive me. With You nothing is impossible. Amen.

SEPTEMBER 28
READ: JEREMIAH 9:12-22

NO ONE KNOWS WHEN THEY WILL DIE!

For death is come up into our windows, and is entered into our palaces, to cut off the children from without, and the young men from the streets.

~ Jeremiah 9:21

As I grow older, my attention turns to the obituary pages a little more often. I've always read them, as I know too well that death hits where it is least expected and at any age. Granted, most of the people in the obits are sixty or older, but there are always two or three that are much younger. Unexpected diseases, accidents, abuse, the causes vary as much as the ages.

Jeremiah tells us that "death is come up into our windows;" it sneaks in and is no respecter of persons. Just today I read a sad article about five teenage boys dying from carbon monoxide poisoning. What started as a celebration of life turned into their final chapter, a tragedy unexpected and with families unprepared.

Did these young men know Jesus? Do their families have any hope of seeing them again in glory? Statistics indicate no. How sad! I can only hope statistics are wrong in this case. What I do know is that life must not be taken for granted. Are you prepared to meet your Maker? If you were to die today, would you go out with a bang? A bang, that is, for Jesus?

TODAY'S HOT FLASH:

What if death claims a loved one? A child? A mother, brother, sister, father, niece, or nephew? Are you prepared? Are they?

PRAYER:

Father, only You know when our time will end. Prepare my heart for whatever You bring my way. May I boldly speak to those who don't know You. Amen.

SEPTEMBER 29

READ: LUKE 19:1–10

IT'S A SAD WORLD AFTER ALL

For the Son of man is come to seek and to save that which was lost.

~ Luke 19:10

My husband and I went out to dinner last night. We went to one of our favorite Italian restaurants where the food is always good. We weren't disappointed, the food was great, but something in the atmosphere was disparaging. We were sitting in the midst of discord. Screaming and slamming sounds reverberated from the kitchen.

As I unavoidably listened, it occurred to me that the majority of people in the world are unhappy. I didn't feel perturbed over their unprofessional behavior; I felt sad. Because I once again was confronted with the fact that it is a sad world after all.

It is easy to sit snugly in our comfortable homes, with our comfortable lives, enjoying the prospect of eternal life with a loving Savior, while most of the world languishes, lost and hopeless. But is that what we are supposed to do? Jesus said He came to seek and to save the lost.

Sadness is universal; we don't have to go far to find it. Yes, it is a sad world, but we have light to share, the light of Jesus, and we can shine Jesus' love brightly, one person at a time.

TODAY'S HOT FLASH:

This sad world needs happiness that only people with eternal hope can offer. Spread the love of Jesus and help remove this veil of sadness that permeates the world.

PRAYER:

Lord, my heart breaks for all the sadness in the world. Use me to spread Your joy, Your hope, and Your love. May I make a difference for You. Amen!

SEPTEMBER 30
READ: EXODUS 20:1-16

ARE YOU TAKING THE LORD'S NAME IN VAIN?

Thou shalt not take the name of the Lord thy God in vain; for the Lord will not hold him guiltless that taketh his name in vain.

~ Exodus 20:7

I learned the Ten Commandments at a young age. I prided myself on my ability to keep God's rules and pointed my finger when someone else failed. It wasn't until many years later that I realized I had no clue as to their full meaning, especially "thou shalt not take the Lord's name in vain."

I was taught not to say "O my God" outside of prayer or use Jesus' name in any way other than specifically talking about Him. But God isn't concerned with my language. He's concerned with my life.

God isn't simply commanding us not to misuse His name verbally, though it is disrespectful; I believe He is warning us to count the cost of our faith. If I claim Jesus as Lord, then my life better honor and glorify Him. To tell the world I am a Christian and then live like a heathen is to claim His name in vain. To sin against God's Word when I have committed to keep His Word is to take His name in vain. It's not simply about what I say. It's all about how I live my life. Are you taking the Lord's name in vain, living a life contrary to God's moral laws? He doesn't take it lightly, and neither should you.

TODAY'S HOT FLASH:

If I say I love God, I will live a life that pleases Him. If I don't, I am taking the Lord's name in vain.

PRAYER:

Father, forgive me for when I take Your name in vain. Help me to live a life that is glorifying to You. Amen.

OCTOBER

OCTOBER 1

READ: ECCLESIASTES 3:1–11

YOU ARE BEAUTIFUL!

He hath made every thing beautiful in his time.

~ Ecclesiastes 3:11a

The leaves scatter brightly over the ground: red, orange, green, and yellow. I can't walk through my backyard without crushing them underfoot. Their innocent beauty is destroyed by one dirt-soiled tread. That's okay. They can't feel anything, they don't experience vanity, and they are oblivious to their beauty.

We are not oblivious to our beauty, or lack thereof. In our culture, beauty determines popularity, and thousands of dollars are spent perfecting our "flaws" of nature. For the normal, middle-class, middle-aged woman, it creates an inner dissatisfaction, and she is unable to "fix" it.

This dissatisfaction intensifies as we age. Things begin to "go south," and winter settles on the mountain top. Looking beautiful gets harder with each passing day. Why can't we be more like the transforming leaves that become more spectacular with age?

God divinely and beautifully designed every stage of your life. From birth to death, you are intricately and individually crafted. It doesn't matter what the world says; Scripture says, "He hath made everything beautiful in His time" (Ecclesiastes 3:11a). There are no exceptions.

TODAY'S HOT FLASH:

The time is now! The time is yours! You ARE beautiful! When you start believing it, the rest of the world will too.

PRAYER:

Lord, You have made me beautiful, just as I am. Help me to stop comparing myself to the world's idea of beauty and remain focused on Yours. Amen.

OCTOBER 2
READ: JOB 8:1-13

COMFORT THE GRIEVING, DON'T ACCUSE THEM

If thy children have sinned against him, and he have cast them away for their transgression.

~ Job 8:4

Job lost his children, wealth, and health. He was in the depths of despair, and his good buddies came to comfort him. For seven days they sat in silence, offering him solace and a listening ear if needed. When they couldn't take it anymore, their "wisdom" poured from their mouths in torrents. It was quickly apparent that these supporters were fair weather friends, at best. Once their tongues started wagging, their support turned into accusation, and it goes on chapter after chapter. Through it all, Job remained his godly self, even in the midst of misspoken busybodies.

When a loved one is grieving, the last thing they want to hear is why it might be their fault. If it is, they know it. They don't need us to tell them. As we get older, we will experience the death of loved ones and friends frequently, and we may be the calming force needed to help those left behind to survive emotionally.

TODAY'S HOT FLASH:

Don't point fingers; show the love of Christ by your nonjudgmental and caring attitude. The grief-stricken have enough to deal with right now. Don't add to their grief.

PRAYER:

Father, help me to be a gentle spirit offering hope to the hopeless, not a pointing finger accusing when comfort is needed. Amen.

OCTOBER 3

READ: LUKE 1:34-38

THE POSSIBILITY OF THE IMPOSSIBLE

For with God nothing shall be impossible.

~ Luke 1:37

There's something about hormones. They magnify every itty bitty feeling, embellish every reaction, and make the smallest irritation seem monumental. We don't want to be crabby old women, but something inside of us clicks and—whammo!—we've lost it again.

Of course, it doesn't end when menopause ceases. We are still human, and reactions are not perfect for the best of us. Even when we think we've made it to the other side of this menopausal mountain, problems don't just go away.

When things go wrong, we still feel bad; when others make us angry, we may say things we don't mean. At all stages of life, challenges abound. The question is how will we react now and how will we react later.

As much as we would like to blame our bad behavior on hormones, there must be a level of integrity even in during the most violent of hormonal surges. It's hard, sometimes downright impossible. But in the midst of the severest of circumstances, there is one thing to remember—with God all things are possible—especially when they seem totally impossible.

TODAY'S HOT FLASH:

Integrity is important in the worst of circumstances. How one reacts in the impossibility of a situation reveals the true worth of their character.

PRAYER:

Only You, Lord, have the power to create within me the ability to react godly in dire circumstances. Keep my eyes focused on Your precious Son. Amen.

OCTOBER 4
READ: ISAIAH 31

WHO CAN YOU DEPEND ON?

But I trusted in thee, O Lord: I said, Thou art my God.

~ Psalm 31:14

Life is unpredictable. You think you have everything under control today, and tomorrow it turns upside down. Maybe a death in the family, a sickness, a spouse unexpectedly walking out of a relationship, possibly a teenager gone awry, house burned to the ground, or a bone crushing accident. It could be anything. Life's comforts are wishy-washy at best.

With so few sureties in life, what is there to set our hearts on? Who in this life is so dependable that we dare leave everything in their capable hands? I love my husband, and my children are totally loyal to me, but they are human. And with every human being comes the curse of imperfection.

There is only one person I can go to when everyone has let me down. There is only one I can rely on to listen to my every heartfelt plea. There is only one place I can go to hide even in the middle of a crowd. And that is to the precious throne of grace where Jesus my Savior waits for my communication. He won't let me down. He's never too busy. He understands me fully. I can trust Him with my secrets completely.

TODAY'S HOT FLASH:

When I talk to Him, my business isn't spread all over the world. He keeps it to Himself. Therefore, I will trust in Him and Him alone.

PRAYER:

Teach me, Lord, to trust fully in You in every circumstance. Sometimes life hurts, and I need Your help to make it through. You are my sanctuary, O Lord. Amen.

OCTOBER 5
READ: PSALM 31:1-14

SHAME ON ME

In thee, O Lord, do I put my trust, let me never be ashamed: deliver me in thy righteousness.

~ Psalm 31:1

When I was a child, I overheard an adult relative talking to a close friend. In all my wisdom, I decided it must be something important. The first chance I got, sitting at a table full of adults, I boasted her secret: "Shirley has hemorrhoids." My clue that I had said something wrong was written all over their faces. First, silence, then laughter, except for Shirley, who sat with mouth agape and face beet red. Oops! I slithered from my chair and out of sight.

This was an extreme case of embarrassment, but it was not a case of shamefulness. Embarrassment is caused by unintentional mistakes; shame is what I feel when I have deliberately sinned against God or my fellow man. A repentant adulterer experiences shame. A godly woman who loses her temper and spouts a few not-so-nice words experiences shame.

Every Christian experiences shame when they know they have sinned against God or others. This shame is a necessary part of the forgiveness and healing process. The problem arises when we can't let go of it. For some, their penitence is their shame.

TODAY'S HOT FLASH:

Don't stuff your shame into a backpack and carry it around with you wherever you go. If you don't like the feeling it brings, vow never to do it again.

PRAYER:

Father, You know I've experienced the pain of shame many times. Help me to learn from my mistakes so I may never have to go to that awful place again. Amen.

OCTOBER 6
READ: PSALM 46

EVERYONE HAS A CRUTCH. WHAT'S YOURS?

God is our refuge and strength, a very present help in trouble.

~ Psalm 46:1

I've been told my faith is a crutch. And you know what? It absolutely is. After all, what is a crutch? Something that holds you up when you can't go it alone. If my leg is broken, I need some extra help to do even the most menial tasks throughout my day. Without this added help, I am useless to myself and everyone else.

Jesus is my crutch. When I am broken, He gives me the added help I need to make it through my day. Instead of curling up in a ball and giving in to my self-pity, I can say, "Jesus, you are my refuge and strength, a very present help in time of trouble." He is all I need.

How sad to think of those people who do not have the safety crutch of my Jesus. When they are down, who will lift them up? When they are broken, their only hope is a doctor offering them pills to cover up the problem.

The truth is that everyone has a crutch they cling to. We were created to fill our void with Jesus. If not Jesus, then food, cigarettes, drugs, alcohol, sleep, even exercise and work are replacements for the One who truly belongs there.

TODAY'S HOT FLASH:

Everyone has a crutch. Something or someone that helps them through when times get rough. I choose to depend on Jesus. He is 100% dependable.

PRAYER:

Father, I am not ashamed of needing You. I am helpless without You. Thank You that You are ever faithful and fully dependable. Amen.

OCTOBER 7
READ: HEBREWS 11:8-29

IS THERE A SEPARATION NEEDED IN YOUR LIFE?

By faith Abraham when he was called to go ... obeyed.

~ Hebrews 11:8a

Abraham separated himself from his country and kinsmen. Paul separated himself from the high position and firm beliefs he lived by. Noah separated himself from his good name to build an ark only he believed in. Rebecca separated herself from her family to marry a stranger. They all forfeited their comforts and securities and separated themselves to an unknown life, all because of the promises of an unseen God.

Do you believe in the promises of God, so much so that you are willing to separate yourself from your comfortable lifestyle for His kingdom? Maybe you need to trade your favorite TV shows for time in God's Word, your favorite restaurants for giving more in the offering plate, or your favorite activities for more volunteer work.

Whatever God is asking from you, are you willing to make the separation? This world has a lot to offer, but none can compare to what God offers us. As the Scripture asks, "What good is it to gain the whole world if in the process we lose our soul?" (found in Matthew 16:26)

TODAY'S HOT FLASH:

Is there anything you are not willing to give up? This is the one thing you have replaced God with. Hold on loosely, lest God feel He must take it away.

PRAYER:

Father, all that I have is Yours; You give and You take away. You are my reward, and I long to be with You. I will glorify You with all of my days. Amen.

OCTOBER 8
READ: GALATIANS 5:17–23

BE CAREFUL WHAT YOU PRAY FOR; YOU MAY GET IT!

But the fruit of the Spirit is love, joy, peace, longsuffering, gentleness, goodness, faith, meekness, temperance: against such there is no law.

~ Galatians 5:22–23

My weight has been a bone of contention all my life. The funny thing is, I have never been overweight, and to those who are, I must sound ridiculous and slightly obsessive. In fact, many might say I have OCD tendencies. Much of my "avoirdupois" (excess weight) is solely dependent on my hormones and how I perceive things at the time. Today I might believe I am the Goodyear blimp, and tomorrow I will think I'm looking pretty good.

On my bad days, I spent a lot of time praying that God would change me, that He would shut my mouth so I couldn't pour food into it. I'd murmur and complain because He was not giving me the strength I needed to overcome my lack of self-control.

About a year ago, I lost all sense of taste and smell. It didn't stop me from eating. Suddenly, I realized I was the problem, not God's lack of attention. Stubborn as I am, it was discovered recently that I have a food intolerance to almost everything. Guess what! I am no longer pigging out on everything I can find.

TODAY'S HOT FLASH:

Be careful what you pray for; you may get it. God revealed to me my self-control problem and how it bleeds over to every area in my life.

PRAYER:

Father, thank You for doing what's necessary to get my attention. Help me to listen more closely to Your still small voice. You are great and worthy of praise. Amen.

OCTOBER 9

READ: 2 CORINTHIANS 5:1–10

AM I PLEASING THE SAVIOR?

Therefore we make it our aim, whether present or absent, to be well pleasing to Him.

~ 2 Corinthians 5:9

I confess. I have trouble with Christians who get so caught up in their emotions and self-centeredness that they couldn't give a rip about God's opinion in the matter. What they want may not be wrong, but their attitude and how they get it speaks volumes to those around them.

When I know I have displeased my Savior, I am heartbroken. When I allow myself to spout self-righteously with little regard to those around me, I am ashamed.

When I develop a plan without regard to the significant people in my life, I have decided I am more important than they are. My plans are almost always not God's, and to push forward like an unstoppable bulldozer will only bring grief.

If God has blessed me with answered prayer, I must give thanks and cautiously go forward, lest I throw his blessing back in His face. I am not the most important person in God's plan, or even in my own life, and when I believe I am, heartache is sure to come.

TODAY'S HOT FLASH:

Thank God for answered prayer, but proceed cautiously in your blessing, lest you step on the toes of the very people who love you the most.

PRAYER:

Father, forgive me when I get caught up in my own agenda. Help me to take my many blessings and use them to bless others. This is well pleasing to You. Amen.

OCTOBER 10
READ: JAMES 4:7–10

DOES YOUR HEART NEED TO BE BROKEN?

Draw nigh to God, and he will draw nigh to you. Cleanse your hands, ye sinners; and purify your hearts, ye double minded.

~ James 4:8

"A vengeful, hateful attitude toward others shows us that our own self-righteous hearts need to be broken by the countless wrongs we too have committed against God and others. Let's be thankful that God's offer of mercy is still available to us today" (Jeff Olson). When you find yourself dwelling on the wrongs done to you, grab a sheet of paper and measure them against the wrongs you've done to Christ, i.e. every sin you've ever committed. When we've failed so miserably, what choice do we have but to forgive?

Circumstances, hormones, and other people are not the cause of our harsh words and misbehavior. God gives us the grace to break through the barrier of our sinful flesh and remain godly in spite of how we feel. Whenever I fail in my attempt to remain godly, I realize I have not spent time with Jesus. How can I draw nigh to Him if I am not even opening the pages of my Bible or petitioning Him for His mercy and grace? Unfortunately, it happens way too often in my life. I think it's time I purified my heart before God has to do it for me. How about you?

TODAY'S HOT FLASH:

When is the last time your heart was broken over your sin? Or do you save it all for how you feel when others offend you? Purify your heart and live for Jesus now!

PRAYER:

Father, forgive the vengeful, hateful attitude I show at times. May I daily draw nigh to You so I am not tempted to attack others. Amen.

OCTOBER 11

READ: REVELATION 1:9–17

PUT GOOD IN, GET GOOD OUT

> *I, John ... was in the isle that is called Patmos, for the Word of God, and for the testimony of Jesus Christ.*
>
> ~ Revelation 1:9

You are what you eat; practice what you preach; what goes up must come down. We've all heard these clichés, and they are true. Watching a commercial the other day, I heard a new one: "Put good in, get good out." When I eat right, my body reflects it. When I practice my skill, I improve, and when I spend time meditating on the Word, my attitude brightens.

Who wouldn't feel good after sitting at the feet of Jesus for a while? Who wouldn't enjoy conversing with the Creator of the Universe on a one-to-one basis? In this world of sci-fi fanatics, how much more "out-of-this-world" can you get?

As we get older, we have a tendency to take less in, choosing to regale others with our vast knowledge instead. But that is never what God intended. Apostle John, at a ripe old age, still had numerous truths to learn from the Savior. Just think of the implications if He had spent more time rambling on about what he already knew rather than listening to the new revelations of Jesus Christ.

TODAY'S HOT FLASH:

Before we can put good stuff out, we must let it in. God's Word is good stuff; fill yourself with the knowledge of the Savior, and you will have good stuff to share.

PRAYER:

Father, I know I don't spend enough time filling my heart with Your Word. Encourage my heart to desire Your Truth above all else. Amen.

OCTOBER 12
READ: ROMANS 14:7-12

IN THE EYE OF THE BEHOLDER

Every knee shall bow to me, and every tongue shall confess to God.
~ Romans 14:11b

Did you know that in some cultures still today, big voluptuous women are considered beautiful? I was watching a documentary on bats not too long ago, and those on the program described these "creatures" as beautiful. I almost gagged. The Museum of Modern Art displays "masterpieces" I will never understand or appreciate.

I don't find huge holes in the ears, lips, or nose becoming, and body piercing really turns me off. A baboon, in my eyes, is one of the ugliest animals alive. I find owls disgusting, but my husband doesn't agree. What I find beautiful, you may find repulsive, but there is one thing all Christ-lovers can agree on. That is the beauty of Jesus Christ.

Charles Spurgeon says it this way: "As for us, my brethren, the beauty of Christ is such that if we go into a barn to worship, we are quite as satisfied as though it were a cathedral with grained arches and glowing windows."

One day every knee will bow and every tongue will confess that Jesus is Lord. And you know what? It will be a pleasure to bow down before He who is the most beautiful of all.

TODAY'S HOT FLASH:

Most beauty is subjective. For Christians, the beauty of Christ is absolute and undeniable; all else pales next to Him.

PRAYER:

Beautiful, wonderful Savior, fill my heart and eyes with Your beauty as I travel through my day. This will help me keep all else in perspective. Amen.

OCTOBER 13

READ: ACTS 2:1-13

IF YOU MUST BE DRUNK, BE DRUNK WITH THE HOLY SPIRIT

Others mocking said, these men are full of new wine.

~ Acts 2:13

It was the day of Pentecost; the apostles were waiting for their sign from God. "Suddenly there came a sound from heaven as of a rushing mighty wind, and it filled all the house where they were sitting. And there appeared unto them cloven tongues like as of fire, and it sat upon each of them" (Acts 2:2-3). What happened? They were instantly filled with the Holy Spirit and began speaking in other languages. The people were astonished. "Aren't these the Galileans?" they questioned. In other words, the rednecks? The uneducated roughnecks? They heard it. They understood it. But in their disbelief, they assumed that "These men are drunk, full of new wine."

The people weren't that far off; they were drunk, filled with a new wine, the consuming, inebriating presence of the Holy Spirit. Strange things happen when the Holy Spirit gets involved. Normal, uninteresting people, filled with this new power, come alive. Alive to Christ, that is. Maybe you've been unspectacular all your life; you're older now, bolder, and ready to take daring steps into the future. Don't be afraid to let others see the "new wine" in your life. They may question it at first, but when they learn the truth, they will be amazed.

TODAY'S HOT FLASH:

The apostles were nobodies who became somebodies through the new wine of the Holy Spirit. Grasp the truth of this and see what God can do through you.

PRAYER:

Father, all my life I've been weak and afraid. Help me to allow the Holy Spirit full reign in my life that I might boldly reach others for You. Amen.

OCTOBER 14
READ: JOHN 21:12-17

KEEP FOCUSED ON THE BIG PICTURE

And Jesus went into the temple of God, and cast out all them that sold and bought in the temple, and overthrew the tables of the moneychangers, and the seats of them that sold doves.

~ Matthew 21:12

Three new kids joined our brood temporarily, and it raised our household number to ten. My older children think we have lost our noodles and believe intervention may be in order. Nonetheless, we have survived the barrage of events and continue to thrive.

Have we lost our noodles? Many thought Jesus had a few screws loose. He lost it with the moneychangers and ranted about destroying and building up a temple in three days. He prepared to feed five thousand with five loaves of bread and five fish. He called Himself God, outraging people with His audacity. Most insane of all, Jesus, God Himself, allowed humanity, His creation, to abuse Him and nail Him to a cross. He truly could have called "ten thousand angels" to set Him free, but He endured to the end for a greater cause than most could see.

When you are misunderstood, when family and friends think you have lost your mind, keep focused on the Big Picture. Nothing is too menial or too great when it glorifies the King.

TODAY'S HOT FLASH:

What seems insane to the world may be perfectly sane in the realm of Christ. Trust God above others no matter what, and do what you know you are called to do.

PRAYER:

Father, help me not to second-guess myself when I know You are involved. You are the only one I need to please. Thank You for each opportunity. Amen.

OCTOBER 15

READ: EPHESIANS 2:1-7

STILL NOT WHERE I NEED TO BE

Wherein in time past ye walked according to the course of this world, according to the prince of the power of the air, the spirit that now worketh in the children of disobedience.

~ Ephesians 2:2

You would think that after fifty years, I'd do and say a lot fewer stupid things than I used to. But that isn't always the case. In a self-righteous tirade, I tried to convince my husband that what he was doing was wrong. He looked at me as I was playing the "if you loved me" card and said, "You are a very manipulating woman." I knew he was right, but it made me mad anyway.

Why do I push and nag and point the finger? It would do me well to remember where I have been. I am not where I used to be, but I am still not where I need to be. When my sinful self is revealed for all to see, I am confronted with the reality that I have too much work to do to point the finger at another's flaws.

Paul states that "in times past we walked according to the course of this world" (Ephesians 2:2). Unfortunately, our past has a way of catching up to us, and we realize we are not as "righteous" as we think we are. This is a humbling pill to swallow, but a much needed pill if we are going to move from where we are to where the Father desires us to be.

TODAY'S HOT FLASH:

We need people in our lives who will tell us the truth. Without them, we develop too high an opinion of ourselves and forget we still have a long way to go.

PRAYER:

Father, forgive me for being a manipulator. I know this is not whom You want me to be. Teach me to focus on my own problems and trust You with everyone else's. Amen.

OCTOBER 16

READ: JEREMIAH 1

DIFFICULT TIMES CALL FOR DEDICATED PEOPLE

But the Lord said unto me, Say not, I am a child: for thou shalt go to all that I shall send thee, and whatsoever I command thee thou shalt speak.

~ Jeremiah 1:7

Jeremiah was a young lad when God chose him for a difficult task. Most young people would run, but not Jeremiah. God knew who He was calling, and Jeremiah's sensitive spirit and tender heart revealed his deep care for his people. He accepted God's challenge.

Shamefully, had I received such a calling at a young age, I would have bolted. At twenty, I wasn't ready; I was self-absorbed and concerned with survival. Now that I am almost fifty, I like to believe I am up for any challenge God brings my way. I am desperate to make up for lost time.

We live in a world drowning in its own misery. Hearts full of anger, sadness, guilt, and self-absorption limp through life with nothing to show for it but unhappiness. Like never before, people need to hear the truth of God's Word. We live in difficult times, and difficult times require dedicated people—people who will proclaim the truth, people who will weep for the lost souls, and people who will rise to the challenge no matter the cost. Will you be one of them?

TODAY'S HOT FLASH:

If you call yourself Christian, this challenge is for you. Millions of lost people need to hear about the love of Christ. Be a missionary in your own back yard.

PRAYER:

Father, I know I have neighbors I haven't told about Jesus. Fill me with a boldness to practice what I preach. Amen.

OCTOBER 17

READ: 2 KINGS 22:1-7

MOTHER ON A MISSION

And he did that which was right in the sight of the Lord.

~ 2 Kings 22:2a

King Josiah did what was right in the eyes of the Lord. How did that happen? How did an eight-year-old king learn right from wrong? With no fatherly guidance, it fell to one person: his mother, Jedidah. We also learn that his father was an evil man. Chapter 21 verse 22 states that he "forsook the Lord God of his fathers, and walked not in the way of the Lord."

Reading between the lines, we can learn a lot from these verses. For instance, Jedidah was a godly woman married to an evil man. How she must have grieved her husband's wicked influence on her son. As terrible as it sounds, she must have sighed with relief when he died. Josiah became Jedidah's mission in life.

Maybe your children or grandchildren are exposed to ungodly influences in their home. Never underestimate your influence. Regardless of what you are going through, always remember that your children are watching and learning. Hormones, emotions, and circumstances are all opportunities to prove your faithfulness even in the worst of circumstances.

TODAY'S HOT FLASH:

Are you a mother on a mission? Do what's right and become a guiding light to your family. They are watching you, and you can make the difference.

PRAYER:

Lord, may I never forget that I am still an influence to my grown children. Keep me walking the narrow path for my loved ones' sake. Amen.

OCTOBER 18
READ: MATTHEW 26:30-41

TAKE THIS CUP FROM ME

Then saith he unto them, My soul is exceeding sorrowful, even unto death: tarry ye here, and watch with me.

~ Matthew 26:38

Had I known the difficulty of my menopausal years, I would have borrowed Jesus' Gethsemane prayer way ahead of time as preparation. "O my Father, if it be possible, let this cup pass from me; nevertheless not as I will, but as thou wilt" (Matthew 26:39b). Granted, the coming onslaught of treacherous hormones is like strawberry fluff compared to the horrendous events Jesus faced. But there were times survival seemed unlikely.

During the height of my menopausal symptoms, my marriage suffered, my children suffered, my family and friends suffered, my mental ability to cope suffered, my ministries suffered, and my health suffered. God did not see fit to remove my "cup" from me; neither did He see fit to lessen the impact of my hormonal surges.

I am forever grateful for the trial of this "cup." I have climbed the jagged sides of the mountain and reached the top. Had it not been for the trial, how would I have known the extent of God's strength? I am a better person because of it. God knew what He was doing after all.

TODAY'S HOT FLASH:

True faith is determined by our reaction during the trial. We can't know the strength of our faith until we've faced hard times and unwelcome circumstances.

PRAYER:

Thank You, Lord, for this "cup" You've allowed me to partake of. May I continue to remain faithful regardless of my circumstances. Amen.

OCTOBER 19

READ: MATTHEW 7:15-23

COMPLETING YOUR ASSIGNMENT

Not everyone that saith unto me, Lord, Lord, shall enter into the kingdom of heaven; but he that doeth the will of my Father which is in heaven.

~ Matthew 7:21

Have you ever worked your fanny off on a school assignment only to find out you did it all wrong? You were expecting an "A," but an "F" took its place. Our Christian walk is an earthly assignment. When we first come to Jesus, the excitement of our new spiritual romance with the Savior overrides everything else, and the "Go" becomes a natural byproduct of our newfound emotions. Over the years our excitement wanes, and we lose focus. In the busy-ness of our "good" activities, we stray from the assignment.

Many "good-deeds" people will stand before Jesus and hear the fateful words, "I never knew you." When the church doors opened, they were there. They sang in the choir and taught Sunday school, but in the end, it amounted to naught. Why? Because the assignment was not completed. This Jesus, whom they were to go and tell others about, became a busy activity. They didn't get to know Him. They thought they earned an "A", but their report card shows a great big "F." Don't let this happen to you!

TODAY'S HOT FLASH:

Motive matters. Saying the words does not salvation bring. Living the life assigned to us out of love for the Life-giver is the goal. What's on your report card?

PRAYER:

Oh Lord, keep my eyes focused on what's most important. Sharing Jesus with a lost world. Let that be my motive for everything I do. Amen.

OCTOBER 20

READ: MATTHEW 10:1–15

HOW DID WE GET TO THIS PLACE?

Freely ye have received, freely give.

~ Matthew 10:8b

How did we get to this place? We don't think about the physical and emotional struggles of the elderly as we struggle through life. It is uncomfortable to allow oneself to experience another's pain. Empathy is lost on the young. Yet, here I sit, in a hospital, waiting for my husband to return from heart surgery. He's getting a pacemaker today. It is tangible proof that we are getting older. With every passing hour, life as we know it is passing us by.

It is not a scary thought. It doesn't change a thing. But it is a sobering thought. How could I have wasted so many days doing nothing? Why can't we grasp this truth when we are young? I've spent too many days angry, lazy, uncaring, and stuck in monotony while lost and dying souls drowned in their own misery and the elderly struggled to survive, hoping for a caring soul to take notice.

Lord willing, I still have quite a few years left on this earth, and I don't intend on wasting another minute. I am going to love with a passion I never exhibited before and reach out to those who need someone to care. God forgive me if I fail to do my part!

TODAY'S HOT FLASH:

Jesus came into this world and gave of Himself freely and unconditionally. How can we do any less? Don't waste another day focused on yourself.

PRAYER:

Father, I have been so selfish, only thinking about myself, my needs, and my desires, while others die lost and lonely. Forgive me. Lead me to the needy. Amen.

OCTOBER 21

READ: EXODUS 17:14-16

WRITE IT FOR A MEMORIAL

And the Lord said unto Moses, Write this for a memorial in a book.

~ Exodus 17:14a

How long will we continue to murmur and complain when things don't go as we desire? How long will we demand a sign from our Lord that He is there and taking care of us? Time after time He is faithful, and time after time we forget.

It's even easier to forget when our minds are fighting daily, hourly, even every second of every day at times, to stay controlled and sane. Hormones mixed with fear make a devastating pair.

How wise of God to tell Moses to write everything down. Every miracle, every faithful act, every deliverance recorded for future generations, but not just future generations, as a reminder to them as well. When doubt invaded, they had only to read and remember.

Many of us would do well to write down what God has done for us, how many times He has been faithful, the miracles accomplished, the comfort given. Then when those sneaky little misgivings and worries crowd in, we too will remember and offer praise rather than murmurings.

TODAY'S HOT FLASH:

Write it, read it, remember it—your story of God's great intervention. It is the greatest legacy you can pass down from generation to generation.

PRAYER:

Lord, May I never forget what You have done for me: the cross and the blood and Your saving grace at Calvary. Amen.

OCTOBER 22

READ: GENESIS 45:1-15

THE POWER OF FORGIVENESS

And he wept aloud: and the Egyptians and the house of Pharaoh heard.
~ Genesis 45:2

After more than thirteen years spent separated from his family, Joseph exhibits a quality most of us would do well to learn from. Hated by his brothers, sold into slavery, forgotten; still, when face-to-face with the agents of his misery, Joseph is consumed with compassion, and his heart can do nothing but forgive. When face-to-face with his brothers, Joseph wept loudly. The feeling of release overwhelmed him as he understood God's plan. His brothers did him evil, but God's plan was much bigger. He forgave them, and years of tension and anger dissolved into healing.

Who do you need to forgive? In this time of emotional overload, bitterness creates only greater discourse. Amazingly, it has been proven that deep emotional release heals. Cry some tears of forgiveness and let the healing begin.

TODAY'S HOT FLASH:

Tears heal: they clean our eyes, kill bacteria, remove toxins, elevate our mood, and lower stress. Yes, God created even tears for a great purpose.

PRAYER:

Merciful Father, my unforgiving heart burns within me and makes me a miserable person. Bring my heart (and eyes) to tears that I may be thoroughly cleansed inside and out. Amen.

OCTOBER 23

READ: 2 TIMOTHY 1:1–12

FOOLISHNESS OF FEAR

For God hath not given us the spirit of fear; but of power, and of love, and of a sound mind.

~ 2 Timothy 1:7

I see them wherever I go: fifty, sixty, and seventy-something's fighting (without success) the assault on their looks that can never be undone. Wrinkles, sagging "parts," thinning hair, brown spots . . . need I go on? You can always recognize them. Dyed hair, long, red fingernails, lush (wrinkly) red lips, miniskirts, skimpy shirts, and an overabundance of stinky smelly stuff. They all have one thing in common. They are afraid to grow old. They try to look and act like teenyboppers and end up looking ridiculous instead. Rather than face their fear, they hide behind their foolish disguises.

Eleanor Roosevelt once said, "You gain strength, courage, and confidence by every experience in which you really stop to look fear in the face. . . . You must do the thing which you think you cannot do."

Have you looked fear of aging in the face? Once you do, you will realize it's not such an ugly monster after all. God in His wisdom has not given you the spirit of fear, but of power, love, and a sound mind. Grab hold of that truth and live in confidence today.

TODAY'S HOT FLASH:

"Courage is fear that has said its prayer" (Dorothy Bernard).

PRAYER:

All-powerful Father, turn my fear into courage, that I might face all things knowing You are by my side and will never leave me or forsake me. Amen.

OCTOBER 24
READ: HEBREWS 4:9–16

TOO MANY, YET NOT ENOUGH

Let us therefore come boldly unto the throne of grace, that we may obtain mercy, and find grace to help in time of need.

~ Hebrews 4:16

I've always been an advocate of prayer. My answer to almost everything is "let's pray." But it hasn't been until recently that I've realized how much prayer is needed and how much I fall short of that mark. It has put me in a real conundrum.

With a husband, eight children, fifteen grandchildren, a grown foster son, an entire church family, and a desperately fallen country, how can I possibly, purposely, and personally pray for everyone and everything needing intercession? I don't dare assume someone else will fill in the gap; I am consumed with the need to pray.

I haven't found the answer to this dilemma, but I have noticed something quite spectacular. When I spend every spare moment coming "boldly before the throne of grace," I tend to get into less trouble. There is no time for pettiness, negativity, and slothfulness when my heart is facing heavenward, and hatred, frustration, and bitterness are pushed out of the way when in desperation we intercede for those around us.

TODAY'S HOT FLASH:

"Work as if you were to live a hundred years. Pray as if you were to die tomorrow" (Benjamin Franklin).

PRAYER:

Dear Father, thank You that I have the assurance that You hear and answer my prayers. Burden me daily with a need to pray for all who touch my life today. Amen.

FOR SANITY'S SAKE
OCTOBER 25
READ: 2 CORINTHIANS 1:1-11

DÉJÀ VU

Who comforteth us in all our tribulation, that we may be able to comfort them which are in any trouble.

~ 2 Corinthians 1:4a

I never could have imagined that just as my menopausal symptoms are coming to an end, I'd be ministering to my daughter whose symptoms are violently crashing in on her. She is only in her early thirties and already wakes up two or three times a night in a bed soaked with sweat. She's spoken to her doctor, and he won't even contemplate the idea that she is in the beginnings of peri-menopause. It truly is déjà vu!

Her mood swings, night sweats, and inability to lose weight match what I went through, symptom to symptom. I have no doubt what is going on. Her doctor has prescribed anti-depressant medications because he feels she is suffering from a bout of mild depression.

I had no one to help me, and I struggled terribly for years. It was in writing this book that I finally came to an acceptance and some control over my situation. I am not totally at the bottom yet but close, and looking back and then forward, I am so thankful my daughter has someone to help her in the difficult times.

TODAY'S HOT FLASH:

Be open and share your menopausal experiences with your daughters and younger female friends. It will be the first step you take to helping them through the hard times when it is their turn.

PRAYER:

Father of grace and mercy, I am so thankful that I have this experience so I can minister to other women in their time of need. You truly do know best. Amen.

OCTOBER 26
READ: HEBREWS 5:11-14

IS YOURS A SHALLOW FAITH?

For everyone that useth milk is unskillful in the word of righteousness: for he is a babe.

~ Hebrews 5:13

While going through the worst of my menopausal years, I was faced with a disturbing truth: my faith was shallow. I was upset at God for not stopping all these horrible symptoms and refusing to give me the strength to avoid sin. I'd pray, then sin, ask forgiveness, pray, and sin again. The cycle almost drove me mad.

As a pastor's wife, I prided myself on being *mature* in my faith. I was wrong. Had I been mature, my faith would have sufficed in all circumstances. How do we know if our faith is shallow? Stormie Omartian, in her book, *The Power of a Praying Woman*, gives a list of five ways to tell if your walk with God is shallow. In short, here it is: if you are concerned only about what God can do for you; if you pray only during hard times; if you get angry with God; if your love is determined by His actions; and if you feel you have to beg God for an answer—your faith is shallow.

Can you find yourself in any of these statements? Is your walk with God shallow? Is your dependence on Him only on an as-needed basis? If you answer yes to these questions, you are missing out on the very best He has for you.

TODAY'S HOT FLASH:

Dig deep—in His Word, in your heart, in every possible way, until God alone becomes your lifeblood. You will be a changed woman.

PRAYER:

Oh, my dearest Father, draw me into a deeper relationship with You so I may know You more fully, love You more abundantly, and desire the things You desire. Amen.

OCTOBER 27

READ: ISAIAH 53:4-10

THE UGLY TRUTH ABOUT MYSELF

All we like sheep have gone astray; we have turned every one to his own way; and the Lord hath laid on him the iniquity of us all.

~ Isaiah 53:6

I hate to break it to you ladies, but what you see in the mirror and those parts of you that you don't like . . . they speak the truth. We are and always have been less than perfect. There's just something about menopause that brings every dirty detail out in blazing colors. It's like flashing a neon sign that says, "Look at me! See how horrible I am!" and there doesn't seem to be any way to stop it. I just want to run to my room, jump in my bed, and pull the covers over my head. But I can't. Life prevents it.

I have good news for you. This refining fire of menopause is but for a season, albeit a long one. The woman who emerges on the other side of this fiery trial is entirely up to you. Add in the extraordinary power of the Holy Spirit and, boy oh boy, we can surely become someone great.

TODAY'S HOT FLASH:

"He bare the sin of many, and made intercession for the transgressors" (Isaiah 53:12b). Victory comes through One person—Jesus! Hallelujah!

PRAYER:

Go ahead, Father, refine me, mold me, reveal everything, so that at the end of this journey, I can be all that You want me to be. Amen.

OCTOBER 28
READ: HEBREWS 9:23-28

WE ONLY LIVE ONCE

And as it is appointed unto men once to die, but after this the judgment.
~ Hebrews 9:27

Why is it important that we get it right in this life? Because this is the only chance at mortality we will experience. There are no ghost whisperers, and we won't come back as a toad, cow, or famous movie star. The truth of the matter is we won't come back at all. There are no second chances. There are no third and fourth dimensions, so there isn't another you living somewhere in another world. History is unchangeable; we can't undo wrong deeds, evil actions, or bad decisions. What's done is done, and our history quite often determines our future.

There is one thing secular history cannot foresee and one thing that can change all of the future for every individual. Actually, it is not a thing; "it" is a He, and He is Jesus Christ. Now is the day of salvation. Now is the time for change. Now is the time to live life to its fullest through Christ Jesus. Many factors in our lives make this life difficult, to say the least, such as hormones, tragedy, old age, and disease. There will come a day when we finally meet Jesus face-to-face and realize it was all worth it.

TODAY'S HOT FLASH:

Once in heaven, if given the chance to a re-life, I am sure most would say no way. It was too hard. But we will be so glad we finished strong in the end.

PRAYER:

Father, protect my mind from the TV shows that want me to believe that Hebrews 9:27 is a lie. Help me trust Your truth and deny the lies of the world. Amen.

OCTOBER 29

READ: JONAH 3:10-4:13

KICKING AND SCREAMING

But it displeased Jonah exceedingly, and he was very angry.

~ Jonah 4:1

Our five-year-old adopted daughter can be as sweet as maple syrup, wooing and winning every soul she meets with her beautiful blue eyes and innocent countenance. What a surprise it is to everyone when, unannounced and unsuspecting, she crosses her arms, plops on the floor, scrunches her face, kicks her feet, and lets out a shriek that would scare the mightiest of warriors. Once begun, there is nothing to do but wait it out.

There is always a reason: someone bumped her, pulled her hair, scolded her, ate the last cookie, or some other minor infraction. Whatever the reason, she didn't get her way, and she makes sure the whole world knows about it.

I have to admit that there are times I throw my own little hissy fit. Something didn't go my way, maybe an unexpected change was made, and the next thing you know, I am kicking and screaming. The only difference between her fit and mine is that hers is done on the outside, but I keep mine safely hidden inside myself.

Wacky hormones magnify the slightest irritation ten-fold, making it very hard to remain in a sweet, sweet spirit mode. When this happens, I am reminded of a truth I would rather forget: I really am a Jonah! I would bet you are too!

TODAY'S HOT FLASH:

Jonah was a chosen man of God, yet he had some serious flaws. God uses us in spite of our brokenness; that way, He alone gets all the credit.

PRAYER:

Oh Father, my life is full of cracks and broken pieces. Thank You for using me as I am. In Your strength, this broken vessel can and will serve You fully. Amen.

OCTOBER 30

READ: MATTHEW 20:16–34

BUT NOW I SEE

So Jesus had compassion on them, and touched their eyes: and immediately their eyes received sight, and they followed him.

~ Matthew 20:34

On May 10, 1748, while trying to navigate his slave ship through a treacherous storm, John Newton cried out, "Lord, have mercy upon us," and the rest is history. He suddenly realized the truth he'd been running from all his life — there is a God! And life for Newton and the rest of the world would never be the same. In a great moment of inspiration, while pondering on the great mercies of God, he wrote one of the most famous hymns of all time, "Amazing Grace."

The two blind men in Matthew 20 cried out to Jesus in their distress. "Have mercy on us, O Lord" (vs. 30). While others tried to shut them up, Jesus did a wonderful thing—He stood still! He listened to their heartfelt desires, and compassion flowed through him. He touched their eyes, and they received their sight. Life was never the same for these two former blind men. They once were blind, but now they see! Glory Hallelujah!

TODAY'S HOT FLASH:

"Have mercy upon me, O Lord!" Something about those words brings out the great compassion of our Savior. He stops in his tracks, and the rest is history.

PRAYER:

Father, where would I be had You not stopped in Your tracks and heard my cry? I once was blind, but now I see, was lost but You found me. I am forever grateful. Amen.

OCTOBER 31

READ: PSALM 37:1-13

CEASE FROM ANGER

Cease from anger, and forsake wrath: fret not thyself in any wise to do evil.

~ Psalm 37:8

I've been having a struggle lately with my anger. It's extra distressing because my anger is geared toward my son. I *love* him unconditionally, but in a less-than-godly moment, I want to slap him silly, scream at him, punch him in the face, and lock him in his room. Mind you, he's thirty and doesn't live with me. But still.

He knows the Lord, has served him for years, and then POOF! Without warning, he threw it to the wind. You can't talk to him. He claims he is doing nothing wrong. So what do I do? I pray and pray and pray. And most of the time I trust God—that is, until those dreaded hormones take over, and I don't think God is working fast enough. It is in those moments my mind does crazy things.

When this happens, I have to force myself to turn to Psalm 37:1. The first two words are the hardest, "Fret not." Well, I don't know about you, but where my children are concerned, I find this almost impossible. Then I am challenged with verse eight, which says, "Cease from anger, and forsake wrath, fret not thyself in any wise to do evil." Of course, God is always right, and his solution in verse seven truly is the answer.

TODAY'S HOT FLASH:

"Rest in the Lord and wait patiently for him" (Psalm 37:7a). I know how hard this is, but it is the only way to receive peace during your time of anguish.

PRAYER:

Father, forgive my anger; help me to cease from anger and trust that You have everything under control. The one I fret over is Your child too. I know You love him. Amen.

NOVEMBER

NOVEMBER 1
READ: PSALM 70

MY DELIVERER

But I am poor and needy: make haste unto me, O God: thou art my help and my deliverer; O Lord, make no tarrying.

~ Psalm 70:5

I've been thinking about the many names of God and how they pertain to me where I am today. The one I seem to connect most with is "Deliverer." When my mind won't focus and I seem to wander aimlessly about, I cry out to my Deliverer. When my foot is inserted into my mouth one too many times and I can't seem to shut it on my own, I cry out to my Deliverer. When my heart aches over my children and my grandchildren and I am helpless to intervene, I cry out to my Deliverer. When hormones take over and everything seems too much to bear, I cry out to my Deliverer. I cry out, He delivers—dozens of times a day. He never tires of my neediness.

How about you? Do you need the great Deliverer active in your life? He might not pull you out of the circumstance, but He will strengthen you for the battle. He will help you make it through one day at a time, and sometimes that is all our mind can focus on. You don't have to go it alone. The Deliverer is ready and able to help in your time of need.

TODAY'S HOT FLASH:

God specializes in needy people. It isn't until we become needy that we finally realize our need for a Deliverer. Cry out! He will deliver!

PRAYER:

Merciful Father, I am poor and needy, just like David. Make haste unto me, for You are my help and my Deliverer. Help me never to forget that. Amen.

NOVEMBER 2
READ: EXODUS 3:4-10

WHO LIKES TO CHANGE?

Come now therefore, and I will send thee unto Pharaoh, that thou mayest bring forth my people the children of Israel out of Egypt.

~ Exodus 3:10

It is interesting that menopause is often called "the change." I mean . . . who among us really likes to change? We want to see it, we know we need it, but we don't like it; it's hard and often uncomfortable.

A doctor may tell us we need to lose weight lest we become susceptible to diabetes and heart disease. We know it is true, yet our love for food outweighs our need to conform. Eventually, we will suffer the consequences of our bad decision.

We can embrace the changes happening in our lives, or we can allow them to destroy us. We can live like the best years of our lives are behind us, or we can follow Moses' example, who at 80 years old changed every aspect of his life, took up his cross, and followed God into his greatest adventure.

With change come challenges, and with challenges comes a time of decision. It is in this time of decision that we will alter the course of our lives for good or bad.

TODAY'S HOT FLASH:

Are you going to be a Moses and embrace these changes head on, or are you going to bitterly cling to what was, destined to ignore God's greater plan for your life?

PRAYER:

Oh, Father, I don't like change any more than the next person. Help me to submit to Your will in my life, regardless of where it may take me. Amen.

NOVEMBER 3
READ: PHILIPPIANS 1:1-6

PITY PARTY

Being confident of this very thing, that he which hath begun a good work in you will perform it until the day of Jesus Christ.

~ Philippians 1:6

I have many days that I feel worthless. I think, *what good am I?* It really has nothing to do with age. I've struggled with this off and on my whole life. I am sure, though, it is embellished by overactive hormones.

I'm a terrible house cleaner, a not-so-great mother, sporadic in my devotional life, and only a so-so cook. I am always busy but have nothing to show for it. I have a million unfinished projects; my son does a million chores just so I don't have to. I am glad he has a pleasing spirit. I try to run a business and am lousy at that too!

Well, are you tired of listening to my pity party? This is what I sound like when my eyes slip away from the Supreme focus and dwell on the "me" focus. I become self-absorbed and petty. I believe God has a purpose for my life even when I cannot see it, for Paul tells me in Philippians 1:6 that "he which hath begun a good work in you will perform it until the day of Jesus Christ." Another version says, "He is faithful to complete it." I like that translation better, as I know I am far from "completed." It gives me hope. It should give you hope as well.

TODAY'S HOT FLASH:

It is good to know that I am not "completed" yet; otherwise, I would be quite worried. God must know what He is doing!

PRAYER:

Merciful Father, forgive my times of self-pity. Remind me every day that You are still molding me into Your masterpiece. Thank You for the hope this gives me. Amen.

NOVEMBER 4
READ: MARK 14:12-21

WE CAN'T SAVE THEM ALL

And as they sat and did eat, Jesus said, Verily I say unto you, One of you which eateth with me shall betray me.

~ Mark 14:18

I am a sucker for the neglected kitten, puppy, or child, and I love underdog movies like *Angels in the Outfield* and *The Blind Side*. Unfortunately, real life doesn't always have a happy ending, and I have had to learn that I can't save them all.

Even Jesus had to let go and let fate take its course. Judas served with Jesus for three years. For three years he watched as Jesus healed the sick and brought the dead back to life. For three years he listened to Jesus' teachings. Still, when all was said and done, he betrayed the very One he claimed to love.

Sometimes we receive very damaged young people into our home. We hope and pray that we can make a difference, but not all of them want help. After much time and effort, we finally have to let them go. I feel like a failure when I do this, but I've learned to recognize God's leading and step out of the way.

Is there someone you need to "let go" of? Someone you have tried to help but to no avail? Maybe God is saying, "Get out of the way and let Me do my God thing."

TODAY'S HOT FLASH:

Letting someone go is one of the hardest things we ever have to do. But if we don't, they may never make it to where they are destined to be.

PRAYER:

Father, help me to realize that hope and help may not always come through me. Keep me in Your will so I won't be in Your way. Amen.

NOVEMBER 5
READ: JOB 40:1-5

MANIPULATION

Shall he that contendeth with the Almighty instruct him?

~ Job 40:2

My girlfriends and I joke about how to get what we want from our husbands. Even in the marriage classes, we talk about manipulating them by our sweet, gentle ways rather than nagging and fighting with them, and most of the time it works. But what may work for our husbands does not work for God!

Have you ever tried to manipulate God? I have! I've said, "Now, God, this is what I need, so I am going to pray, or fast, or behave, or get up every morning at 5:30 to do my devotions until You answer my prayers." Two weeks later I am disillusioned, frustrated, and depressed because God is not biting. What went wrong? Why hasn't God blessed me in the way I thought He should?

The answer lies in the motivation of my actions. I cannot tell God what to do. "But, God, You've said You will give me the desires of my heart!" No, God says, "Delight thyself also in the Lord; and he shall give thee the desires of thine heart" (Psalm 37:4). You see, when we delight in the Lord, we do all these things out of love, not manipulation. The funny thing is, when we do it because we love Him, His desires become our desires, and all we need is more of Him!

TODAY'S HOT FLASH:

Patsy Clairmont once asked, "Have you ever tried to counsel God?" Then she goes on to say, "I wouldn't recommend it!" Let His desires become your desires.

PRAYER:

Lord, I've tried to manipulate You by my actions. As Job said, "I am vile; what shall I answer thee?" Forgive me; make my desires Your desires, gracious One. Amen.

NOVEMBER 6

READ: ISAIAH 55:6–13

THIS IS NOT WHAT I HAD PLANNED!

For my thoughts are not your thoughts, neither are your ways my ways, saith the Lord.

~ Isaiah 55:8

Had you asked me five years ago what my plans were for the future, I would have laid it all out in detail: travel, relaxation, out to dinner every night, new clothes and furniture, and NO DOGS! But nobody asked me, especially not God!

It wasn't my plan to adopt three young, damaged children. It wasn't my idea to adopt a hound so our son would have a companion. Little did I know, it was my husband who needed it more than our son. It wasn't my idea to start homeschooling again after all my children had left the nest. I had no plans to potty train again, live in a constantly messy home, spend $200 a week on groceries, and feel exhausted at the end of the day. I mean, it just isn't right, is it? I'm in my fifties, for Pete's sake.

God doesn't ask us what we want. He knows what we need and even more importantly, who needs us. For all my complaints, I don't doubt God's wisdom and wouldn't change a thing. Yes, I am tired, and there are numerous moments I feel I can't do it, and then I remember . . . I CAN'T DO IT! But God can do it through me, and I will cling to that.

TODAY'S HOT FLASH:

Maybe it's not what I had planned, but my plan was selfish and benefitted no one but myself. God's ways are not my ways, but they are always better.

PRAYER:

Father, give me the strength to make it through each day in Your strength. Thank You that You overruled my selfish desires for Your better way. Amen.

NOVEMBER 7
READ: PSALM 23

NO OUTLET

Yea, though I walk through the valley of the shadow of death, I will fear no evil: for thou art with me; thy rod and thy staff they comfort me.

~ Psalm 23:4

Bordering Jordan on the east and Israel on the west lies one of the world's saltiest bodies of water, the Dead Sea. Its high salinity content and absence of any outlets is lethal. Nothing can survive in it. It is 1,237 feet deep, stagnant—dark—void of all life.

Without an outlet, we too remain stagnant and without viable life down to our very soul. Without a divine outlet, healing may never come. Have you ever been in the depths of despair? Overwhelmed by a pain so torturous that you buried it in the very depths of your soul? My friend, emotional pain buried makes outer life empty. It is through the pain that life begins. Buried pain creates stagnancy and death. It is only as we walk through the valley that we can find freedom from the very thing that sucks the life out of us.

We need an outlet for the pain. David found that outlet in God, and so can you. That is why he could say, "Though I walk through the valley of the shadow of death, I will fear no evil."

When we deny the existence of emotional pain or downplay its effect, we cut off the only outlet we have to insure our safe arrival to the other side: God!

TODAY'S HOT FLASH:

Face your emotional monsters with calm assurance that with God, there is nothing to fear. Free yourself from your pain and live!

PRAYER:

Oh, Father, the pains buried so deep seek to destroy my life. Walk me through them, Lord, and bring me freedom that comes only from You. Amen.

NOVEMBER 8
READ: JOB 19:25–29

ONE THING I KNOW

For I know that my redeemer liveth, and that he shall stand at the latter day upon the earth.

~ Job 19:25

It's been a Jonah month. If my life were based on the past few weeks, I'd have to admit to complete failure in everything I do and touch. Sales are way down, housecleaning is nonexistent, and my voice can't hit a C if my life depended on it. I've been diagnosed with the flu and a staph infection, and anything I touch seems to go to pot. Have you ever had one of those weeks?

I keep plugging along, doing everything I am supposed to do, but with little heart. The only consistency in my life at this very moment is God, and what a comfort He has been.

I may not know what today will bring. It could throw leaky ceilings, defiant kids, depleted finances, hormonal turmoil, or some devastating disaster at me. There is only one thing I know: "My redeemer liveth, and . . . he shall stand at the latter day upon the earth." This I know—this I believe beyond a shadow of a doubt—and though all of life may topple around me, this truth remains firm. Because of that, I will go on. Because of that, I will persevere. Because of that, victory is already mine!

TODAY'S HOT FLASH:

Job was in the midst of devastation, yet without hesitation he proclaimed, "I know that my redeemer liveth." Do you know that your Redeemer lives?

PRAYER:

Father, I trust You to carry me through the dark days. You have said, "I will never leave you or forsake you." Thank You for that promise. Amen.

NOVEMBER 9
READ: SONG OF SOLOMON 7:6–13

BEAUTIFUL

How fair and how pleasant art thou, O love, for delights!
~ Song of Solomon 7:6

When you think of beauty, what comes to mind? For me, it's the puffy white clouds on a brilliantly blue sky, the changing leaves in mid-October, the smiling and often mischievous faces of my fifteen grandchildren, a newborn baby fresh from the womb. In all the evil of this sin-filled world, I believe there is still much beauty to be found. When I think of beauty, the one thing I never think of is—me.

I have knobby knees and gargantuan thighs, unruly hair and brown spots on every part of my body. I definitely would win an ugliest toes contest; mine are downright horrendous!

Did you know that, statistically, only two percent of women think they are beautiful? I definitely am not part of that small percentage. More than likely, neither are you.

The Romancer in Song of Solomon considers His bride fair and pleasant. He is mesmerized by her. Many scholars believe, and so do I, that the Romancer is a type of Christ, and the bride is His church. It is a revealing of Christ's feelings toward His church, or bride. He thinks we are beautiful. The greatest King of all desires us.

We are beautiful to Christ. Once we grasp that truth, our self-worth will soar beyond infinity, and nothing will be able to convince us otherwise.

TODAY'S HOT FLASH:

The world says I have to be a certain size and a certain age to be beautiful. Isn't it great that the only One who matters finds us ravishing and irresistible at all times and every age?

PRAYER:

Father, when I am feeling old and ugly, imperfect and undesirable, remind me that I am beautiful in Your eyes and that I am the honored Bride of Your Son. Amen.

NOVEMBER 10
READ: JOSHUA 22:1-9

TAKE HEED

But take diligent heed to ... love the Lord your God, and to walk in all his ways, and to keep his commandments, and to cleave unto him, and to serve him with all your heart and with all your soul.

~ Joshua 22:5

When we are young, we often feel invincible and ignore the warnings of wiser adults. How many times as teenagers were we told, "That's dangerous; don't do that! You better listen to me. I'm warning you." But to no avail.

Moses, Joshua, and the many leaders after them experienced the same kind of rebellion from their people. Only these were adults, people who experienced first-hand the miraculous intervention of God. Still, when discontent encompassed their hearts, they willingly and knowingly forgot the warnings of the prophets.

I am older now and oftentimes have acted just like those rebellious Israelites. I've seen God's miraculous hand in my life; nonetheless, I've chased after the leeks and garlics of my past. I am not proud of this, and my heartfelt desire is to never go that way again. This can only be accomplished if I keep my eyes focused in one direction—forward, to the cross. I can do this in God's strength alone. Help me, God!

TODAY'S HOT FLASH:

I am so glad Jesus didn't act on a whim, feeling, or temptation. If He had, we'd all be doomed to hell!

PRAYER:

Ever-forgiving Father, You are merciful and patient. Help me to stay strong and keep my eyes looking to the cross so that I may not fail You again. Amen.

NOVEMBER 11
READ: JOHN 8:12-29

WWJD

I am the light of the world: he that followeth me shall not walk in darkness, but shall have the light of life.

~ John 8:12

WWJD has become clichéd and nothing more than unfulfilled statements from times past. I choose to live it literally.

When I'm exhausted and prefer to relax and watch a TV program, knowing I haven't spent time with the Father, I ask myself, "What would Jesus do?" When frustrated and ready to pull my hair out because my son is not cooperating with me, rather than call him names and scream, I ask myself, "What would Jesus do?" (Well, most of the time.) I am by no means perfect! When I'm in the middle of my planned project and the phone won't leave me alone, I ask myself, "What would Jesus do?" When tempted to gossip or give my opinion in a matter (after all, my opinion counts, doesn't it?), I ask myself, "What would Jesus do?" I am reminded that Jesus never gave opinions, only truth, for He is the Truth, the Way, and the Life.

When I follow this little statement, my days flow effortlessly and my attitude remains peaceful. Unfortunately, I forget more often than not. What I can say: "For today, I am resolved to ask in everything, 'What would Jesus do?'"

TODAY'S HOT FLASH:

The words "What would Jesus do?" roll off the lips quite easily. The actions, however, take much resolve and unswaying determination to fulfill.

PRAYER:

Father, to be like Your Son, that is my desire, regardless the cost. Take my life today and let it be consecrated, Lord, to Thee. Amen.

NOVEMBER 12

READ: ACTS 17:16–21

HAS YOUR SPIRIT BEEN STIRRED?

Now while Paul waited for them at Athens, his spirit was stirred in him, when he saw the city wholly given to idolatry.

~ Acts 17:16

What stirs your spirit? Does the visual discomfort of once-prominent men living in cardboard boxes stir it? How about the knowledge that millions of babies are aborted every year—does that stir your spirit? Did you know that until recently in China, many female babies were left to die because of the one-child rule? Does that stir your spirit?

I viewed a photo the other day of a newborn, one hour old—dead, beaten to a pulp by the very person who brought him into this world. That, my dear friends, stirred my spirit. I wept for that child.

Paul's spirit stirred over the sin that engulfed the people of Athens. It thrust him into immediate action. He could do nothing but react—speak out—try to make things right.

When I was young, I was too self-absorbed, too busy surviving to even notice many of the atrocities around me. I am older now, and I wonder how I lived so long blinded by my own tunnel vision. I must act—react—try to make a difference. What else can I do?

TODAY'S HOT FLASH:

Take time to see things. When we take notice, our spirits stir within us and call us to action. That's God speaking. It's time to take notice and take action.

PRAYER:

Father, forgive me for my self-absorption. I've wasted so much valuable time. Don't let me waste another minute. I will take action for Your glory! Amen.

NOVEMBER 13

READ: ACTS 23:12-22

WHAT POWER! WHAT PASSION!

And when it was day, certain of the Jews . . . bound themselves under a curse, saying that they would neither eat nor drink till they had killed Paul.

~ Acts 23:12

What power the name of Jesus wields, that forty men would vow to starve themselves to death rather than allow Paul to live. His crime? Proclaiming the name of Jesus! What passion this servant of the Most High must have exhibited to set on fire the hearts of so many men to the point of extreme retaliation! They were determined to shut his mouth at the cost of their very lives.

It is a rare Christian indeed that boldly proclaims the truth, regardless the cost. For most, the need to be accepted outweighs our passion to preach Christ uninhibited. Throughout his epistles, Paul pleads Christ's cause; he speaks in earnest, his spirit is so stirred he cannot help but tell this great news, yet everywhere he goes, he meets opposition. The ruler of this world did not want Jesus preached to lost souls, and he doesn't want Him preached now. He will stop at nothing to break down the faith of believers and to keep them from sharing the Good News with exceeding earnestness.

TODAY'S HOT FLASH:

How has Satan challenged your voice for Christ? Do you fear retaliation? Gird up your loins and go boldly forth in His name.

PRAYER:

Father, take away my fear and inhibitions. Give me strength and resolve to go boldly forth to where I have never gone before, proclaiming the name of Your Son. Amen.

NOVEMBER 14
READ: ACTS 20:17–24

LISTEN, THEN OBEY

But none of these things move me, neither count I my life dear unto myself, so that I might finish my course with joy, and the ministry, which I have received of the Lord Jesus, to testify the gospel of the grace of God.

~ Acts 20:24

If you can't tell by now, I love the Apostle Paul. He was a man of action. Even before his conversion, he relentlessly pursued his convictions. It is obvious to me that God chose Paul for the very characteristics that made him a great Christian persecutor. He believed in his cause, and nothing could hold him back.

It only stands to reason that after his conversion, that same zeal would drive him, but in a different direction. Once convicted of a great truth, Paul set out to accomplish his goal, regardless the cost. My guess is that he was twice as gung-ho as before; he had the weight of his actions in times past as a constant reminder.

Most of all, Paul loved with tremendous passion. He loved his fellow believers, and he loved Jesus most of all. I want to be like Paul! I want to think nothing of my own life and finish my course with joy. I want to act in obedience without counting the cost. I can do it, and so can you. We first have to listen, and then we must immediately obey. We need to squash feelings of discomfort and move without question. If not today, tomorrow may be too late!

TODAY'S HOT FLASH:

"We can disobey God if we choose, and it will bring immediate relief to the situation, but we shall be a grief to our Lord" (Oswald Chambers).

PRAYER:

Mighty God, make me a mighty warrior for the cause of Jesus Christ. Teach me to listen and to obey without hesitation. Amen.

NOVEMBER 15
READ: EZEKIEL 24:15-24

RISE UP IN THE MORNING

So I spake unto the people in the morning: and at even my wife died; and I did in the morning as I was commanded.

~ Ezekiel 24:18

To live is to experience heartbreak, tragedy, and devastation. No one is exempt from it; no one can escape its grasping tentacles. It is our handlings in the midst of grief that determine who we are and whom we serve.

Ezekiel preached God in the morning. By evening, his wife was dead. God deliberately took away "the desire of his eyes" and warned him not to "mourn nor weep." Our first instinct when we read this passage is to accuse God of being heartless. But that wasn't Ezekiel's reaction. "And I did in the morning as I was commanded." He arose and obeyed God. He didn't take a sabbatical; he didn't wallow in self-pity. He arose, dressed, and continued in his calling.

As Christians, we have the ability, through the Holy Spirit, to continue on in spite of the pain. If we don't have that, what can we possibly offer this world full of hopelessness and tragedy? What is your reaction to tragedy? Are you illuminating Christ in your pain, or hopelessness in your agony?

TODAY'S HOT FLASH:

"The great God wants our conspicuous crisises to be occasions of conspicuous testimony; our seasons of darkness to be opportunities for the unveiling of the Divine" (J.H. Jowett).

PRAYER:

Father, don't let me fail You. When pain comes, when devastation strikes, may I do as Ezekiel did: arise in the morning and continue to live in obedience to You. Amen.

NOVEMBER 16

READ: ACTS 18:1–5

PRESSED IN THE SPIRIT

Paul was pressed in the spirit, and testified to the Jews that Jesus was Christ.

~ Acts 18:5

Have you ever been pressed in the spirit? I have been—many times. Unfortunately, it hasn't always been for the right reasons. When my hackles rise and I am sure everyone else is wrong, I push my opinion. When my husband has offended, I give him a piece of my mind. Yes, I've been pressed in the spirit, but regrettably, I often mistake my fleshly uprisings for a poke from the Holy Spirit. Before I know it, I've stuck my foot in my mouth—again.

Paul was pressed in the Spirit, by the Spirit, to speak of Jesus Christ. He didn't depend on emotions, opinions, or self-righteous attitudes to guide his path; he was one with his Savior. Nothing could keep him from passionately sharing his heart's desire—Jesus Christ.

I pray that one day my puny opinions and insignificant remarks fade to nothingness and only that which glorifies my dear Savior radiates from me. My desire is that one day, when I am pressed in the spirit, I will know that it is truly His Spirit, and Jesus alone will receive the glory for the words that pour from my mouth.

TODAY'S HOT FLASH:

When the urge rises within you to have your say, make sure it is the Holy Spirit and not last night's dinner making a reappearance. Opinions don't count.

PRAYER:

Lord, too often I've pushed my opinions and attitudes. Remove that from me. Press upon my spirit Jesus and Jesus only. Then my life will glorify You. Let it be so. Amen.

NOVEMBER 17

READ: ROMANS 11:26-33

UNSEARCHABLE JUDGMENTS

O the depth of the riches both of the wisdom and knowledge of God! how unsearchable are his judgments, and his ways past finding out.

~ Romans 11:33

The penalty for adultery was death, yet David received mercy. Death did come over and over again through his children, but he was spared. The Ten Commandments say, "You shall not lie," but Abraham lied twice, putting his wife in jeopardy and displaying his cowardly character. Adam and Eve deliberately disobeyed their Creator, and although punished, in His mercy God clothed them and opened an avenue of deliverance through sacrifice.

The stories of undeserved deliverances of God's people saturate Scripture, but we don't have to think long or hard to bring to mind His magnificent mercy poured out on us. I can't count on my fingers the evils I've done and commandments I've broken. Triple offenses have occurred in times of hormonal uprisings, yet in His great mercy and unsearchable judgments, He held back His mighty hand.

I don't deserve it. David didn't deserve it. Abraham didn't deserve it. You don't deserve it. Nonetheless, His mercy flows through our lives like God ordained pollen to flow through the air, reaching its destination and guaranteeing new life.

TODAY'S HOT FLASH:

This new life is guaranteed us as well, if we but turn our hearts to Him in genuine repentance. His mercy is new each and every day. Thank you, Jesus!

PRAYER:

Wonderful, merciful Father, I don't deserve mercy; I deserve the full measure of the law. Your ways are not my ways, and I am ever grateful. Amen.

NOVEMBER 18
READ: 2 CORINTHIANS 2:1–13

LOVE DOES THE HARD STUFF

For out of much affliction and anguish of heart I wrote unto you with many tears; . . . that ye might know the love which I have more abundantly unto you.

~ 2 Corinthians 2:4

Paul wrote a letter to the Corinthians. It wasn't an ooey, gooey, soft letter; it stung like a swarm of bees on the attack, confronting them in their sin. "My heart was broken, and I wept bitterly over having to do this" (my paraphrase), he told them.

I've often thought about writing heartfelt letters to my children as they went through crises, especially crises of their own making. Not through e-mail or texting; just me, a piece of paper, and pen. The kind of letter that says, "You are worth my time."

They hear the same words from my lips time after time. But my words don't seem to penetrate. I don't want to nag and condemn them for their wrong actions. I want to reveal to them clearly God's feeling on the matter and the damage that can occur if they continue on their chosen path. I want them to feel and see the anguish their sin causes me and, more importantly, the anguish it causes God. I want it written so they can come back to it as often as necessary and, hopefully, stop short before taking the same rocky path again. If you'll excuse me, I think I will go write a letter!

TODAY'S HOT FLASH:

Words tumble from our mouths, and it's too late to take them back. In a letter, we can carefully—and prayerfully—construct what we need to say.

PRAYER:

Father, I ask that you might give me Your words for my children. Open their hearts to hear the truth in love so they may choose to follow You in all they do. Amen.

NOVEMBER 19
READ: PSALM 76

I KNOW YOU ARE!

Thou art more glorious and excellent than the mountains of prey.
~ Psalm 76:4

Finally, the first snow of the season. I am all for the fluffy white stuff ... as long as I can appreciate it from inside my house. It is another reminder of God's greatness and His magnificent flair for beauty.

Consider the vastness of the ocean, or the infinity of the stars. The V-shaped migration form of geese traveling south for the winter. The change from summer to fall, the sunset on a midsummer's eve, a single rose given as a token of love, celebrations of marriage, birthdays, and, yes, even death.

At every turn I am reminded of the Almighty. At every turn He uses His Creation to nudge my conscience into remembrance of Him. With every breath I am thankful, with every word my loved ones speak, I am reminded how fortunate I am. I wouldn't trade my life for anything, and if it ends tomorrow, I am content.

Nothing or no one can take from me the assurance I have that He *is*—He always will be—and one day I will be with Him in glory. My God, My King, My All in All.

TODAY'S HOT FLASH:

It is my fervent hope that you find comfort in the little things as well as the grandiose. God is visible in almost everything when one is truly looking.

PRAYER:

Father, thank You for opening my eyes to Your presence in my life. It brightens my day and lightens my load knowing You *are* and always will be. Amen.

NOVEMBER 20
READ: MARK 13:32-37

ARE YOU READY?

But of that day and that hour knoweth no man, no, not the angels which are in heaven, neither the Son, but the Father.

~ Mark 13:32

If you knew Christ was coming tomorrow, would it change your actions for today? Do you know Christ is *not* coming tomorrow?

In my deep spirituality, my greatest fear was that He would return in clouds of glory while I was sitting on the toilet. Admit it; you've thought it as well. I've also thought about His return while I was sinning, but it didn't change my behavior for that moment.

Now I realize the pettiness and selfishness of these thoughts. The "toilet" never comes to mind (unless I'm writing, obviously), and I tremble as I realize how much more I loved myself than God. Standing before Jesus as He examines my life will not bring visions of sitting in the bathroom—or any other silliness. It will bring sorrow over wasted time, hurtful words said, deeds left undone, souls left untouched.

Are you sowing regrettable seeds? When you look into the face of Jesus, will shame fill your heart? Jesus tells us, "No man knows the day nor the hour of My return." In verse 37, He sums it up with one word: WATCH!

TODAY'S HOT FLASH:

What will the Savior find you doing when He returns for His Church? What have you left undone? What if it were today?

PRAYER:

Father, may I not do anything today that I will regret tomorrow, if Jesus were to come. May I do all I need to do and not waste one minute. Amen.

NOVEMBER 21
READ: MARK 16:1-8

FAITH UNSURPASSED

And when the sabbath was past, Mary Magdalene, and Mary the mother of James, and Salome, had bought sweet spices, that they might come and anoint him.

~ Mark 16:1

I've often wondered how Mary Magdalene, Mary the mother of James, and Salome planned on getting past the stone and into the tomb where Jesus' body lay. They were sure of their actions; they brought sweet spices with the intention of using them. Still, there was the dilemma of how to get into the tomb.

What sweet and vulnerable faith these women had. They knew the odds of accomplishing their goal was slight. Yet they went, believing it would happen. They were driven, probably beyond their own understanding. As we see the scene rolled out before us, we know it is by divine intervention that they were propelled toward that grave. In their love for Jesus, they were blessed with the first discovery of Jesus' empty tomb.

God expects us to have this same sweet vulnerability where He is concerned. He pricks our hearts to a task beyond our capabilities, and we have a choice. We can ignore the pricking or throw ourselves into His leading. It isn't easy stepping out boldly in faith. But when we do, the rewards are greater than we could possibly imagine.

TODAY'S HOT FLASH:

What is God leading you toward? Are you holding back because you can't see the possibility of it? Step out in faith and be blessed.

PRAYER:

Dear Father, You know my fear of stepping into the unknown. Take my hand and lead me wherever You want me to go. I will leave the details to You. Amen.

NOVEMBER 22
READ: 2 SAMUEL 24:18-25

WHAT DOES YOUR FAITH COST YOU?

And the king said unto Araunah, Nay; but I will surely buy it of thee at a price: neither will I offer burnt offerings unto the Lord my God of that which doth cost me nothing.

~ 2 Samuel 24:24

How much does your faith cost you? Is it a sidebar in the stream of life, conveniently placed and easily adjusted when necessary?

David refused to take Araunah's threshing floor as a gift. Earlier in the book of 2 Samuel, he refused to drink of the water that was painstakingly retrieved for him at the cost of human life. He would not drink for the great sacrifice made. He would not offer burnt offerings without a price.

How much does your faith cost you? Does God receive your leftovers? Spare time, money, and efforts? Our love for God is determined by the sacrifices we make. We sacrifice our lives to raise children, build careers, and do the things closest to our hearts. Where do God and His Son fit into the picture?

God loves us so much that He sacrificed the life of His only Son. He gave up the most precious part of Him, knowing He would receive little in return. We give little or nothing, knowing we will receive everything.

TODAY'S HOT FLASH:

Is God getting your leftovers? Put Him on the top of your to-do list. The rest of the stuff will get done after His work is accomplished.

PRAYER:

Father, forgive me for putting You at the bottom of my list. You sacrificed all for me; help me to do the same for You. Amen.

FOR SANITY'S SAKE
NOVEMBER 23
READ: EPHESIANS 5:15-21

THANK YOU, LORD

Giving thanks always for all things unto God and the Father in the name of our Lord Jesus Christ.

~ Ephesians 5:20

It's 1:30 in the morning, and I can't sleep. I lay for a few hours tossing and turning, willing myself to fade into oblivion, but to no avail. I've said for years that if you can't sleep, you can pray. In this early morning quietness, I feel an urge to give thanks. So that's what I'll do.

Father, thank You for giving us Your answers to all the world's problems, and more personally, thank You for giving me the answers to all mine. I need only go to the Book, Your Book! Thank You for prayer. Who could have imagined that the Creator of the universe wants to communicate with me personally? You are Almighty God, yet You care about what I think and feel. Thank You, Lord, for my children; may each one choose to live a life of service for You.

Time and space do not allow for me to name all the things I am grateful for; there are too many to count. Lord, in my times of stress and need, I thank You for Your Son, my family, and godly counselors. How can I ask for anything more than what You have already given?

TODAY'S HOT FLASH:

Pull out a piece of paper and begin your list of 100 things you are thankful for. Come back to it throughout the day until you have completed it.

PRAYER:

Lord, Your blessings are numerous. Don't let me take anything for granted. You are the Master Giver, and I praise You for that. Amen.

NOVEMBER 24
READ: 2 SAMUEL 13:23-39

DO WHAT'S RIGHT, ALL THE TIME!

And, ye fathers, provoke not your children to wrath: but bring them up in the nurture and admonition of the Lord.

~ Ephesians 6:4

A mixture of love and guilt blinded David to Absalom's arrogance and weakened his ability to make wise decisions in dire circumstances. After all, he hadn't been the greatest of parents. We know from Scripture that David was a passionate man. When he sinned, he sinned passionately. When he loved, he loved passionately. When he warred, he warred passionately. Good or bad, he never did anything halfheartedly. Except when it came to dealing with his children's sin!

Amnon, David's son, raped his sister, Tamar. In her grief, she cried to Absalom, who then went to his father, the king. Severe consequences should have followed, but David wavered. He did nothing.

Absalom, infuriated with his father's indecision, grew bitter. And this bitterness grew until hatred consumed him. He decided to take justice into his own hands.

Do you frustrate your children? Do you practice what you preach, or do you live a life of hypocrisy? We learned the tragic consequences of David's decisions; what will they be for you?

TODAY'S HOT FLASH:

Our faith must not waver, even as we chastise our children. If they see a crack in our veneer, they will split it wide open. Then what? Another Absalom?

PRAYER:

Father, help me stand strong against the sin of my adult children, no matter the cost. Better they hate me for a season than their hearts be lost to me and You forever. Amen.

FOR SANITY'S SAKE

NOVEMBER 25

READ: 2 SAMUEL 14:7-33

HERE WE GO AGAIN

And when he had called for Absalom, he came to the king, and bowed himself on his face to the ground before the king: and the king kissed him.

~ 2 Samuel 14:33

First Amnon gets away with rape (for a season), and now Absalom gets a free pass on murder. He was banished for a while, but that wasn't God's judgment. Death should have been the consequence for his sin. But David couldn't do it!

Murder wasn't going to be the last great sin of Absalom. Consumed by love for his son, David missed the writing on the wall. He couldn't bring himself to believe that his very own son hated him. This was a costly mistake.

Right under David's nose, Absalom stole the kingdom. He began to do the king's work, right at the main gates. Didn't David notice fewer and fewer people were coming to him with their problems? Did he really think he was so great a king that he had solved all the issues of the kingdom? This went on for years, until Absalom's following became so great that he rebelled and took over the kingdom.

What kind of parent are you? Do you know what's going on in your children's lives? Do you hold them accountable for sin? God expects us to do it. If we don't, we will live to regret it.

TODAY'S HOT FLASH:

What's right is right all the time, and God expects us to hold our children accountable!

PRAYER:

Merciful Father, help me to fear for the souls of my children far more than my relationship with them. Help me stand up for what is right, all the time. Amen.

NOVEMBER 26
READ: JOHN 4:14–38

I MISSED THE BOAT!

Behold, I say unto you, Lift up your eyes, and look on the fields; for they are white already to harvest.

~ John 4:35

A new foster boy entered our home about three weeks ago. We've grown apathetic in our reaction to many of them. They're here and gone, almost like they never came. Just today I realize the great travesty in this.

Without much ado, this young man came to me last night and said, "The youth leader was talking to me about Jesus and salvation and that stuff, and he gave me a Bible."

"Oh yeah? Well, that's nice," I said and continued with what I was doing. He quietly scuffled off to his room. About four in the morning, I woke up. I couldn't sleep. Something was bothering me. And then it hit me. Did I totally ignore the fact that this troubled young man accepted the Lord into his life? I couldn't believe it.

When I awakened him for summer school, I questioned him more thoroughly. "Did you tell me that you asked Jesus into your life last night?" I asked.

"Yes," he said. I proceeded to let him know how excited I was and that it was a great thing. But I certainly missed an opportunity to rejoice in the moment when the news was fresh.

TODAY'S HOT FLASH:

What are you missing in your apathetic state? Have you forgotten God works miracles in spite of us?

PRAYER:

Father, I am so ashamed. Have I lost the excitement? Have I lost the reason for living? Revive my heart, O God, and renew a right spirit within me. Amen.

NOVEMBER 27

READ: DANIEL 9:3-16

WHAT ARE YOU HOLDING ON TO?

This evil is come upon us: yet made we not our prayer before the Lord our God, that we might turn from our iniquities, and understand thy truth.

~ Daniel 9:13

Daniel, in desperation, beseeches God on behalf of the Israelites. Confessing the guilt of his people, he is broken-hearted over their rebellion. Time after time, God rains mercy upon their heads and exhibits His miraculous wonders; still they choose to worship self over God.

Even though horrific things continue to happen to the Israelites, in their hard-heartedness, they refuse to comply. Their fleshy desires override God's law.

How much pain must a nation—a city—a company—a church—an individual— have to endure before they fall to their knees and surrender all to the one and only God of all? How much pain do we have to bear before we get it? Some of us learn quickly, others—not so much.

Is God asking you to surrender your life completely to Him? What are you holding on to? Unforgiveness? Anger? Self-sufficiency? Control? Cigarettes? Don't you think it's time to let go and experience the blessed life He has waiting for you?

TODAY'S HOT FLASH:

Fall on your knees and surrender all to the God who wants to lavish you with unspeakable blessings. When you do, you will wonder why you waited so long.

PRAYER:

Father, it's so hard to let go of my fleshly desires. I am afraid I am going to miss out. Help me to understand that what You offer is so much better than good. Amen.

NOVEMBER 28

READ: MARK 7:6–23

INCAPABLE ON MY OWN

There is nothing from without a man, that entering into him can defile him: but the things which come out of him, those are they that defile the man.

~ Mark 7:15

What comes out of your mouth? What actions and thoughts come out of your heart? I have struggled throughout my entire menopausal experience with keeping my mouth shut. I'd pray, "Lord, You said, 'Greater is He that is in me, than He that is in the world' (4 John 1:4). And Lord, You said that if I ask anything in Your name, You will do it, so I am asking." For the few minutes I prayed, everything was great. That is . . . until someone walked into the room, then Whammo! What? Did I just do it again? Right after praying? What gives? Why can't I get this right?

My next reaction is to start blaming God for not giving me the needed power to persevere. It took a while for me to understand. He that is in the world has nothing to do with it. There is enough sin in my flesh that Satan doesn't need to step foot in my house. I am more than capable of screwing things up on my own. This was a "me" problem. It was far deeper than I had ever realized. It is my sin problem—my love problem. My love for self outweighed my love for my Savior. Ouch! There was only one answer—total surrender to the will of the Father. How about you? Have you surrendered all?

TODAY'S HOT FLASH:

Jesus set the example when He resisted temptation to the point of sweating blood. He won the battle. Maybe when we start sweating blood, victory will be ours as well.

PRAYER:

Father, forgive my self-sufficiency. On my own, I can do nothing. Help me to realize my insufficiency so I can depend totally on You. It's hard, Lord; give me the strength. Amen.

NOVEMBER 29

READ: ROMANS 1:12-17

BOLDNESS FOR CHRIST

For I am not ashamed of the gospel of Christ: for it is the power of God unto salvation to every one that believeth; to the Jew first, and also the Greek.

~ Romans 1:16

Recently, I attended a seminar led by Kirk Cameron. Yes, that's him, the kooky, sexy heartthrob Mike Seaver of *Growing Pains*. According to his autobiography, he came to know Jesus at the age of 18, and life as a star changed. Still, I was skeptical; the statistics for lasting Hollywood conversions are not high. The seminar was called "Love Worth Fighting For."

I was impressed. God had changed this teenage icon into a kingdom warrior. Not long after, I read an article where Kirk appeared on a TV show and was asked his views on homosexuality. He could have been vague, said half-truths, and moved on to the next question, but he stood his ground and spoke his convictions. What was my reaction? "You go, Kirk!"

I pray that God gives me an avenue for boldness and that I will not shirk my responsibility as a Christian. I want to step forward and speak boldly like Kirk did without fear. Will you step out and speak the truth, regardless the cost?

TODAY'S HOT FLASH:

When you step forward, make sure your boldness is backed by God's truth, not strongly felt opinions or highly felt expectations.

PRAYER:

Ever-loving Father, make me a bold and outspoken witness for You. May I be found faithful, no matter the cost and no matter the audience. Amen.

NOVEMBER 30
READ: LUKE 1:26-33

LET THE SEASON BEGIN!

The angel went to her and said, "Greetings, you who are highly favored! The Lord is with you."

~ Luke 1:28

Every year on November 29, the Rockefeller Center in New York City puts on a big Christmas tree lighting celebration. Almost from the moment the tree is lit, the hustle and bustle begins. Baking, buying, parties, and programs will consume us for the next twenty-five days. By Christmas Day, we will find ourselves exhausted and sighing in relief that it is finally over.

Mary's pre-Christmas hustle and bustle was nothing like ours. When Gabriel announced God's intentions, her life became an unfamiliar whirlwind of events. But through it all, this very young woman handled it with unbelievable maturity. With the possibility of rejection or even death, Mary rose to the challenge and stayed focused on the outcome.

May I rise to the challenge of keeping Christ in my focus throughout this season, not only in word but in deed as well. It's easy to say, "Jesus is the reason for the season." The hard part is living it when the world is crashing in around you.

TODAY'S HOT FLASH:

Don't fret the small stuff. Jesus IS the reason for the season. Keep focused on Him, and the rest will fall into place.

PRAYER:

Father, it's easy to tell others what to do, but it's hard sometimes to practice what I preach. Keep my eyes and heart on glorifying Your Son this season. Amen.

DECEMBER

DECEMBER 1

READ: JOHN 13:2-12

MODEL THE MASTER

After that he poureth water into a bason, and began to wash the disciples' feet, and to wipe them with the towel wherewith he was girded.

~ John 13:5

We don't have to wake up in the morning and question God's plan for our lives. Scripture is clear about our daily duties. In three self-sufficient words: Model the Master.

Jesus lived among the people as an example to the people because He loved the people. They were, after all, His creation, His workmanship. The Creator lived among His creation and became part of them as an example to them. When the Master took the towel and basin and began to wash His disciples' feet, they were dumbfounded. Peter could barely stand it and at first refused to allow it. But when Jesus said, "If I wash thee not, thou hast no part with me," Peter replied, "Lord, not my feet only, but also my hands and my head."

The Master became the servant. To be like Him is to serve as He served. This holiday season is the perfect time to begin. Find someone you can serve and get busy.

TODAY'S HOT FLASH:

Peter had to let go of his pride and humble himself before he could serve. How about you? Do you have to let a little pride go yourself?

PRAYER:

Father, forgive the high and mighty attitude I have at times. May I model the Master in every way, every day, for Your glory alone. Amen.

DECEMBER 2
READ: 1 JOHN 5:1–8

I DID IT!

For whatsoever is born of God overcometh the world: and this is the victory that overcometh the world, even our faith.

~ 1 John 5:4

If you have read this devotional for some time, you may have noticed that I struggle with this little thing called self-control. You'd think by now I'd be an expert on the subject. Not!

I do have days when victory meets me in the bedroom, and I can look back on the day and realize—I did it! Unfortunately, it is in my realization of "I" that my wall crumbles, and failure is just around the corner.

Victorious living is not based on what "I" can do. If it is, it will be short-lived. On my own I am impulsive, uncontrolled, self-sufficient, and proud. "I did it!" "Look at me!" Wham! I have set myself up for failure, and it is devastating.

It is only in the absolute strength of Jesus that I can accomplish anything. When self-sufficiency prevails, discouragement and failure are always around the bend.

It's been a hard lesson, but slowly I am learning that without God's direction, strength, and unfailing grace steering me, prodding me, guiding me, I will fall flat on my face. You'd think after tripping up so much, I'd learn the lesson once and for all.

TODAY'S HOT FLASH:

Pride and self-sufficiency are a universal problem. It isn't until God breaks this destructive cycle of selfishness that we can truly begin to follow the Lord in blind faith.

PRAYER:

You alone give me the needed strength to persevere. Oh, Lord, help me never to forget this truth and to remember to draw all my strength from You. Then victory will come. Amen.

DECEMBER 3

READ: EPHESIANS 4:1-3

WHAT IS YOUR WORK?

I therefore, the prisoner of the Lord, beseech you that ye walk worthy of the vocation wherewith ye are called.

~ Ephesians 4:1

Everyone has work to do. Society views some jobs as more important than others and some people of more worth. But that is not God's view.

It doesn't matter if you pump gas at the local "Gas-N-Go," are the CEO of a large corporation, deliver newspapers, stay at home with your children, babysit, telemarket, deliver pizza, sing in the opera, serve in the armed forces, scrub toilets, or volunteer. Your work is important! Whether the whole world recognizes you or only a few individuals, what you do is important, and God has a purpose for your life.

Often our roles change through our golden years. Life changes and so must we. As our parents age, we are faced with a reversal of roles. Grandchildren often need a stabling force in their lives, and the elderly may just need a friend who cares. How are you doing in these roles?

These are the greatest of opportunities to let Jesus' light shine through you. They are also more important than any six-figure income. Are you doing what God has called you to do?

What's stopping you?

TODAY'S HOT FLASH:

Are you lacking joy and fulfillment in your life? Then get busy loving someone who desperately needs you, family or not.

PRAYER:

Father, show me where I am needed today. Let Your light shine through me for all the world to see. Then I know fulfillment and joy will be mine. Amen.

DECEMBER 4
READ: EPHESIANS 1:1–6

WORTHINESS IN CHRIST

For to me to live is Christ, and to die is gain.

~ Philippians 1:21

In a culture that defies everything Christ teaches, how do we find our worthiness in Him alone while blocking out the world's views? There's nothing harder than being in the world but not of it. Let me help you.

1. Although working and making money is important to survive, we must always remember that God provides for His children. David said, "Yet have I not seen the righteous forsaken, nor his seed begging bread" (Psalm 37:25).

2. You are God's workmanship. He will not stop fashioning you until you reach His ultimate goal (Ephesians 2:10).

3. God loved you so much that He sent His Son to die for you (John 3:16).

4. God finds His pleasure in you (Ephesians 1:5).

5. The only expectations you have to meet are God's (Matthew 6:33).

When you feel pressured to cave in to the world's way of thinking, remember these timeless truths and your perspective will fall into place. God only, ever, and always! Relinquish control of your life to Him, and He will take care of the rest.

TODAY'S HOT FLASH:

Nothing you ever say or do can thwart God's ultimate plan for you. Give Him the reins of your life; then sit back and bask in His calm, ever-present security.

PRAYER:

Father, help me to remember that You have everything under control. I don't and can't fix things; only You can. I gladly hand over my life to You. I trust You, Lord. Amen.

FOR SANITY'S SAKE

DECEMBER 5

READ: MARK 9:14-29

A CAN-DO CHRISTIAN

Jesus said unto him, If thou canst believe, all things are possible to him that believeth.

~ Mark 9:23

What misery, agony, and turmoil this family in our Bible passage must have suffered. Ever since their son was a young child, demons plagued him. They tore at his body and threw him in fires and deep waters. It was the true definition of today's horror flick, with a villain, a foaming mouth, and everything else terrifyingly imaginable. But this was no flick; it was reality.

In desperation, the father cried for help and hope. Jesus' reply? "If you can believe—all things are possible to him that believes."

That is the greatness of Christianity—the beauty of Christ—the hope that only those who follow Jesus possess. We have the ability to persevere in every circumstance. His power alone will see us through. We don't have to wallow in defeat, our negative emotions, or our hormonal surges. HE makes it possible to be godly in spite of what we are going through.

God didn't present us with a can't-do, no good, impossible, not good enough scenario. With Him we become can-do Christians. That is His promise to us. "If you truly believe—all things are possible."

TODAY'S HOT FLASH:

In God's can-do world, nothing should ever drag you into the depths of despair. For there is nothing God cannot do.

PRAYER:

O Father, I know I can't make it through this on my own. I will believe that You can do the impossible. And that impossibility is to keep me godly in spite of myself. Amen.

DECEMBER 6
READ: MATTHEW 8:28-34

GOD FIRST . . . ALWAYS!

The whole city came out to meet Jesus: and when they saw him, they besought him that he would depart out of their coasts.

~ Matthew 8:34

Two men possessed of devils cried out to Jesus, "What have we to do with thee, Jesus, thou son of God?" Jesus, with undisputable authority, freed the poor souls. And those pesky demons? He sent them into a herd of swine. Those pigs, not knowing what "got into them," went bonkers and ran off a cliff into the sea below.

Where was the praise for rescuing these possessed men from their ill-fated life? The people were so self-focused they couldn't see the miracle for their own greed-stricken view. No swine, no money! No one cared about the two lives saved.

How many times have we rejected our Lord over possible financial or personal gain?

As women already suffering from fluctuating emotions, help comes in decisiveness and predetermined commitment. Make the right decisions during the sane times. Then when hormones flare, God will remain at the top of our list.

TODAY'S HOT FLASH:

God first . . . always! Take care of His business and He will take care of yours.

PRAYER:

Father, great Giver of gifts, help me to choose the right thing even when my emotions say otherwise. Help me to honor You. I know You will take care of the rest. Amen.

DECEMBER 7

READ: MATTHEW 8:22–26

O YE OF LITTLE FAITH

And he saith unto them, Why are ye fearful, O ye of little faith? Then he arose, and rebuked the winds and the sea; and there was a great calm.

~ Matthew 8:26

How are you today? Did you wake up this morning? Did you eat a good breakfast? Get dressed? Was your cable working, your lights on? Did any of your worries of yesterday change a thing for today?

As women of faith, we need to cling to every blessing set before us by our great Creator. What is it that causes you to fret? What puts you in panic mode? Unpaid bills? Calls from collection agencies? Wayward children? Sickness or disease? An unexpected tragedy? A storm or weather report? The upcoming visit of your mother-in-law? For some of us, it doesn't take much to magnify our insecurities.

Jesus' words to His disciples ring true for us today. "Why are you fearful, O ye of little faith? Don't you know what manner of man this is that even the winds and the sea obey Him? Be still and know that He is God!"

This same Jesus that spoke the world into existence has your life nestled in the palm of His hands. He cares, He sees, He knows. Stand back and let Him be God! He will never fail you.

TODAY'S HOT FLASH:

The more we know we need God, the more our desire to draw near to Him and trust Him in our time of trouble.

PRAYER:

Jesus, my Deliverer, I can't always see answers and the way out of bad situations, but I know You are with me and You will never leave me or forsake me. I'm trusting You! Amen.

DECEMBER 8
READ: MARK 4:35-41

PEACE, BE STILL

And he arose and rebuked the wind, and said unto the sea, Peace, be still. And the wind ceased, and there was a great calm.

~ Mark 4:39

The storm battered the ship, tossing it to and fro. Would it sink? Would it topple? Was the fierceness of the wind too great a burden? The disciples thought it was, and fear overwhelmed them. Trembling and frightened, they scurried to their sleeping, unworried Master. He realized their fear and with calm assurance said, "Peace, be still."

Maybe you or someone you love has been diagnosed with a terminal disease. Fear overrides any semblance of rationality. Then you hear that still, small voice; "Peace, be still."

Maybe your children have turned their back on you and all you believe in, thumbing their noses at your precious Savior. Your heart is broken, and you cry out to the Lord. His reply? "Peace, be still."

Does your husband want a divorce? Are bill collectors knocking on your door? Do you face eviction, homelessness, disease, loneliness? "Peace, be still." "Peace, be still." "Peace, be still."

TODAY'S HOT FLASH:

What happened when Jesus spoke these spectacular, life-changing words? The wind ceased, and there was a great calm. He will do the same for you.

PRAYER:

Oh Father, my heart breaks for the sadness and pain in my loved ones' lives. Say Your words over their lives, Lord, "Peace, be still," and give them that miraculous calm. Amen.

DECEMBER 9

READ: MARK 9:42-50

DO YOU TAKE JESUS SERIOUSLY?

And if thy hand offend thee, cut it off: it is better for thee to enter into life maimed, than having two hands to go into hell, into the fire that never shall be quenched.

~ Mark 9:43

Statistically, more people believe in heaven than in hell. But God is blunt and descriptive and leaves no doubt in His Word of its existence. Hell is an agonizing, everlasting burning furnace created for Satan and his demons. There is no relief in hell. It is a torture chamber that lasts forever and ever; the pain exists, yet the body is never destroyed.

If you wind up in hell, you will replay your life over and over. It will be exceptionally hard because you called yourself Christian. Maybe you lived the life, but your heart remained defiant and unchanged. You will wonder how you fooled yourself into believing you were saved and safe when you never gained victory over the sin that so easily beset you.

You will wonder why you berated and chided those fanatics who hounded you about changing your life. Who warned you about your bitter heart and unforgiving spirit, who prayed endlessly for your mean tongue to exhibit fruit of the Spirit.

If there is no change on the inside, and no victory in your life, don't you think it's time to take Jesus seriously? We are coming down the other side of this mountain. Don't wait too long. Surrender all now!

TODAY'S HOT FLASH:

There are no second chances after death. Don't fool yourself into hell.

PRAYER:

Lord, I know at times I am just playing the part and just saying the words. Help me to fully surrender myself in all areas of my life. I want to make You Lord over all my life. Amen.

DECEMBER 10
READ: EPHESIANS 1:1–7

MERCY AND GRACE

To the praise of the glory of his grace, wherein he hath made us accepted in the beloved.

~ Ephesians 1:6

Mercy: God withholding from us what we deserve.

Grace: God giving us what we don't deserve.

Dr. Jeremiah gave these definitions of mercy and grace during one of his radio broadcasts. The simplicity yet the profoundness of it amazes me. "The wages of sin is death." I should be dead. You should be dead. My children, parents, and friends should all be dead—physically and spiritually. Yet we live! Why? Because of the five-letter word *grace*. God giving to me what I absolutely, positively do not deserve.

What did He give me? Eternal life through His Son! This is amazing grace. What did He withhold from me? Eternal damnation and punishment for my sin. This is His undeniable mercy.

Each and every day, when I am faced with my sin once again, I thank God for His precious gift of mercy, and I praise Him for His amazing grace.

When life seems nothing more than a hollow fallen log, empty and useless, I am reminded of God's grace, and I can once again live, love, and laugh.

TODAY'S HOT FLASH:

Without God's grace and mercy, all seems hopeless. With it, life thrives, hope prevails, and peace and joy are a natural state of being.

PRAYER:

Caring Father, thank You for the mercy and grace You have given me. I know I don't deserve it, but gratitude consumes me because You gave it to me anyway. Amen.

DECEMBER 11

READ: PROVERBS 15:25-33

THE UNIMPORTANCE OF MY OPINIONS

The fear of the Lord is the instruction of wisdom; and before honour is humility.

~ Proverbs 15:33

When my hormones are raging, I often shoot off my mouth before thinking. I shout, scream, stomp, and argue my opinion, even when I know I am wrong, because my attitude will not allow me to back down. Something seems to shut my mouth, though, when a known authority on the subject arrives. Humbled and embarrassed, I know I cannot win this knowledgeable person by my aggressive argument. He is an expert. I refuse to argue with him, because deep down I know I was just being cantankerous and ornery. I was exalting myself no matter the cost.

The disciples walked with Jesus, and still they argued over which one of them would be the greatest. God Almighty was walking with them, and they were arguing over such frivolities? Is it just me, or do you too find it unbelievable that these "Christ followers" would argue such nonsense in the presence of a holy God?

Isn't that what we do? We voice our opinions loudly, argue our case, allowing our self-importance to swell up inside of us while forgetting one important fact: we are in the presence of the Master.

TODAY'S HOT FLASH:

How great can we fathom ourselves when measured against a holy God? The disciples needed humbling, and shamefully, sometimes I do too.

PRAYER:

Father, forgive my presumptuous attitude and self-righteous opinions. Help me to throw my opinions to the wind and stand alone on Your Word. Amen.

DECEMBER 12
READ: 2 SAMUEL 4:9-12

WHY TELL?

How much more, when wicked men have slain a righteous person in his own house upon his bed?

~ 2 Samuel 4:11

Have you ever done anything bad for a good reason, justifying it in your own mind as a necessary action? For instance, telling Joe's wife you saw him kiss the waitress at Sid's Café? Instead of taking the righteous approach (according to Matthew 18:15: go and tell your brother his fault), you intuitively rush to warn the perceived injured party. What was your motive for telling? In the process of your justifiable act, you shatter a heart, possibly misinterpret a situation, and place a marriage in jeopardy. In your high and mighty self-righteousness, you can't see the damage done.

Rechab and Baahah ambushed Saul's son while he lay in bed and killed him (see Scripture reading). They cut off his head and with prideful hearts delivered it to David, expecting praise and recognition.

That praise never came. David was furious. Instead of their desired reward, they died. Not only did David kill them, but he also hung their bodies over a pool in Hebron, their final humiliation and a warning for everyone else.

It is never okay to step outside of God's standard for any reason. When you do, it is always harmful, damaging, and unnecessary. Let God do His job and keep your nose out of it.

TODAY'S HOT FLASH:

Whenever we begin to take matters into our own hands or give information that is not ours to give, we commit sin. I am not God, and neither are you.

PRAYER:

Father, forgive me when I try to take circumstances into my own hands. Forgive me when I have played God in the past. Help me never to do it again. Amen.

DECEMBER 13

READ: MARK 6:45–56

DON'T LET HIM PASS BY!

And he went up unto them into the ship; and the wind ceased: and they were sore amazed in themselves beyond measure, and wondered.

~ Mark 6:51

Wow! In the midst of the storm, struggling to survive, they (the disciples) look into the dark sea, and behold! Jesus was walking on the water. Scripture says He "would have passed by them." I never really saw that statement before. I always assumed He was walking to them, but He wasn't.

In the midst of their crisis, Jesus presented Himself to them. He was the answer to their desperate situation, but they had to call out to Him, lest He pass them by. In their fear, they cried out to Him. Seeing, but not quite believing. Immediately, Jesus came to the rescue! Immediately, Jesus acknowledged their cry of distress. Immediately, He answered them. "Be of good cheer: it is I; be not afraid!" (Mark 6:50b).

I don't know all the storms that weigh you down and threaten to sink your boat, but be assured, Jesus is walking beside you, just waiting for you to cry out in your distress. He will immediately come to your rescue. He will immediately answer you. His words to you are no different. "Be of good cheer; it is I, be not afraid."

TODAY'S HOT FLASH:

Don't let Him walk on by. Jesus is presenting Himself to you right now! Call out to Him. He is waiting for His invitation to enter into your circumstance.

PRAYER:

Wonderful Father, I can't carry these burdens alone, and my hormones make them even harder. Come to me. Calm my soul. And help me to "be not afraid." Amen.

DECEMBER 14
READ: MARK 6:32-34

THE GREAT SHEPHERD

And Jesus, when he came out, saw much people, and was moved with compassion toward them, because they were as sheep not having a shepherd.

~ Mark 6:34

Do you ever feel like a sheep without a shepherd? Sometimes even a lamb without its mother, helpless, hopeless, without a clue? Your mind is distracted or befuddled to a point of uselessness. I have experienced this often over the past few years. Along with the anxiety derived from these feelings comes discouragement and frustration.

Praise God for the Great Shepherd whose expertise is leading hopelessly lost souls to Him. His compassion exceeds all human experience. His leadership soars higher than any living being. His mercy is unfailing, unending, and undeniable. His love is of greater depth than the deepest seas.

On the days when you feel shepherdless, stop fretting and forcing yourself to be okay when you are not. Cling to the Shepherd's staff for a while. Relax and let His compassion fall freely over you. Realize He just wants to love you with a love beyond our understanding.

The only expectations you're not meeting are your own. God would rather you rest in Him until the stormy weather of your mind passes.

TODAY'S HOT FLASH:

When your mind is incapable of rational thought, befuddled and exhausted, and you can't think one sane thought, think only one word—Jesus!

PRAYER:

Lord, there are so many days I can't seem to think straight. Help me to think of only Jesus until He alone saturates my mind. Amen.

DECEMBER 15

READ: 2 SAMUEL 4:5-8

WHAT'S SNEAKING UP ON YOU?

... who lay on a bed at noon.

~ 2 Samuel 4:5b

I always knew lounging in bed all day could be disastrous. I have this inner clock that refuses to let me stay in bed too long in the morning. If someone comes or calls while I am still in bed, I feel lazy and useless. I just can't do it.

Life is too short to waste time lounging in the middle of the day (there are reasons and exceptions, of course), but 2 Samuel 4:5-8 proves my point. Why do you think it was even mentioned that he lay in bed at noon? It's an add-on to the sentence: and, oh yeah, did I mention he was in bed at noon?

Had he been up, going about his business, doing the work that needed to be done, he would have been alert and vigilant. The evildoers probably would have failed in their assassination attempt.

We can learn a lot from this story. Sleep is good and necessary, but for everything there is a time and a place. Sometimes, when raging hormones invade our sanity, it seems better to escape to solitude, sometimes sleep. But this is not usually the answer. It is time to get about your business, hormonal or not, and do what needs doing in spite of how you feel.

TODAY'S HOT FLASH:

Be alert and vigilant, lest the evils of this world sneak up on you and lay their trap.

PRAYER:

Oh Lord, forgive my laziness and help me to stay alert and be vigilant every moment of every day. Prick my spirit when I need to be reminded. Amen.

DECEMBER 16
READ: MARK 6:32-44

DO YOU "SEND THEM AWAY"?

Send them away, that they may go into the country round about, and into the villages, and buy themselves bread: for they have nothing to eat.

~ Mark 6:36

The disciples didn't see it; they hadn't experienced the desert place of loneliness yet. Nearsighted and narrowly focused, they suggested an unfathomable action for Jesus to take. "Send them away," they told Him. Can you imagine? In their humanity, they counseled Jesus (which I advise you never to do). As needy as these people were, the disciples only saw their own interests. They were tired, hungry, and unwilling to share their measly tidbits, so they wanted relief—from the responsibilities of the people.

Jesus saw in His chosen few that very same neediness. His very character would not allow Him to send them away. His mercy would not allow them to go hungry. His unfathomable compassion refused to take the easy way out. His reply? "Give ye them to eat." They were once again confronted with their minuscule measure of faith.

Send them away? It was and is an impossibility. They needed Him, and He would not let them down, nor will He fail you.

You need Him, I need Him, and when we seek Him, He can always be found. Whom have you sent away in your desire to be left alone or in your weariness and eagerness to rest?

TODAY'S HOT FLASH:

It is always easier to turn our back on the needy. They take time, effort, and compassion. If Christ-likeness is our goal, we must replace our desires with their needs.

PRAYER:

Oh Father, I have let You down so many times. I've turned my back on others in need because their need was inconvenient for me. Let it never be so again. Forgive me. Amen.

DECEMBER 17

READ: 1 JOHN 5:9-19

UNANSWERED PRAYERS

And this is the confidence that we have in him, that, if we ask anything according to his will, he heareth us.

~ 1 John 5:14

Andrew Murray once said, "Prayer has power according to the life. A life in line with God's will can ask according to God's will."

Many people become disillusioned with God because of unanswered prayer. They don't realize that there are conditions to be met. If He is to answer our prayers, we must first obey His Word. 1 John 5:3 says, "For this is the love of God, that we keep his commandments." Answered prayer is dependent on the life we live. If there is no obedience, there will be no answered prayer.

For the person living in rebellion, God only desires one prayer and that is the prayer of repentance. Psalm 66:18 says, "If I regard iniquity in my heart, the Lord will not hear me."

Scripture promises answered prayer when we meet the requirements of the "ifs" and when we ask according to His will. We know God's will through His Word and through our personal relationship with Him. If we are not living the life, we will not experience the power of prayer.

TODAY'S HOT FLASH:

Why do we expect things from God when we refuse to give what He expects from us?

PRAYER:

Father, thank You for Your blessings of answered prayer. Keep my heart in tune with You, that my prayers may not be hindered. Amen.

DECEMBER 18
READ: JAMES 2:21-26

GOD IS NOT SANTA CLAUS

Abraham believed God, and it was imputed unto him for righteousness: and he was called the Friend of God.

~ James 2:23

Abraham lied and told the king that Sarah was his sister. He also took matters into his own hands and bore a son through Hagar. At times he acted out of fear, and other times from impatience, but in the end, "he believed God." In spite of his failures and moments of weakness, he believed God would do what He said, and God honored his belief.

David was not the greatest father; he was egotistical at times and often made bad decisions. He committed adultery with Bathsheba, sealing the fate of their firstborn son. Still, God described David as a "man after His own heart" and honored him for his belief.

Sometimes we feel we've done too much bad for God to love us. We can't let go of our sin. God is not Santa Claus. He is not making a list and checking it twice. He doesn't judge according to whether we were naughty or nice. "Abraham believed God, and it was imputed [credited] unto him for righteousness: and he was called the Friend of God." Are you a friend of God? Do you believe He will do what He says?

TODAY'S HOT FLASH:

David and Abraham failed many times, but eventually, they learned obedience and trust. They were works in progress, and so are you.

PRAYER:

Father, I desire to be a woman after Your own heart and to be considered Your friend. Teach me Your ways, that I may honor You in all that I do. Amen.

DECEMBER 19
READ: LUKE 17:11-19

THE ART OF RECEIVING GIFTS

And Jesus answering said, Were there not ten cleansed? but where are the nine?

~ Luke 17:17

While passing through Samaria, Jesus encountered ten lepers. "They lifted up their voices, and said, Jesus, Master, have mercy on us." Jesus heard their cries and instructed them to show themselves to the priest, and they were immediately cleansed.

They were outcasts, set apart from family and friends with no hope of change. Then Jesus comes, and everything changes. Amazingly, only one returns to Jesus. Only one is so full of gratitude that he must return to the healer and offer praises of thanksgiving. The remaining nine were not gracious in the acceptance of their gift.

Gracious gift receiving is an art form many of us have not learned. Children are notorious for their lack of gratitude. I've also seen many adults plop their gifts down, unimpressed and without a word of gratitude. What a slap in the face to the givers.

The nine lepers received a most precious gift and couldn't be bothered to thank the Giver. The only one who returned received a final blessing. "Arise, go thy way: thy faith hath made thee whole."

TODAY'S HOT FLASH:

Do you excel in the art of gift receiving? Graciously accepting that which is given you, regardless of the gift? There are blessings in receiving as well as giving.

PRAYER:

Lord, make me a gracious gift receiver. After all, if they care enough to give, I must care enough to receive graciously, regardless of the gift. Amen.

DECEMBER 20
READ: JAMES 5:12–17

FESS UP!

Confess your faults one to another, and pray one for another, that ye may be healed. The effectual fervent prayer of a righteous man availeth much.

~ James 5:16

I teach the ladies in my group how to handle stress. I convince them that they have the greatest power in the universe to stave off momentary lapses and stress-filled anxiety. I spout, "Jesus is the reason for the season," but then I become so embroiled in the season that I barely have time to honor the One it's all about.

I am here to confess my faults to you, in hopes that it brings healing and renewed commitment. This has not been a good week; temper tantrums, depression, exhaustion, and self-pity have consumed me. My mind whirls with all the things I should do, desperately seeking to choose which is the most important. I should bake cookies, clean house, put my Sunday school lesson together, and comb my hair.

I did it again, didn't I? God is missing from my list; it is time to pick up my Bible and bask in my Savior. Maybe after a little time with the most necessary of all, I'll gain perspective and everything will fall back into place.

TODAY'S HOT FLASH:

How about you? Do you need to stop everything and start listening to Jesus? Only in Him can we remain focused on Him during this season for Him.

PRAYER:

Father, I've not been very good this week. Nothing is going right, and my attitude stinks. Forgive my neglect of You. Keep me focused for today. Amen.

DECEMBER 21

READ: JOHN 3:11-21

GROWN-UP CHRISTMAS LIST

For God so loved the world, that he gave his only begotten Son, that whosoever believeth in him should not perish, but have everlasting life.

~ John 3:16

"What do you want for Christmas?" I've been asked this a hundred times. Sure, there are material things I wouldn't mind having. But while my Christmas list truly is unconventional and most likely unattainable, still I can dream—and hope. After all, isn't that what Christmas is all about—hope?

If I could have anything I wanted this Christmas, I would pass out hope to the hopeless: the homeless, the sick, the weary, and the grief-stricken. I would lavish on them these most wonderful words: "Fear not: for, behold, I bring you good tidings of great joy, which shall be to all people" (Luke 2:10). These words don't apply to only a few; they apply to ALL people. In every station of life, in every corner of the world, wherever people are found, the hope of Jesus rings true.

Hope opens the door for healing and a renewed vigor for life. This is my grown-up Christmas wish. What's yours?

TODAY'S HOT FLASH:

What is your grown-up Christmas wish? Is it selfishly motivated or divinely inspired? Seek and you shall find a way to offer hope to the hopeless this Christmas.

PRAYER:

Father, sometimes I can be very selfish. Bring me to the hopeless souls that need to see the love of Jesus this Christmas. May I not only see, but act as well. Amen.

DECEMBER 22
READ: PROVERBS 17:1-8

THE MOST LOVED RECEIVES THE MOST GIFTS

A gift is a precious stone in the eyes of him that hath it: whithersoever it turneth, it prospereth.

~ Proverbs 17:8

I've denied it with every breath, but it's true, I am afraid. My husband spoils me. All month long he has bombarded me with early Christmas gifts. First, he bought me a new Crockpot, then a digital camera. If that wasn't enough, I received a package in the mail with the very Christmas dress I had admired in a catalog. It didn't stop there; the other day he came home with the Susan Boyle Christmas CD I wanted, and yesterday he bought me the Elvis CD I asked for as well. I'd be content if I never received another gift, but I know on Christmas Day I will discover more gifts under the tree.

My husband's gift giving is visible proof that he loves me. Do I need these material reminders? No, but it sure does make it easier to believe.

How much do we give to the greatest gift-giver of all time? If giving gifts is proof of our love for someone, doesn't it stand to reason that if we love our Lord more than anything or anyone, He will receive the bulk of our giving?

TODAY'S HOT FLASH:

Is God's gift pile small or large in comparison to everyone else's? Have you honored the Birthday Boy first or set Him aside to receive the leftovers?

PRAYER:

Father, help me to focus on the One whose birthday we celebrate. It's all about Jesus. May I never forget that. Amen.

DECEMBER 23

READ: MATTHEW 1:18-25

GIMME, GIMME, GIMME

She will give birth to a son, and you are to give him the name Jesus, because he will save his people from their sins.

~ Matthew 1:21

I love giving gifts, but I must admit that I love getting them every bit as much. Sometimes I am guilty of the dreaded "gimme disease." Even more so now that menopause has kicked in. I struggle with the "it's all about me" attitude.

My mental list grows long as the sales catalogs start arriving in the mail. I conspicuously place them around the house, hoping someone will catch the hint.

It is when I am in the "gimme" mood that I need to be reminded of Jesus. I need to be reminded that He is the most precious gift ever given to this undeserving world—more personally, to undeserving me. Just as wonderful is the wonderful truth that no matter how horrible I become, He never withdraws His precious gift. He loves me that much!

This Christmas, instead of contemplating what I can get, I will ponder on what I have already been given: absolute forgiveness.

TODAY'S HOT FLASH:

What can I possibly give that compares to God's gift of His Son? Absolutely nothing! But I am going to try with every fiber of my being anyway.

PRAYER:

More-than-wonderful Father, You gave up Your only Son—for me—and I didn't deserve it. I want to give back to you because of what you gave to me. Amen.

DECEMBER 24

READ: MATTHEW 5:1-12

BLESSED ARE THEY THAT MOURN

Blessed are they that mourn: for they shall be comforted.
~ Matthew 5:4

It started weeks ago. As if on cue, with the beginning of Halloween and the onset of the holiday season, old personalities began surfacing in my children. What we've worked two years to "fix" is suddenly broken again. Temper tantrums and misbehavior at school are again a daily occurrence. I realize now that it will probably recur for many years to come. They can't control it; they can't even understand it. They only know that the life they once knew is gone; they have experienced the ultimate rejection, and that is hard to recover from.

For many, the rejection and abuse experienced in their youth continue to haunt them. They hide it most of the time, but with the onset of the holiday season, something clicks and the pain and hurt resurface. Suicides rise, mental hospitals fill, and bars are jam-packed. Hurting people doing whatever it takes to shut off the leaky faucet of painful memories.

We can help. Jesus said, "Blessed are they that mourn: for they shall be comforted." Comforted by whom? By those of us who have overcome because of one little Baby who entered this world to offer hope.

TODAY'S HOT FLASH:

God's love is a bottomless well of refreshing water. Share it generously. It will never run dry.

PRAYER:

Loving Father, I've been there. I've experienced the pain of loneliness and hurt. Help me to reach out and comfort those who mourn as I have been comforted. Amen.

DECEMBER 25
READ: JAMES 1:13-21

THE GREATEST GIFT OF ALL

Every good gift and every perfect gift is from above, and cometh down from the Father of lights, with whom is no variableness, neither shadow of turning.

~ James 1:17

I love receiving well-thought-out gifts. When someone takes time to hunt for the perfect present, I feel loved. They could pick up the nearest pair of fuzzy socks or buy a five-dollar bottle of perfume, but instead they search out and settle for nothing less than the "just right" gift.

When I was younger, I only cared that everyone received a gift. Now that I am, well, not so young, I realize the significance of a wonderful gift given. I begin thinking about who gets what months ahead of time with the intent of giving every person on my list the perfect gift.

No matter how hard I try, I can never outgive the Father of lights. More than 2,000 years ago, in a little town called Bethlehem, His perfect gift arrived in the form of a tiny Baby wrapped in swaddling clothes, lying in a manger. That perfect gift represented love, peace, forgiveness, redemption, hope, and eternal life. The amazing part is—it's a gift that keeps on giving and will continue to do so for eternity.

TODAY'S HOT FLASH:

What great love the Father must have for His children to relinquish His only Son to an ungrateful world. Jesus was and always will be the greatest gift ever given.

PRAYER:

Father, my gifts can never match Your most precious gift. May I pass on the greatest gift of all this Christmas season—Jesus! Amen.

DECEMBER 26
READ: 1 KINGS 3:4-14

IF YOU COULD HAVE ONE WISH

In Gibeon the Lord appeared to Solomon in a dream by night: and God said, Ask what I shall give thee.

~ 1 Kings 3:5

If you had one wish, what would it be? Would you wish for world peace? For unity among the countries, ensuring the return of our sons and daughters? Would you wish to be the richest person in the world? Oh, what you could do with all that money. Give to the poor, meet all the needs of your church, travel, live in a mansion (I'd prefer a castle of extreme proportions). Would you choose fame over fortune?

God, the Creator of the universe, the owner of everything that exists, the Deliverer, the Great I Am, granted Solomon one wish. And Solomon came through with flying colors. He didn't ask to be conqueror of all nations; he didn't desire all the treasures of the world; he desired wisdom, and his humble request pleased the Almighty.

Wisdom is the ability to discern what is true and right, and to know exactly what to do with that knowledge. Godly wisdom is to know what the Lord desires and live in obedience to it. Of all he could have asked for, this seems to be the wisest choice of all.

TODAY'S HOT FLASH:

Given the choice, would you choose a characteristic or something tangible? Would you choose what best suits you or what best suits your role in God's kingdom?

PRAYER:

Lord, teach me to make wise decisions. Help me to make the choices that best serve Your interests, not mine. It is You alone I want to please. Amen.

DECEMBER 27

READ: MARK 6:32-44

JESUS HAPPENED!

And they did all eat, and were filled.

~ Mark 6:42

When Jesus sets out to accomplish something, He does it completely, fully, and with no loose ends. He cannot make mistakes; He cannot fail. The multitude was hungry. The disciples had five loaves of bread and two fish when they began lunch; still, more than 5,000 were fed. They all ate and were filled, every single man, woman, and child.

You may feel like you're less than a person, useless and unneeded. Menopause has robbed you of the little bit of control you used to have. The girlish figure you cherished and the ability to have children have evaporated. What's left?

My friend, hold on tight; just as the disciples felt the situation was hopeless—Jesus happened! They worried and fretted for a time—then Jesus!

You are experiencing this time of confusion and questioning, the "what now's" of your future, but God is molding you into His great workmanship, unimaginable to the human mind.

The people ate and were filled! Sister, Jesus will fill you completely with worthiness and purpose. You are destined to do great things for His kingdom. Menopause happened—then Jesus!

TODAY'S HOT FLASH:

When Jesus happens, life gets exciting! Your only requirement? Open your heart, mind, and availability to the One who wants to use you to do great things.

PRAYER:

Oh, Father, I feel useless and unworthy. I worry about what's next in my life. Help me to totally trust and believe that You are going to make it far greater than it was before. Amen.

DECEMBER 28
READ: HOSEA 2:14-23

THEN CAME JESUS

Therefore, behold, I will allure her, and bring her into the wilderness, and speak comfortably unto her.

~ Hosea 2:14

There was a time in my life when I had lost all hope. I grew up knowing the truth, but I walked away from it. During those wilderness years, I experienced defeat in many ways: a bad marriage, single motherhood, babysitter struggles, lack of finances, and so much more.

Then came my "savior," a man who seemed to have his act together. He swooshed me off my feet. But my wilderness experience didn't end there. My guilt and hurt of the past boiled within until it exploded, almost destroying my marriage.

For more than thirty years, I struggled with my self-worth, looks, and baggage from the past. THEN CAME JESUS! I thought I knew Him; after all, I am a pastor's wife, a Sunday school teacher, and a music director. I was wrong. I didn't have a clue.

It's hard to explain, but when Jesus truly touches your life, you realize how untouched you'd been in the past. I also thought I was a new creature in Christ until I truly experienced HIM! It was then that I saw myself for who I really was—a wretched sinner, unworthy and inexcusable. My wilderness experience turned to restoration. My wilderness blossomed into a vineyard exploding with life. My guilt, into a joyous song. Thank you, Jesus!

TODAY'S HOT FLASH:

Only Jesus can turn a wilderness into a blossoming vineyard. Have you ever experienced true redemption? It is a feeling like no other, and it changes your life forever.

PRAYER:

Oh, Father, I cannot thank You enough for what You have done in my life. I truly am a new creature, and my life is bursting with Your grace and mercy in every area. Amen.

DECEMBER 29

READ: PHILIPPIANS 4:1-7

THE SINCERITY OF WORDS

Therefore, my brethren dearly beloved and longed for, my joy and crown, so stand fast in the Lord, my dearly beloved.

~ Philippians 4:1

Paul was bold and unbending in his confrontations, but he also cared deeply for his fellow saints. That is why, when hard words were necessary, people listened. His letters are prime examples of his extraordinary use of words. Endearments such as "dearly beloved and longed for" and "my joy and crown" leave no doubt as to his feelings toward the recipients. He watched over his converts with passionate zeal. When they failed or chose to walk away, he reacted immediately. Through his letters, he pursued them, challenged them, and warned them of upcoming judgment.

How much do you love your fellow saints? Do your words display your love? Do you remind them, challenge them, and warn them when they falter?

We are our brothers' (and sisters') keeper. Paul looked after the saints entrusted to his care. We are to do the same. Words of sincerity are needed as we minister to those within our reach. Speak the truth in love as you meet the needs around you.

TODAY'S HOT FLASH:

Words are important. What we say. How we say it. Every word matters. Use your words wisely to encourage, provoke, and challenge others to righteousness.

PRAYER:

Gracious Father, take my words and use them for Your glory. May they truly be acceptable in Your sight. Use them to lift up and encourage fellow saints. Amen.

DECEMBER 30
READ: ECCLESIASTES 6

THE FUTILITY OF RESOLUTIONS

For who knoweth what is good for man in this life, all the days of his vain life which he spendeth as a shadow? for who can tell a man what shall be after him under the sun?

~ Ecclesiastes 6:12

All my life I've struggled with guilt because of unfinished lists and failed resolutions. One would think I'd learn and stop the damaging cycle, but no, every year I'd start all over again—until now, that is. I don't know what has changed, but I assume it is the wisdom and limitations age brings. Finally, after many years of failure, it doesn't matter anymore.

It used to be that I'd set a weight-loss goal every year; now if I keep my weight under a certain number, I am satisfied. I used to resolve to do my devotions every morning before anything else got in the way. Yeah, right! Now I am satisfied to keep focused on my Savior and spend as much time as possible with Him. After all, I am much more legalistic than He is.

Every year I determined to become an organized person; why did it take forty-eight years to realize that God made me this way and that is why I have been unable to change? My family loves me just as I am; it's about time I do the same. How about you?

TODAY'S HOT FLASH:

Resolutions are just a way to set ourselves up for failure. Ask yourself why it is so important to you. Are you trying to alter the very person God made you to be?

PRAYER:

Father, thank You for the revelation that I am who You made me to be. Help me to work on the sin problems and accept those things I cannot change. Amen.

DECEMBER 31
READ: 2 CORINTHIANS 7:1-10

HAVE AN UNHAPPY NEW YEAR

Now I rejoice, not that ye were made sorry, but that ye sorrowed to repentance.
~ 2 Corinthians 7:9

We had a guest speaker visiting our church. In his first speech, he opened with this statement: "I wish you all an Unhappy New Year." What did he mean by this?

Paul desired for his followers to become uncomfortable. His challenging letters pricked the hearts of the readers and either prodded them to righteousness or angered them, revealing their true colors to their fellow Christians. He reveals his motives in 2 Corinthians 7:9 when he writes, "I rejoice . . . that ye sorrowed to repentance."

Many people are content to remain in the "status quo." After all, change is hard. We thrive in our comfort zones and surround ourselves with a great big, impenetrable bubble.

Unfortunately, when we conceal ourselves from discomfort, we close our hearts and minds from hearing God's still, small voice, or for that matter, His thundering boom. If we are going to become all that God wants us to be, we must be unhappy where we currently are. So from our guest speaker, to me, to you, "Have an Unhappy New Year!"

TODAY'S HOT FLASH:

Don't become too comfortable with where you are in your Christian faith. Growth is essential in our spiritual walk. It never ceases until we are dead.

PRAYER:

Father, make me uncomfortable. Reveal to me those areas I need to change. May I boldly take the steps needed to become more like Your Son. Amen.

For more information about
Lisa Arnold
&
For Sanity's Sake
please visit:

www.lisasforsanitysake.com
www.facebook.com/lisasforsanityssake
twitter.com/lisasarnold1

For more information about
AMBASSADOR INTERNATIONAL
please visit:

www.ambassador-international.com
@AmbassadorIntl
www.facebook.com/AmbassadorIntl